Cárdenas Compromised

CÁRDENAS COMPROMISED

The Failure of Reform in Postrevolutionary Yucatán

Ben Fallaw

DUKE UNIVERSITY PRESS   Durham and London 2001

*For my wife, Mónica, and
our daughter, Amy María*

Contents

ACKNOWLEDGMENTS

T HIS BOOK COULD not have been written without the support of a number of people and institutions. As an undergraduate at the University of North Carolina — Chapel Hill, I had the good fortune to study under the historians Leon Fink and Michael Hunt and the political scientist Jeffrey Obler. There I took a class on Mexican history with Gilbert Joseph that introduced me to the subject and changed my life. Since then, he has helped me in too many ways adequately to acknowledge.

During my graduate years at the University of Chicago, Friedrich Katz calmly guided me through the arduous process of fieldwork and writing, never letting me forget the human dimension of history. John Coatsworth's clarity of thought and Sheila Fitzpatrick's direction through the thickets of comparative peasant literature helped me finish my dissertation, "Peasants, *Caciques,* and Camarillas: State Formation and Rural Politics in Yucatán, 1924–1940." I also gratefully acknowledge the support of the Fulbright-Robles Foundation, the Mellon Foundation, and the Center for Latin American Studies of the University of Chicago, which enabled me to research and then write my doctoral research, which formed the basis of this book.

Like many other North American scholars, during my research in Yucatán I crossed many bridges that Gil Joseph built between U.S. Yucatecanists and Mexican scholars. Comments from Alan Knight, Mary Kay Vaughan, and Heather Fowler-Salamini improved various parts of this project. As visiting scholars at the University of Chicago, Neils Jacobsen, Brigada von Mentz, and Guillermo de la Peña shared their insights into Latin American rural history and whetted my appetite for the archives.

In Yucatán, my teacher and friend Hernán Menéndez Rodríguez — whose encyclopedic knowledge of the Yucatecan past is matched only by his boundless enthusiasm for history — offered much hospitality and loaned me priceless sources. Dr. Piedad Peniché Rivero's professional assistance as director of the state archives of Yucatán, as well as her friendship, lightened my load in the field. Alejandra García Quintanilla and Ivan Franco always had time for questions, a cup of coffee, and intelligent conversation. *Profesores* Antonio Betancourt Pérez and Hernán Morales Medina, who have since passed away, provided me with crucial interviews and their own historical interpretations. In Mexico City, I am greatly indebted to the Villanueva Villalpando family and Señora Semiramis Núñez Vda. de Villalpando for making my months in the city so enjoyable. It gives me great pleasure to call them my *suegros* and my *cuñados.* My boundless gratitude, however, is reserved above all for Mónica, my wife.

In Chicago, Kate Bjork, Chris Boyer, Emiliano Corral, Adam Daniel, Robin Derby, Michael Ducey, Peter Guardino, Alex Stern, Richard Turtis, Chuck Walker, and Rich Warren provided sound comments on various parts of this work. Special thanks go to my mother, Sarah Fallaw, who spent hours giving a professional proofreading to the seemingly endless stream of chapters.

At Eastern Illinois University, where my dissertation evolved into this book, my chair, Anita Shelton, and dean, James Johnson, consistently supported my research. The Eastern Illinois University's Council of Faculty Research generously supported two trips to Mexico (in 1997 and 1999) that helped turn this dissertation into a book manuscript. My colleagues at the Eastern Illinois Department of History, above all Chris Waldrep, helped create a challenging and supportive atmosphere for intellectual inquiry. I owe a special debt of gratitude to the interlibrary loan staff of Eastern's Booth Library. And Ronald Finger, of Eastern's Department of Geology-Geography, prepared a fine map for this work.

Judith Ewell, editor of the *The Americas,* kindly gave me permission to reprint part of my article "Cárdenas and the Caste War That Wasn't: Land, Ethnicity, and State Formation in Yucatán, 1847–1937," which originally appeared in the April 1997 issue of that journal. Paula Baker, the editor of *Social Science History,* extended the same courtesy for my article "The Southeast Was Red: Left-State Alliances and Popular Mobilizations in Yucatán, 1930–1940," which appeared in that journal's summer 1999 issue. Tina McDowell, publications officer of the Carnegie Institute of Washington, gave me permission to use a map from George Cheever Shattuck's *The Peninsula of Yucatan: Medical, Biological, Meteorological, and Sociological Studies.* At Duke Press, Valerie Milholland and Justin Faerber helped turn a ragged dissertation into a book. Finally, here at Colby, Shanna Browstein and Cassandra Canfield helped me prepare the book manuscript.

Despite all this support, this work undoubtedly contains errors, and all are my own.

Cárdenas Compromised

Introduction:
Cárdenas, the Mexican Revolution,
and Yucatán

FROM 1911 TO 1920, a series of peasant revolts, coups, and civil wars known as *the Revolution* transformed Mexico. In the subsequent two decades, the nation recovered, and a new state took form. The post-revolutionary regime's longevity and stability have drawn much scholarly attention. Its paradoxical combination of popular mobilization and lack of a competitive, multiparty political system has been characterized as an experiment in one-party democracy by a North America political scientist, compared to the "soft dictatorship" (*dictablanda*) of Spanish strongman Primo de Rivera in the 1920s, and lauded by an admiring Mario Vargas Llosa as the perfect dictatorship.[1]

The key features of the postrevolutionary state in Mexico emerged during the presidency of Lázaro Cárdenas (1934–40): presidentialism (extreme concentration of power in the hands of the executive, limited only by the president's six-year term), corporatism (integration of society into the party organizations by sectors), populism, and a "third way" of economic development balancing state intervention and capitalism. Not surprisingly, the Cardenista period is one of the most studied in Mexican history.

Three distinct theoretical currents have shaped our understanding of the Revolution, Cárdenas, and Cardenismo, defined here as the project of political inclusion, social transformation, and economic nationalism implemented by the president and his key collaborators. The first generation of generally prorevolutionary scholars focused on land reform, education, and (to a lesser extent) politics, arguing that Cardenismo was fundamentally a populist phenomenon. In the 1970s and 1980s, a wave of revisionists challenged the populist consensus by revealing how caciquismo (boss rule), corruption, and other undemocratic practices survived the Mexican Revolution and flourished in the postrevolutionary era, including the Cardenista era. Often working from a Marxist perspective, the revisionists generally assumed that the Revolution overthrew the old dominant landowning class only to bring a new, petit bourgeois ruling class to power.[2]

Recently, many scholars armed with more advanced theoretical approaches and carefully conducted regional and local research have corrected the excesses of the revisionists and underscored the genuine popular support that the Mexican Revolution and Cárdenas enjoyed among many social sectors. In particular, Gilbert Joseph and Daniel Nugent have challenged scholars to rethink revolutionary state formation by taking into account both popular culture and social movements. Several members of this third generation of scholars, generally known as the neopopulists, posit that the Revolution and Cárdenas nurtured a new national political culture that legitimized itself in no small part by addressing popular demands.[3] One neopopulist scholar, Jennie Purnell, has used a new concern for the interplay of social and cultural factors to profoundly analyze, not only popular support for the postrevolutionary state, but also genuine popular opposition to it—a huge gap in modern Mexican historiography, especially in light of the election of 2 July 2000.[4]

This study tests revisionist and neopopulist interpretations of Cardenismo by asking four questions. First, who were the Cardenistas, and who opposed them? Second, to what extent did Cárdenas truly succeed in mobilizing popular support and building an enduring base for the postrevolutionary regime among the workers and peasants by meeting popular demands (the core of neopopulist arguments)? Third, how much success did Cárdenas have in centralizing power on the national level (an achievement long assumed by the revisionists to be the cornerstone of the postrevolutionary state)? Fourth, what did Cardenismo change? Did it represent the culmination of state building that froze the process of revolutionary change, or was it an opening during which political institutions and social structures were called into question?

This study focuses on the regional as opposed to the community or national level to avoid the idiosyncrasies of local analyses while not losing sight of important phenomena that can be seen only on the grassroots level, such as changes in political culture and the degree of popular support enjoyed by Cardenismo.[5] It analyzes Cardenismo in Yucatán because that state and the northern, cotton region of La Laguna (northern Durango and southern Coahuila) were the two areas where Cárdenas tested land reform on the largest scale.[6] It is only a slight exaggeration to say that Yucatán was Cárdenas's TVA; more resources were spent there on agrarian reform than in any other place except for La Laguna for most of his presidency.[7] While there are several regional studies of Cardenista-era Mexico, there is no other archive-based history of Yucatán during the period, in spite of its importance as a Cardenista revolutionary laboratory.

Moreover, the Cardenista project in Yucatán extended far beyond land reform. Cardenismo crafted a greatly enlarged, progressive national government to foster a more productive, more patriotic, and somewhat less patriarchal society. As federal engineers oversaw a massive land reform in the henequen zone of the northern half of Yucatán, federal teachers and doctors sought to reform and modernize rural society. National Cardenista politicians sought to root out the influence of the old landowning oligarchy and the regional bosses of the native Socialist Party of the Southeast (Partido Socialista del Sureste, or PSS) and create a mass base for the modern Mexican state.

Yucatán seemed to offer Cárdenas the perfect place to forge a new Mexico. It boasted a revolutionary tradition dating back to the governorships of conquering northern general Salvador Alvarado (1915–17) and homegrown radical Felipe Carrillo Puerto (1922–24). The division between the so-called Divine Caste, a small number of white families that still dominated the state's economy, and the poor, Maya-speaking majority gave the Cardenistas the opportunity to mobilize a revolutionary social base along ethnic and class lines. The southeastern state was, in short, the best place to realize what Cárdenas believed was the promise of the Mexican Revolution. Consequently, a consideration of Yucatán is crucial if we are to gauge the effect of Cardenismo on Mexico as a whole.

Until now, the paucity of archive-based investigations and the distortions of contemporary political polemics have hampered our understanding of Cardenismo in Yucatán. The right-of-center opposition Party of National Action (Partido de Acción Nacional, or PAN) built a strong base in Yucatán in part by blaming all regional problems on meddling presidents and federal bureaucrats. The most hated of the carpetbaggers from the Mesa Central was none other than Lázaro Cárdenas, whose program of agrarian reform was compared by one Yucatecan critic to Stalin's collectivization.[8] PANista Ana Rosa Payán, former mayor of Mérida and at the time of writing senator from Yucatán, expressed the bitterness toward Cardenismo that animates much of the regional and national Right when she claimed recently, "Economically, [the national government] sunk us. This was a very rich state until 1937, when the all-powerful Mr. Lázaro Cárdenas came to destroy the wealth of this state, and since then things have only gotten worse; if we are subsidized, it is because it [the national government] has taken our wealth."[9] On the other hand, the postrevolutionary state and its political extension, the PRI, have mythologized Cárdenas, echoing the eulogists of Cárdenas's own day, who styled him a crusader who delivered the promise of the Revolution to the people.[10]

Most recent historiography on Cardenismo in Yucatán has reflected these misconceptions: historians sympathetic to the postrevolutionary regime attribute far too much power to Cárdenas and the national government — a position facilitated by much theory but backed by little empirical research — while revisionists often uncritically restate conservative attacks on Cardenismo without historical analyses.[11] The Yucatecan historian Hernán R. Menéndez has traced many of the half-truths and omissions to attempts by both the Mexican state and its conservative opponents selectively to interpret history for their own political benefit.[12] Although diametrically opposed in their views of Cárdenas, both official (pro-Cárdenas) and conservative (anti-Cárdenas) scholars depict the national state as an all-powerful entity, thus depriving key Yucatán actors of agency.[13]

Sources, Methodology, and Order of Argument

Moving beyond the polemical discussions of Cardenismo in Yucatán required returning to primary sources. Fortunately, local, state, and national archives yielded rich veins of virtually untouched documentation. In Mexico City, the Archivo General de la Nación's collection of President Cárdenas's papers and the archives of the Secretary of Gobernación (the powerful national ministry charged with overseeing elections and maintaining domestic order) allowed me to reconstruct relations between the national Cardenista regime and Yucatecan officials and the colossal agrarian reform project in the henequen zone. The Archivo General de Estado de Yucatán in Mérida contained many of the records of the gubernatorial administrations of Cardenista-era Yucatán, most importantly, the correspondence between the state government and local authorities. About half the municipal archives in the state had been moved to Mérida as well, which proved very useful in reconstructing local histories. The state's José Maria Pino Suárez *hemeroteca* (periodical archive) in Mérida contained a complete series of the progovernment *Diairo del Sureste* and the opposition *Diario de Yucatán* dailies and the weekly *El yucatanista*, which helped me fill in the gaps in the archival record and provided much political *chisme* (gossip).

Yucatán inspired a prodigious amount of writing by natives and foreigners during the 1920s and 1930s. By reading a seemingly endless stream of guides, amateur histories, ethnographies, travelogues, and fictional works, I fleshed out my understanding of key actors and the social and cultural environment of Cardenista-era Yucatán.

The sheer volume of data mined from archival, periodical, and secondary sources made it difficult to piece together a reasonably sized and coherent narrative of Cardenismo in Yucatán while at the same time explaining the bewildering number of institutions, actors, and structural considerations that explained its evolution and outcome. To that end, I adopted a chronological order of argument and balanced explanations of national- and regional-level processes with short case studies of events in representative or important localities. As explained below, I use the concepts of camarilla and cacique to analyze the interaction between Mexico City, the state capital of Mérida, and the local level.

Consequently, this work challenges the static models of Cardenismo common to disciplines outside history by reintroducing process and careful attention to local variations into the scholarly debate. By showing how political networks or camarillas cut across class, ideological, and ethnic lines, it moves beyond flat structuralist analyses of society and politics. For instance, chapter 3 highlights the ability of the wealthy provincial oligarchy to manipulate the Yucatecan hero cult of "proletarian martyr" Felipe Carrillo Puerto and regionalist sentiment through an alliance with the self-professed Cardenista leader Gualberto Carrillo Puerto.

Similarly, while I argue that Cárdenas's reforms in Yucatán eventually failed, the outcome was not preordained by structural limits. Cardenismo in Yucatán was a historical process that evolved over time; both elite and popular actions affected how it unfolded. Still, reacting to popular mobilizations both for and against the Cardenista project, Cárdenas and his national collaborators made a series of choices that ultimately decided the outcome of reform. Cárdenas did not commit resources needed to fulfill his project in Yucatán until late 1937, over two and a half years after agrarian reform began and popular Cardenista elements started mobilizing in Yucatán (chaps. 1 and 2). Facing strong resistance in Yucatán as well as competing demands from other national commitments on scarce resources (chaps. 3 and 4), Cárdenas abandoned sociocultural and political reform in favor of agrarian reform in a kind of strategic triage (chaps. 4 and 5). Then, only a few months later, faced by the overwhelming economic demands created by oil nationalization as well as fear of a political crisis over his succession, Cárdenas returned control of agrarian reform and electoral politics in Yucatán to state officials (chaps. 5 and 6). Agency, and a combination of elite and popular political conflicts, sealed the fate of Cardenismo in Yucatán (chap. 6).

In the end, Cárdenas's ambitious project for Yucatán was fundamentally compromised on several levels. Both its failures and its successes challenge the revisionist and, to a lesser extent, the neopopulist interpretations of Cardenismo. Contradictions in the Cardenista coalition, the limits of time, and competing national demands on finite political and economic capital forced Cárdenas to abandon his revolution from above in favor of reliance on regional cliques or camarillas. Here, I build on the arguments of Alan Knight and Jeffrey Rubin, who have attacked the revisionist notions of an all-powerful national state (for Knight, "statolatry") and call for researchers to "decenter" (Rubin's word) Mexican historiography.[14] I found that, stung by popular and landowner opposition to reform, the Cardenista national state repeatedly made key concessions to regional politicos that, in turn, greatly undermined most of the planned Cardenista reforms in Yucatán.[15]

Many will undoubtedly find this approach overly political. While social and economic forces influenced the fate of Cardenismo, choices made by Cárdenas and a host of important national and regional elites ultimately doomed the Cardenista reforms and popular Cardenismo in Yucatán to failure. Structural obstacles and resistance by established interests limited Cárdenas's choices and raised the costs of his reforms both politically and economically. But, in the end, Cárdenas chose to abandon Cardenismo in Yucatán, in part to preserve his gains elsewhere.[16]

My conclusions differ significantly from both dominant interpretations of Cardenismo. The revisionists posit a strong, Leviathan-like postrevolutionary state. If this were to be found anywhere, it would have been present in Yucatán during the Cardenista era, where so many federal agencies aggressively intervened. But the Cardenista state was hobbled by economic limits, hampered by infighting, and frustrated for over two years by the effective resistance of the landowning oligarchy and significant popular opposition. When in the fall of 1937 Cárdenas did finally bring the full weight of the national state to bear on Yucatán, the result was, not the clearcut triumph or revolution from above usually depicted, but a series of clandestine negotiations that in the end undid Cardenismo in the state.

This study also challenges neopopulist interpretations of Cardenismo by rethinking who made up the Cardenista base and showing the degree to which that base depended on state support or at least tolerance to survive. While some neopopulists see Cardenismo as the midwife of a true civil society in Mexico, the experience of Cardenismo in Yucatán demonstrates that, at least in that state, pro-Cárdenas popular mobilizations never achieved the level of autonomy or legal protection suggested by the term.

To be sure, local perspectives do reveal a high degree of grassroots mobilization, especially during the first half of Cárdenas's presidency. But the classic urban worker–rural peasant alliance was not the principal base of Cardenismo in Yucatán. Instead, the Left (the Mexican Communist Party and allied popular organizations) formed the strongest component of Cardenismo, with much of its grassroots support coming from young people, women, and the rural proletariat (known as *peons*). On the other hand, urban workers of the major cities of Progreso and Mérida either remained aloof from political struggles or joined with hacendados to oppose agrarian reform. Just as importantly, in the first half of Cárdenas's presidency, conservative landowners successfully used popular mobilizations among peons and urban labor to weaken Cardenismo and national institutions. But these antiagrarian movements also expressed genuine popular grievances over the shortcomings of agrarian reform.

Regional politicos enjoyed similar success in blunting Cardenista mobilizations from 1937 to 1940, the subject of chapters 5 and 6. In the end, as is painfully apparent in chapter 6, the Cardenista grassroots mobilizations that had survived until 1940 withered when denied the protection of the national Cardenista regime. The neopopulist assumption of a strong grassroots base for Cardenismo must be balanced by a recognition of strong and genuine popular opposition to Cardenismo among many peasants, workers, and peons. In addition, when denied the support of the Cardenista state, popular Cardenismo disappeared as a political force in Yucatán.

Caciques and Camarillas

To understand Yucatecan Cardenismo, this study examines the interaction among national-, regional-, and local-level politics.[17] To do so, it looks at key actors and associations that bridged these different realms: the cacique and camarilla.

The cacique, or boss, controls a community, political organization, or labor union through extralegal means.[18] His power derives largely from his ability to mediate between his own base and larger political, economic, and social structures.[19] At times, his authority can be expressed bluntly through violence; at other times, he calls on more paternalistic means, such as granting favors, sponsoring godchildren, or throwing fiestas. Frequently denounced as petty tyrants, caciques were not absolute rulers; if they threatened a large enough segment of the community, even the most despotic bosses eventually faced a challenge from below or from within their own retinues. Their local power, however, depended not only on maintaining at least a degree of support from below, but also on maintaining the favor of patrons from larger political, economic, and even cultural systems. By mediating between the region and their domains, caciques channeled resources to clients while delivering votes or other support to patrons.

Just as caciques often dominated political interchange between local and regional levels, camarillas — networks of informally linked elites controlling regional political and economic resources — mediated relations between the states and national institutions.[20] Because only rarely could a single cacique extend his control over an entire state or region (such a dominant figure was known as a caudillo), camarillas were coalitions more than the vehicle of a single dominant figure.[21] United by friendship, family ties, and mutual political and economic interests, rival camarillas in Yucatán competed for elected office and bureaucratic posts.[22] The fluid political and economic dimensions of camarillas often escaped narrow ideological or social definitions. Wells and Joseph's observation that prerevolutionary camarilla politics was always "permeable and pragmatic," filled with unexpected alliances with enemies for mutual advantage, was still valid after the Revolution.[23] One camarilla might, for instance, include Communists and landowners, while another might unite anarchosyndicalists and conservatives. The fact that political networks spanned ideological, class, and ethnic boundaries (which are often assumed to determine political behavior) underscores the importance of identifying camarillas to explain Cardenista-era politics. As the brilliant Communist writer José Revueltas once noted, "The most extensive ideology in Mexico is that of friendship."[24]

Yucatán: A Regional Overview

The persistent influence of caciques and camarillas was certainly not confined to Yucatán. Yet Yucatán did possess several distinctive regional characteristics. Geographically, historically, and ethnically distinct from the rest of Mexico, Yucatán was perhaps the least Mexican of all the states of the nation. Moreover, Yucatán's history had been altered forever by a spiky, hardy plant that thrived in its dry, rocky soil: henequen. Known by the Maya for centuries, this agave became a cash crop for Yucatán's bourgeoisie in the late nineteenth century. At that time, North American wheat farmers were looking for a durable fiber to bind sheaves harvested by McCormick's mechanical harvester, a need that henequen met. On the outbreak of the Revolution in 1910, almost 100,000 Maya-speaking Yucatecans, as well as thousands of Yaqui Indians deported from Sonora and imported wage laborers from Korea, labored on henequen haciendas in debt peonage often compared to slavery.[25] In these open-air factories, peons (landless rural workers who lived in hacienda communities) cut the sharp leaves of the henequen plant. Fiber was then pressed out of the leaves in a mechanized "rasping train" on the hacienda grounds, pressed, and then transported to Mérida, where it was woven into twine in cordage factories or simply shipped in bulk. From Yucatán's port of Progreso, ships exported henequen to the United States, Australia, and Europe. By 1910, henequen wealth had brought untold prosperity to Yucatán's capital, the "white city" of Mérida. Paved, lit, and spotlessly clean, it boasted a large and prosperous community of planters and henequen factors who proudly called their home the Paris of the West. But the peons and peasants who worked the henequen fields received few, if any, benefits from the henequen boom.

Socially and culturally, Yucatán guarded a distinctive identity within Mexico as a whole. Outside the capital of Mérida and its port of Progreso, Maya, not Spanish, predominated. While regional landowners and their literary panegyrists celebrated its distinctive Maya-Spanish heritage, the Maya-speaking peasantry did not share the romantic provincialism of the landlords.[26] And, despite their historical tradition and shared experience of racial oppression, no strong pan-Maya identity could be found among the peasantry. Instead, it was the municipality that remained the locus of political identity for the Maya-speaking rural poor.[27]

While the municipality claimed strong loyalty, Yucatecan towns and villages were divided between *vecinos* and common folk. For centuries, trade, the professions, and political office had been monopolized by the Spanish-speaking, white or mestizo provincial elites commonly known as *vecinos,* literally "neighbors," for their residence in the center of town. The poorer, politically marginalized majority of Maya-speaking peoples shared a hybrid Maya and Spanish culture and were mainly peasants, although a fair number were artisans, smallholders, and ranchers.[28] To be sure, marriages and unions outside marriage had blurred the racial line between vecinos and peasants, and the two groups had lived cheek by jowl for centuries, and to a great degree, shared a common culture. But, although the distinction was weakened by the Revolution, it persisted through the Cardenista era.[29]

Within Yucatán, important differences distinguished the henequen zone, which included the center, north, and west of the state, from the maize- and cattle-producing south and east. Outside the henequen zone, rural society was less stratified and had no dominant planter oligarchy or large estates. In the henequen zone, on the other hand, powerful hacendados with paternalistic influence over hundreds of employees often overshadowed the power of the town-dwelling vecinos. Henequen municipalities were divided between the villages and towns inhabited by peasants and vecinos and the nearly autonomous hacienda communities made up mainly of peons.

In 1934, some thirty thousand adult male peons and their families lived on hacienda estates. Yucatán's larger henequen plantations were a world unto themselves, boasting their own chapels, stores, and schools; residents rarely interacted with neighboring towns and villages. Landowners used paternalistic loans, gifts, and medical care (and at times schools), along with the social bond of godparentage, to foster loyalty and dependence among peons.[30] Although both village-dwelling peasants and hacienda peons worked for wages in the same fields, landowners reserved the highest-paying jobs, those requiring the most skills, for a better-paid, usually literate group of hand-picked resident laborers who formed the loyal core of estate communities. Even the majority of peons, who were paid less and did jobs requiring little skill, received employment security and other considerations denied peasants.[31] Although the hacienda still dominated much of Yucatán when Cárdenas took office as president, the Mexican Revolution cast a long shadow over its future.

Yucatán in the Mexican Revolution

Between 1911 and 1915, scattered insurgencies erupted to threaten the status quo of insular Yucatán. Yet, during the first years of the Revolution, Yucatecan planters managed to ride out the storm raging across the rest of Mexico with their control over the region intact.[32] In the spring of 1915, the pharmacist-turned-general Salvador Alvarado led the Army Corps of the Southeast into Yucatán on the orders of Venustiano Carranza, head of the Constitutionalist faction. At the time, Carranza was locked in a bloody civil war against Emiliano Zapata and Francisco Villa, and Carranza sent Alvarado to Yucatán to secure henequen revenue for his war effort.[33]

Alvarado's efforts as military governor expanded far beyond simple financial extraction. He abolished debt peonage and corporal punishment, which had bound thousands of peons to their estate owners. Although paternalistic bonds and economic necessity kept thousands of peons on the estates, in the late 1910s and early 1920s many left.[34] To consolidate the postrevolutionary political order, Governors Salvador Alvarado (1915–18) and Felipe Carrillo Puerto (1922–24) sponsored an official party, eventually known as the Socialist Party of the Southeast (PSS).[35] It united elements of the middle class, renegade hacendados, workers, and peasants and organized hundreds of village, neighborhood, and professional leagues under the strict control of a central league. Despite its name, the PSS was far from a Marxist party of class. Instead, its core ideology centered around concepts of individual rights (*libertades*), secularism, and state intervention in the economy. In this sense, Yucatecan socialism owed as much to classical liberalism and anarchosyndicalism as to historical materialism. The PSS linked the reclamation of individual liberties stripped during the prerevolutionary Time of Slavery to the assertion of male honor, which implied equality among men of all social strata. Luis Aboites interviewed old peons and peasants in the eastern provincial town of Espita, who recounted the origins of Yucatecan Socialism. For them, "Socialism brought freedom," and "Alvarado was Socialist because he gave [us] freedom."[36]

In its early years, the PSS supported the empowerment of the poor and disenfranchised. The explicit enemies of the PSS were the old landowning class, the Catholic clergy, and the prerevolutionary *jefe politico,* or district prefect, all blamed for slavery and ignorance. Land reform, cooperatives, education, and secularization promised freedom and development. But, by the late 1920s, Yucatecan Socialism suffered from its very success — the old jefe politico was gone, and the Time of Slavery was increasingly forgotten. A new generation of Socialist caciques spawned new forms of exploitation — protection rackets, arbitrary government, and electoral fraud.[37] While for the most part these Socialist bosses maintained a firm hold over village politics, the peon communities on estates remained largely beyond the reach of the revolutionary regime.

Since 1918, the PSS's leaders had enjoyed regional autonomy in return for supporting national authorities. For years, Yucatecan Socialists had looked to their national protector, Plutarco Elías Calles, president (1924–28) and then *jefe máximo* (maximum chief) (1928–35) of Mexico. In 1929, Calles founded the political arm of the postrevolutionary state, the Party of the National Revolution (Partido Nacional Revolucionario, or PNR), but it failed to create a popular base for the jefe máximo. In 1934, Calles needed to fill the presidency with a politician capable of moderating his conservative policies in order to attract popular support for the PNR. Calles's choice, ex-Michoacan governor Lázaro Cárdenas, had assembled a peasant-worker-intellectual coalition in his home state that would serve as a model for the PNR. He had also repeatedly proved his loyalty to Calles, most recently by disarming the peasant militia of the radical leader Adalberto Tejeda of Veracruz. Not only was the young general the darling of the left wing of the

PNR, but he also had the support of the most powerful generals of the army. At a time of growing economic pressure from the Great Depression and heightened political tension within the PNR, Calles saw in Cárdenas a means of tacking to the left while still maintaining control of the postrevolutionary state.[38] Calles's selection of Cárdenas for the presidency would drastically change all Mexico, but no state would be more affected than Yucatán.

Cárdenas and Yucatán

Even before taking office, Cárdenas sought to restart agrarian reform on the national level and reached out to organized labor. This only increased tension within the postrevolutionary elite because reformers and the conservative arch-Callistas — generals and politically connected entrepreneurs were threatened by Cárdenas's policies.[39] Cárdenas accepted Calles's authority but expected to govern without interference. When Calles publicly criticized Cárdenas's support for organized labor in June 1935, the president exiled his former mentor and began ousting his loyalists from power. Cárdenas would move even further to the left to gather popular support against Calles.[40]

Even before the break with Calles, Cárdenas had begun to steer the revolutionary state in the direction of agrarian reform. On 10 March 1934, Cárdenas's presidential campaign brought him to Mérida, Yucatán, where he announced that almost nineteen thousand hectares of privately held henequen land claimed by peasant villages for over a decade would finally be turned over to them. Not only did Cárdenas champion the claims of peasant communities to land across Mexico, but in Yucatán he also invoked the legacy of the assassinated Socialist hero Felipe Carrillo Puerto to announce that land would be turned over to those who worked it in the form of collective, federally administered *ejidos* (collective, communal land grants farmed by peasant villages). Cárdenas and his collaborators believed that breaking up the old haciendas would not only yield economic benefits, but also create a new class-based consciousness and a feeling of loyalty to the Cardenista regime.[41] While anticipating resistance on the part of the old oligarchy, Cárdenas hoped that by allowing the landowners to keep part of their land, he would avoid a dangerous confrontation or perhaps even a national civil war. Cárdenas also believed, perhaps naively, that the landowners in Yucatán and elsewhere would voluntarily divest themselves of their landholdings and reinvest their capital in more productive parts of the national economy, such as industry.[42]

There was more than land at stake, however. Cárdenas always saw agrarian reform as inseparable from a larger social, cultural, and even moral transformation.[43] To the national Cardenistas, the hacienda, along with the church and the *cantina,* represented Old Mexico, a backward mind-set mired in superstition, ignorance, and sloth. The collective ejido, along with the school, would instill sobriety, patriotism, industry, and secularism.[44] The Jacobinism of Cárdenas's early career, however, was soon discarded in the light of social and political realities.[45] In place of anticlericalism, Cárdenas stressed other aspects of modernization, above all the elimination of the "social vices" of drinking and gambling. At the same time, Cárdenas called for special attention to "the Indian conglomerate" in order to "incorporate it into the national life." Two new national agencies — Indigenous Affairs and Physical Education — reflected the new Cardenista priorities of paternalistic advocacy for Indians and prohibition via sports.[46]

The Cardenista project in Yucatán required an unprecedented degree of federal intervention in a state long suspicious of the national government and jealous of its distinctive regional identity. National Cardenistas, who hailed overwhelmingly from central and northern states, saw in Yucatán much of what needed to be reformed or eliminated to modernize Mexico. Yucatán's physical and historical isolation from the rest of Mexico, the power still wielded by the landowning families, the lack of heavy industry, and the high incidence of Maya monolingualism and rural poverty all added up, from the perspective of the national Cardenistas, to a backward region in need of "Mexicanization" and modernization.

In the minds of the national Cardenistas, negative views and outright stereotypes of Yucatecans coexisted with a mythical vision of the Yucatecan Mayas as a tragically oppressed "race" in need of redemption by the national government. Cárdenas himself clung to a romantic view of the Maya as a proud, stoic folk requiring his government's paternalistic guidance for salvation. Almost two decades after his presidency, Cárdenas spoke of his first encounter with Mayan peasants: "What struck me was their virtues, virtues that many in the interior [Mesa Central] of the Republic completely lacked. They had a grand faith in the Revolution and trusted in the national government to resolve their problems." The widespread belief in the legendary peaceful and hardworking qualities of the Maya among other Mexicans was given a new gloss by Cárdenas, who believed that "the peasant population [of Yucatán] still conserves elements of their ancient and advanced civilization, as demonstrated by their work ethic, cleanliness, and respect for life."[47]

These innate virtues, the Cardenistas believed, could shine through only if the Maya were saved from an oppressive, unjust provincial social order. Carlos M. Peralta, a northerner and head of the agrarian bureaucracy, told Cárdenas that the Yucatecan peasants "do not know Spanish and have been intellectually degraded as a result of centuries of relegation in the most terrible misery; they remain powerless and inert in the rude class struggle convulsing the state."[48] Accordingly, revolutionary change would have to come from above, not below.

The belief in a "quiescent" Maya requiring redemption from the national government was strongly held by the national Cardenistas. The corollary notion that Yucatán's politicos were corrupt Callistas who had to be eliminated influenced national policy just as strongly. The views of Narciso Bassols, a leader of the left wing of the PNR that rallied around Cárdenas, were typical. According to Bassols, the long-suffering Maya had been forced to witness "hundreds of infamies, deceptions, Socialist mystifications, mass murders, immoral and ostentatious corruptions, banquets of bureaucrats, and Roman orgies all practiced by 'Socialist *compañeros.*'"[49]

The national Cardenistas believed that the revolutionary process in Yucatán had been started by Felipe Carrillo Puerto, to one Cardenista the president's Juan the Baptist, and it would be fulfilled by Cárdenas.[50] While Cárdenas himself was never as vocal in his criticism of Yucatecan politicos as were many of his key advisers, he had little faith in the homegrown leadership of the state.[51] Gualberto Carrillo Puerto, Felipe's brother, had been among the first in Yucatán to endorse Cárdenas and at times had the president's ear. But the only Yucatecan whom Cárdenas truly trusted was his close friend and former chief of staff General Rafael Cházaro Pérez, who would be Cárdenas's main intermediary in the state until his untimely death in an aviation accident in January 1936. After campaigning in March 1934, the president would not return to Yucatán for over three years. Until the fall of 1937, Cárdenas would rely on trusted lieutenants and the federal agencies in Yucatán to implement his project and build a popular base. No item on the Cardenista agenda would be more important than agrarian reform.

1

Agrarian Cardenismo, the Rise of the CGT, and the Fall of Governor Alayola, 1934–1935

As a presidential candidate in March 1934, Lázaro Cárdenas pledged to carve dozens of collective henequen ejidos out of the haciendas of Yucatán. Even before Cárdenas took office, the federal agrarian bureaucracy had been planning an "energetic offensive" to achieve the "social liberation of the Yucatecan peasantry."[1]

This chapter considers land reform and its political and social ramifications from the beginning of the Cárdenas presidency to the overthrow of Governor César Alayola Barrera in a general strike in September–October 1935, an event usually (and somewhat erroneously) considered as a victory for Cardenismo over its enemies in Yucatán. The first part considers the institutional means employed by the Cárdenas regime to try and create collective henequen ejidos. It then turns to the political effect of agrarian reform, principally the rise of the agrarian camarilla. I will then consider the reaction against agrarian reform — the rise of anarchosyndicalist peon unions sponsored by hacendados. The rise of strong opposition to land reform in the henequen zone played a major role in toppling Governor César Alayola.

The Mechanics of Agrarian Reform

To fulfill his "solemn promise" of land reform, Cárdenas created a special committee to oversee the new Mixed (joint federal-state) Agrarian Commission just instituted in April in Yucatán. In December 1934, he promised (but had not yet allocated) 7 million pesos to the new federal National Bank of Agrarian Credit (soon to be the National Bank of Ejidal Credit). The Agrarian Bank would provide credit to peasant-run collective ejidos in the form of "advances" against future earnings, in cooperation with the recently created Autonomous Agrarian Department, which would provide technical support and management expertise.[2]

To head the agrarian bureaucracy in Yucatán, Cárdenas dispatched Candelario Reyes, a native of the northeastern state of Tamaulipas and protégé of fellow Tamaulipeco Emilio Portes Gil. The latter was a former president and a powerful member of Cárdenas's inner circle. Unlike many other federal lieutenants sent to Yucatán, Reyes stuck to his orders and refused bribes from landlords and local politicos, which led to his reputation as *intocable* (untouchable).[3] The fact that an unelected outsider wielded so much power over Yucatán's fortunes rankled the regional oligarchy as well as many average Yucatecans; taxis carried signs saying, "This car will not pick up Candelario Reyes," and many cafés and restaurants put signs in their windows reading, "In this house Candelario Reyes will not be served."[4] Although Reyes was personally honest, he wielded his power and large budget like a veteran political player.

It was understandable that many Yucatecan officials remained ambivalent about land reform. For starters, the Agrarian Bank's numbers simply did not add up. It planned to take 20–25 percent of all the henequen acreage in the state from haciendas to create ejidos. But even if officials divided *all* the haciendas' henequen land, the daily per capita income of the *ejidatarios* (peasants with rights to join collective ejidos) would have been 1.27 pesos, well below the barely adequate 2.50–4.00 pesos daily average.[5] The Agrarian Bank anticipated planting henequen on vacant land to make up the difference—but that meant subsidizing ejidos for the seven years needed for the young sprouts to mature.[6] Moreover, the process of dividing up planted and fallow fields among eligible pueblos proved to be a task worthy of Solomon. In an attempt to give ejidos convenient access to nearby raspers (the machinery that processed henequen leaves on haciendas) and fields, some haciendas were spared, while others were almost completely divided up among two (or even more) ejidos, creating confusion and disputes among ejidos and resentment among hard-hit hacendados.[7]

Even more problematic was the situation of the peons, the rural workers who lived on the haciendas. Cárdenas promised to give the henequen fields to those who worked them. But agrarian law and federal policy generally excluded peons and privileged peasants, who lived in towns and villages and worked on henequen plantations as day laborers. The peons, an estimated half of the sixty-thousand-person workforce in the henequen zone, found themselves shut out of the new ejidos. Cárdenas encouraged them to form labor unions to raise wages through federal arbitration, but, again, the numbers did not add up: land reform left many haciendas with lower labor requirements and therefore many peons unemployed. As we shall see, the mobilization of the peons proved to be a formidable factor in regional politics, although not in the way in which Cárdenas intended.

The fate of federal teachers under agrarian reform presented another unexpected obstacle for the Cardenista agrarian project. When hacendados lost land to ejidos, they stopped paying the federal teachers to educate the children of peons, as required by Article 123 of the Constitution of 1917. When the Agrarian Bank took over private henequen land, neither the bank nor the state government would assume responsibility for the schools, leaving the children of the peons without schooling and the teachers without work.[8] The fact that federal teachers organized the peons into unions and that unemployed teachers blamed the Agrarian Bank both for their predicament and for the exclusion of peons from land grants drove a wedge between teachers and peons, on one hand, and the Agrarian Bank and the Cardenista agrarian project, on the other.

To make matters worse, the combination of disorganization and underemployment on the ejidos and layoffs on the haciendas proved disastrous for the rural poor. Peasant villagers still depended on work on the declining haciendas, and estate-dwelling peons resented their exclusion from agrarian reform. Governor Alayola fruitlessly petitioned the national Cardenista authorities for a suspension of agrarian reform, arguing that the lack of work and hunger provoked riots. Protests by hacendados, complaints by state officials, and the threat of rising social instability in the henequen zone led Cárdenas to convene a series of meetings with all interested parties in Mexico City. In May 1934, and once again in October 1935, Alayola, the state's official party (the PSS), and the state PNR forwarded an alternative agrarian plan that would transfer much less land, do it more slowly, and involve far less government supervision than did the federal blueprint for agrarian reform.[9]

Even when faced with growing resistance and escalating costs, Cárdenas stood by Reyes and the original, much more aggressive federal agrarian reform plans. His determination was in no small part due to the fact that, while his solemn promise of agrarian reform had antagonized many groups, it had also given new hope to some peasants across the henequen zone. Cárdenas hoped that an agrarian Cardenista base would be mobilized among villagers demanding land in the henequen zone.

The Rise of Agrarian Cardenismo

Since the Mexican Revolution, many Yucatecan villages had been using legal channels to try to recover land seized by hacendados and planted with henequen during the Porfiriato (the dictatorship of Porfirio Díaz, 1877–1910). Despite the wave of petitions from rural communities, only a handful of grants affecting henequen land had been authorized since the end of the radical Carrillo Puerto administration (1922–23). Having already waited for years, many peasant communities did not stand by for official sanction to reclaim their land once Cárdenas took office. Long-running boundary disputes between hacendados and communities flared up in the tense atmosphere of early 1934 in places like Cacalchen.[10] In October and November 1934, at least seven villages legally laid claim to the land of neighboring henequen haciendas.[11]

Despite mounting tension in the countryside and some eruptions of popular Cardenista agrarianism, federal agrarian authorities made little progress in establishing functioning henequen ejidos during the waning months of 1934. The next year, however, they redoubled their efforts to establish two model henequen ejidos in the towns of Cacalchen and Motul.[12] Despite hacendado resistance in the form of destruction of henequen fields and refusal to negotiate access to raspers, by the end of April 1935 five new henequen ejidos functioned: Komchen, Chuburná, Dzununcan, Seye, and Mococha. To address growing resentment among peons who feared unemployment should their haciendas be turned over to ejidos, the Agrarian Bank promised them (unspecified) aid in the future. Reyes even held out the prospect of financial independence from the federal government by setting aside a percentage of each year's harvest to be put toward a social fund for the future needs of ejidatarios, such as schooling, medical care, and pensions. The Agrarian Bank chose May Day 1935, traditionally a high holiday of leftists and organized labor in Mexico, to promise 1.3 million pesos in credit to nine new henequen ejidos.[13]

As Cardenista authorities forged ahead, both state officials and hacendados raised further objections. More ominously popular complaints increased and were gleefully reported by the *Diario de Yucatán,* the Mérida daily that often acted as the mouthpiece of Yucatán's business and landowning classes. For instance, on 1 May 1935, federal officials granted the peasants of Tixpeual land. But, much to the dismay of federal agrarian engineers, most of Tixpeual's peasants refused to accept the entry of henequen fields on the bank's conditions, realizing that with the mandatory federal credit came debt and dependence. Federal officials pressed ahead and created the ejido anyway, but, in July 1935, peasants demanded land without outside interference. That same month, a bomb, apparently planted by aggrieved peasants, went off outside the ejidal headquarters while visiting federal inspectors were meeting inside.[14]

Similarly, federal engineers received a hostile reception in other communities. Rumors spread that census taking and mapping were preludes to a military draft and the loss of land.[15] Such beliefs fed peasant perceptions of federal officials as authoritarian and unresponsive and reflected a deep-seated suspicion that prerevolutionary debt peonage was to be replaced with a new debt servitude, this time to federal bureaucrats.

Faced with mushrooming peasant resistance and sporadic violence, the federal engineers often overreacted. The ejidatarios of Dzununcan complained that Agrarian Department officials threatened them with five years in prison should they not join the collective land grant. To make matters worse, frustrated agrarian engineers at times called in federal troops to deal with peasant obstinacy.[16]

By mid-1935, popular and hacendado resistance, financial shortfalls, and administrative errors threatened Cárdenas's agrarian plans for Yucatán. But other political and economic commitments — above all, the looming showdown with Calles — occupied Cárdenas. The president could only manage to lean on Governor Alayola to help out the ejidos. In response, the state government grudgingly moved to expropriate raspers so that the ejidos would not have to rent them from hacendados, in the process giving federal agrarian officials a potent weapon to use against recalcitrant hacendados.[17] Landowners promptly blocked these measures with the ubiquitous *amparo,* an appellate court's judicial stay issued on constitutional grounds.[18] Consequently, the pace of agrarian reform further slowed.

The Agrarian Bank originally had planned to organize some 236 ejidos (about half henequen, half corn) by the end of 1935, but by mid-September even optimistic figures showed that only 11,816 of 53,778 eligible peasants had enrolled in the Agrarian Bank's local credit societies. This meant that over three-fourths of peasants eligible to receive land either had not been organized or refused to cooperate. While the Agrarian Bank claimed to have sown some 90,900 mecates (one mecate is twenty by twenty meters, or one-twenty-fifth of a hectare) of henequen by mid-September 1935, some two years later bank jefe Candelario Reyes admitted that only 4,361 mecates were actually sown during that entire year. During 1935, only three of the thirty-one ejidos that should have been planting henequen actually did so, despite outlays of some 190,000 pesos toward that end.[19] An estimated 30 percent of productivity was lost through deficient management (poor cutting, badly timed burning) of henequen ejidos by federal engineers. An additional unknown percentage was lost through fraud. Moreover, it seems that federal spending never came close to matching Cárdenas's promises and Reyes's plans.[20]

Agrarian Cardenismo as Camarilla: Ejidal Caciques and the New Notables

Federal agrarian reform unintentionally created a powerful new regional group referred to here as the agrarian Cardenista camarilla. It was made up of the federal agrarian officials themselves and ejidal caciques, community leaders who supported agrarian reform to increase their own power. These local power brokers, who would play an important role in local and state politics in the coming years, came to exert influence, ironically enough, because of the centralized nature of Cárdenas's agrarian plan.

In theory, the Cardenista doctrines of popular empowerment and economic justice entrusted the management of ejidos to a locally elected *comisariado ejidal,* or ejidal commissary. But in practice, the agrarian bureaucracy proved unwilling actually to turn over management of the ejidos to peasant representatives. Agrarian engineers generally held sympathetic but patronizing attitudes toward the peasants, believing them incapable of running the complex agricultural and industrial process of henequen production. Because the Agrarian Bank considered Maya-lingual peasants "helpless" owing to their supposed political inertia and inability to speak Spanish, lower-level Agrarian Bank officials created their own network of pliable intermediaries to control the ejidos.[21] Patron-client ties between federal engineers and so-called ejidal caciques undergirded the operation of federal agrarian institutions. The Agrarian Bank's field agents, predominantly native Yucatecos despite their federal positions, used these petty agrarian bosses to carve out their own political bases. The agrarian reform bureaucracy, sent to free Yucatán from control by the landlords and Callista officials, paradoxically created a new system of caciques.

The political and economic clout of the federal agrarian engineers and the arbitrary power exercised by their loyal ejidal caciques created a great deal of popular resentment. Residents of Tixkokob complained that the president of the local ejido had already been robbing the people for more than fourteen years as an elected local official and that those who complained were denied land.[22] In nearby Homun, peasants denounced Maximiliano Pacheco for controlling its ejido for six years, extorting illegal rents, denying land to an opposition mayoral candidate, and illegally enrolling medium-size landowners and the unemployed on the ejido's rolls. Pacheco's exploitation and violation of the "noble principles" of the ejido, they complained, was sanctioned by the Agrarian Bank chief, Reyes, who "decidedly supported this individual, whom he converted into the cacique of the ejido."[23] To be sure, minority factions of peasant communities mastered the use of the discourse of caciquismo (boss rule) to try to provoke government intervention on their behalf, but there is ample evidence that many ejidos fell under the control of the same person or clique for years on end with the complicity of Agrarian Bank personnel.

The emergence of ejidal caciques like Maximiliano Pacheco was closely linked to federal agrarian officials, whose prominence in regional affairs led one analyst to label them *the new notables*.[24] The zone chiefs (subregional supervisors) and lower-ranking Agrarian Bank employees like accountants and clerks were almost all Yucatecans qualified, Reyes claimed, by their competency and ideological correctness.[25] This screening did not prevent many old Socialist Party politicos from colonizing the new network of federal offices in search of wealth (loans, kickbacks, graft) and political patronage. Humberto Centeno, whose family ruled the eastern town of Valladolid under Callista-era governor García Correa in the early 1930s, now ran the Agrarian Bank branch in Peto after acting as bank accountant in Espita. Veteran Socialist political operator José Jesús Barceló found a second career as a federal agrarian official. Notables like these served agrarian reform poorly: Barceló allegedly held up land transfers in return for money from hacendados, and Centeno was eventually fired for fraud.[26]

Despite federal regulations strictly prohibiting political activities, the new notables often used positions in the Agrarian Bank as a springboard for elected office: in 1936, Hernando Pérez Uribe used the office of zone chief of Tixkokob to win the mayoral election for Mérida and would go on to campaign with less success for governor. In areas where the federal engineers or ejidal bosses did not hold sway, Agrarian Bank chief Reyes himself often personally intervened to project federal influence. Ejidatarios of Cacalchen ("the first in Yucatán to welcome with the greatest enthusiasm the idea of the ejidos, believing that they would make things better") denounced Reyes as "a true cacique" for poor pay and his mistreatment of peasants.[27] Ejidatarios also charged that Reyes promised them the right to choose their supervisors, then imposed his favorites against the will of the majority.[28]

To counter widespread peasant resistance, Reyes often dispatched federal troops or armed loyal ejidatarios to quell problems, a policy that maintained the bank's influence at the cost of widening local divisions and creating much resentment.[29] In the struggle to create functioning henequen ejidos, the Agrarian Bank and its supporters were increasingly indistinguishable from other regional camarillas, battling for power on the local and regional levels, advancing clients and punishing enemies.

The Problem of the Peon and the
Hacendados' Response

The combination of economic stress and political tension caused by agrarian reform weighed especially heavily on the peons. In the mid-1930s, many peons found themselves caught between hostile agrarian Cardenistas, who considered them reactionary, and coldly calculating hacendados willing to use them as cannon fodder to foil agrarian reform. Peon income dropped as the newly founded ejidos froze them out and hacendados resorted to punitive lockouts of both peons and peasants to increase pressure on the Agrarian Bank to stop land reform.[30]

The volatile situation created by throwing thousands of peons out of work forced Candelario Reyes to try in September 1935 to target land grants specifically for peons. He also urged the ejidos to hire peons to run rasping machinery and give them a "reasonable percentage" of field work to keep them "more or less equal" with the peasant ejidatarios. But it would be almost two more years before local-level federal officials included more than a few hundred peons in the ejidos.[31] The villager ejidatarios were both unable and unwilling to accept peons. Most ejidos did not have enough land in production to employ their existing members fully; most would be waiting seven years until newly planted henequen seedlings came into production to come close to self-sufficiency. Moreover, there was often mutual suspicion between peasant villagers and peons over the latter's close ties to landowners. Given the inability of Cardenista agrarian reform to resolve the plight of rural laborers residing on estates, the hacendados had a popular reservoir of resentment against agrarian reform to exploit.

To no one's surprise, Cárdenas's agrarian proclamation of March 1934 provoked angry protests from most landowners. Hacendados complained that the Agrarian Bank's plan was illegal and would destroy the state's economy.[32] Less alarmist arguments claimed that reform would be too expensive and that peasants were psychologically or culturally unsuited to run henequen production themselves (the one idea that national Cardenistas and Yucatecan hacendados shared).[33] Landowners hoped that the loss of tax revenue caused by the disruption of henequen production and the "starvation wages" received by many ejidatarios would convince Cárdenas to drop agrarian reform. The president stood by his plan. Without any serious national challenge to Cárdenas on the horizon after Calles's defeat, hacendados turned to indirect tactics. Behind all their efforts lay an underlying strategy to raise the costs of collectivization to a level unacceptably high for the president without appearing to challenge him directly. To force Cárdenas to retreat on agrarian reform, the hacendados also brought pressure to bear on the president from a number of different directions.

Attempts to ask the United States to pressure Cárdenas to end agrarian reform in Yucatán proved futile.[34] Landowners tried to find allies in Cárdenas's inner circle, courting one of the strongest and most conservative ministers in his cabinet, Agriculture (not to be confused with Agrarian) Secretary Saturnino Cedillo. Yet Cárdenas did not heed Cedillo's criticism of the ejidos' "improper and uneconomic exploitation of the henequen."[35] Still, hacendados did not want for ways to frustrate agrarian reform.

Their employees routinely sabotaged rasping machinery and overcut their henequen fields rather than turn them over to ejidatarios. Another favorite tactic, when forced to transfer land, was to turn over newly sown, immature fields instead of mature ones.[36] Many landowners threatened not to plant new henequen and refused to hire workers unless agrarian reform was suspended, provoking protest marches (some led by federal teachers) and attacks on federal Agrarian Bank officials.[37]

When Cárdenas still refused to budge, hacendados tried to convince him to accept a compromise plan that would spare most haciendas, allow the federal government to spend less, and at the same time permit the president to improve the precarious position of the peasantry. Under their alternative, the government would buy several haciendas along with vacant land with funds to come from the hacendados themselves. The land and the haciendas would be run as peasant cooperatives, and surplus peasants left without land would be resettled in the south and east to grow maize — once again at hacendado expense.[38] Cárdenas politely heard the proposals but would not swerve.

The final part of the hacendados' strategy, which undoubtedly did the most damage to agrarian reform, was the decision to tap the peons' grievances and mobilize them against land reform. To do so, the hacendados used an unlikely ally against Cárdenas: anarchosyndicalism.

The CGT: Revolutionaries against Agrarian Reform

To mobilize peons against agrarian reform, hacendados funded unions under the aegis of the Yucatecan branch of the anarchosyndicalist General Confederation of Workers (Confederación General de Trabajadores, or CGT). The national CGT was created in 1921, but by 1931, its influence was waning in most of Mexico.[39] It found a new lease on life in Yucatán as hacendados subsidized anarchist leaders to fashion an ideology that claimed to be both popular and revolutionary.

For decades, the workers of Mérida and its port of Progreso nurtured a radical, anarchosyndicalist tradition. It stressed worker control of production, suspicion of the state, and the use of the general strike to fight workers' enemies. Prerevolutionary social transformations — the rapid growth of working-class neighborhoods, the proletarianization of urbanized peasant families, and class discrimination in education and employment — contributed to the spread of anarchist ideas.[40] Although the revolutionary state in Yucatán had tried to co-opt anarchosyndicalist organizations and ideology, Yucatecan Socialism never completely absorbed anarchism.

With the rise of Cardenismo and the weakening of the PSS, anarchist labor recovered, but its revival was linked to opposition to agrarian reform. Old anarchists, such as veteran activist Tomas Pérez Ponce and his protégé Porfirio Pallares, made common cause with hacendados against the Socialist Party and Cardenista agrarian reform, bartering their organizing skills in return for financial support. Pallares and former barber Santiago Capetillo, both of whom had been expelled from another labor federation for their ties to hacendados, quickly took up leading roles in the CGT in Yucatán. In perhaps the most blatant indication of hacendado influence over the CGT leadership, on 19 September 1936 Pallares asked that the federal minimum wage be lowered when the price of henequen fell, thus allowing landowners to cut meager salaries. At times, CGT officials allegedly represented owners in labor arbitration cases. The national CGT's delegate to Yucatán accepted twenty thousand pesos from landowners to go to Mexico City and try to convince Cárdenas to end agrarian reform. Most importantly, the CGT gave the hacendados a means of turning popular support against land reform and, on more than one occasion, of politically destabilizing Yucatán to serve the hacendados' political aims.[41]

Besides working to influence the CGT from the top down by co-opting its leadership, hacendados also controlled many anarchosyndicalist organizations from the bottom up by using trusted employees to form and lead local CGT chapters on their own estates. The CGT on hacienda Xcumpich in Chuburná was led, not by average peons, who were for the most part poorly paid, illiterate, and unskilled, but by its well-paid, literate, and skilled employees (a carpenter, mechanics, and an overseer).[42] Similarly, the CGT Union of Henequen Cutters on the massive hacienda San Francisco in Dzidzantún was organized and led by the estate's overseer and its carpenter. Owners encouraged peons to join the CGT on many haciendas during *chocolomos* — festive celebrations at which hacendados like the Manzanilla family and Felipe G. Cantón distributed beef (an expensive rarity in peasant diets) in a traditional show of paternalistic largesse. Alcohol served as another inducement to join the CGT.[43] Across Yucatán, estate overseers frequently distributed money or rum to CGT unions to encourage their participation in anti–agrarian reform demonstrations.[44] Clearly, it was paternalism and economic self-interest, not Kropotkin, that motivated most of the CGT's peon base.

The cozy relationship between many CGT leaders and wealthy landowners created serious problems for the organization.[45] In response, the discourse of the CGT emphasized its supposed rugged independence and ardent pro-Cárdenas orientation: Manuel J. Cano of the Motul CGT wrote to the president in the name of Motul's peons ("neither ejidatarios nor landlords") and saluted Cárdenas's "noble intentions to resolve the agrarian problem."[46] The CGT tried to justify its opposition to Cardenista agrarian reform ideologically by denouncing the ejido's "bourgeoisification" of the countryside.[47] This failed to convince the CGT's largest single affiliate, the Union of Cordage Factory Workers of Yucatán (Sindicato de Cordeleros de Yucatán, or SCY), which demanded the expulsion of corrupt leaders and eventually walked out of the CGT.[48]

Although hacendados used their considerable economic and social capital to recruit peons for the CGT, the mobilization of hacienda laborers against agrarian reform was not a simple case of manipulation. Some CGT unions, like that on Mulchechen hacienda in Kanasín led by Benito Arceo, did honestly represent peon demands.[49]

Moreover, the CGT enjoyed great success by exploiting the ideological gaps in Cardenismo. The Cardenistas used a rhetoric that caricatured landowners as heartless aristocrats who exploited their workers; agrarian Cardenistas spoke of *esclavitud* (slavery) on haciendas. But the discourse of agraristas was anachronistic by the 1930s. The prerevolutionary whipping post, estate jail, and legally enforced debt servitude had been abolished for almost two decades before Cárdenas's first visit to Yucatán. Since 1915, peons who truly despised a hacendado could leave, resulting in a migration that left behind a more loyal peon population.[50]

Rather than being the huddled serfs yearning to be freed from a feudal regime, peons were generally supportive of landowners because of economic codependence as well as traditional patron-client bonds. In an interview with a North American investigator in 1974, Don Crespín, a resident of hacienda Xcanatún, confirmed the appeal of the CGT to peons and revealed why many opposed the Agrarian Bank. Don Crespín said that, in comparison with the Cardenista ejido, Felipe Carrillo Puerto's 1922–23 reform (which did not include henequen land) "was better . . . because the hacendado kept the hacienda, and the campesino had work. But Cárdenas did a great evil, because he took [the hacienda land] away and gave it to the campesino in name, but actually to the Agrarian Bank." Don Crespín believed—not without reason—that the hacendado had to treat the workers well because their future depended on keeping a loyal labor force, while neither federal engineer nor ejidatario really cared how the ejido ran because neither ultimately depended on its profits.[51]

Was Don Crespín representative of peon opinion? Nicolas Dzul, a peon on the Too hacienda, spoke decades later of its former owners, remembering Don Alfredo Molina Castilla as "good-hearted, very sociable, very caring and friendly with all the workers" during his periodic visits to his estate to hand out gifts and attend church with the peons. Dzul also spoke favorably of the owner because of the good wages paid on the hacienda during the Great Depression.[52]

It was not only that many hacendados played the "good owner" to the hilt: the isolation of the hacienda itself also reinforced peon attachment to the estate and hacendado.[53] It seems most likely that positive (security, godparentage) as well as negative (isolation, stigmatization as inferior by outsiders) factors linked peons to hacendados, and this paternalistic relationship created an environment in which CGT unions could often mobilize popular support against Cardenista agrarian reform.

However, the CGT was not merely reinforcing the traditional cultural and economic linkage between owners and peons, despite the subsidies and support that it received from some of the wealthiest hacendados. The most basic appeal of the CGT's ideology was its articulation of popular resentment of the Agrarian Bank. Although the Agrarian Bank claimed to be merely a lending agency for ejidatarios, its employees ran the ejidos. Because Cárdenas and federal agencies forced hacendados to pay the minimum wage, the CGT encouraged peons and peasants working on ejidos to demand from the Agrarian Bank the minimum wage and other legal entitlements, such as medical care, compensation for work-related accidents, and free schooling for their children. Reyes admitted that the Agrarian Bank simply could not afford to give ejidatarios these necessities. When peons and peasants pressed their demands, Reyes responded "that the land belongs to the ejidatarios, not the bank."[54] But, given that bank accountants paid the workers, and bank-appointed checkers and overseers made work assignments on henequen ejidos, such arguments convinced few.

While the agraristas tried to whip up popular support for agrarian reform by denouncing the hacendados' wealth, the CGT turned the tables on the Cardenistas by pointing out that, while peasants and peons often earned a mere three pesos weekly in the ejido, federal engineers reportedly earned fifty pesos daily, bought shirts worth a hundred pesos, and drove cars worth four thousand pesos.[55] The inability of the ejidos to provide enough work and the discrimination against peons by village-dwelling peasants and by Agrarian Bank officials were other stock themes in the CGT discourse.[56]

There was clearly a deep mistrust of the Cardenista agrarian bureaucracy among supporters of the CGT. Where the national Cardenistas saw a landlord plot to wreck agrarian reform by withholding work, peons and peasants sympathetic to the CGT saw in the ejidos' problems the handiwork of misguided and autocratic agrarian engineers.[57] The CGT's demand that the Agrarian Bank's budget be used to aid unemployed peons and underemployed peasants directly instead of paying bank employees resonated across the henequen zone.[58]

Denunciations of Reyes and ejidal caciques were staples of CGT propaganda.[59] The CGT denounced the Agrarian Bank for allying with corrupt politicians of the PSS, town councilmen, and agrarian leaders. Petty tyrants backed by the Agrarian Bank, claimed the CGT, denied its members local economic and political resources.[60] The intracommunal disputes between the CGT and agrarian Cardenistas often ran along the social fault line between peons and peasants. Even before Cárdenas, estate-dwelling peons were marginalized, effectively denied much input into municipal government and the PSS. Socialist leaders often jailed peons who left the party for the CGT and pressured hacendados to fire workers who joined it.[61] The CGT, then, offered the numerically large but fragmented population of peons a means of banding together for mutual defense.[62]

While the CGT rallied peons by attacking the Agrarian Bank, it had to walk a fine line between criticizing it and directly attacking Cárdenas. To avoid offending the president, the CGT labeled agrarian reform "a Communism that dares not confess its true name," a conspiracy to seize control of all political, social, and economic organizations in Yucatán in order to test Communist ideas that would later be imposed on the rest of the nation.[63] The CGT warned peons that the supporters of agrarian reform would take away their land and that Communist schoolteachers ("pseudo-Communist agitators") would take away their children.[64]

The CGT's solution to the economic problems and political tensions caused by agrarian reform was simple: kick out the Agrarian Bank and replace the collective ejido with small, privately owned plots of land. In the fall of 1936, Yucatán's delegation introduced a resolution at the CGT's national convention, declaring that its members were "totally sincere revolutionaries who truly desire that the revolutionary government [of Cárdenas] enjoy prestige" but asking that Cárdenas end the "economic servitude" of the "official capitalist patron," the Agrarian Bank. In its place, the CGT proposed "truly viable cultivation" of individual plots of henequen.[65] Federal officials feared that, if land were granted to individuals, hacendados would quickly buy out the new class of smallholders and reassemble their old haciendas, just as prerevolutionary hacendados had bought out the peasants' individual plots when the original communal ejidos were broken up in the late nineteenth century and the early twentieth.[66] Nevertheless, the appeal of private ownership of land struck a deep chord with both peons and peasants in rural Yucatán. Peasants harbored a deeply held faith in the individual rights of the *hombre libre* (free man).[67] The CGT juxtaposed the individual liberty to work one's own plot of land against Reyes's "ignominious tutelage."[68]

Unlike the collective henequen ejido, whose kinks were being painfully worked out, the individual plot was a proven alternative. In 1934, a year before agrarian reform began, there were already at least three thousand peasant smallholders growing henequen. The CGT's plan promised to combine individual plots into "ejidal districts," which would coordinate cultivation and processing, thus avoiding the poor organization and faulty centralized planning of the collective ejido.[69] Existing haciendas, obliquely referred to as "henequen units," would be spared total breakup into ejidos, thus lowering the transition costs of agrarian reform by keeping production and employment up.[70]

The CGT's spread in the henequen zone in 1934 and 1935 underscores the popular appeal of its message and the failures of the Agrarian Bank in Yucatán as well as the ability of Yucatán's plantocracy to deploy its formidable economic, political, and social resources. Against the ejido's questionable economic future and undemocratic structure, the CGT promised peasants and peons their own plot and liberty to work it. A close examination of the experience of one rural community, Muxupip, during the period 1934–36 will reveal how the CGT built a powerful popular base in the henequen zone by skillfully exploiting the shortcomings of Cardenista agrarian reform.

Muxupip: Crucible of Agrarian Reform

Muxupip is close to the heart of the henequen zone. It boasted a long history of popular resistance to landowners, a culture of opposition that could trace its roots back to the Revolution. The great Yucatecan Socialist leader Felipe Carrillo Puerto had won his first strong following among the peasants of Muxupip before the Revolution.[71] As governor, Carrillo Puerto rewarded Muxupip with one of the first provisional donations of (non-henequen) land.[72] When Cardenista agrarian reform began, Candelario Reyes sought to graft Cardenismo onto Muxupip's Socialist roots.

Fortunately for the Agrarian Bank, a cadre of active peasant leadership remained in Muxupip almost a decade after the death of Don Felipe. Although the PSS in Muxupip had weakened, revolutionary sentiment persisted.[73] The leader of the agrarian Cardenistas in 1935, Diego Domínguez Tacú, was a thirty-one-year-old peon who had been politically active since his youth. Domínguez remained deeply grateful to Don Felipe for giving him a scholarship to study at the Model Agricultural School in Mérida. The radical tradition of the community nurtured by Domínguez and other veteran Socialist leaders led one resident to describe Muxupip as "100 percent Carrillista."[74]

In organizing the ejido, Candelario Reyes drew on the local Carrillista tradition and the mythic image of Felipe Carrillo as Martyr of the Maya slain by reactionaries. Because many Muxipipeños believed that hacendado Felipe G. Cantón paid to have Carrillo Puerto assassinated in 1924, Reyes told Muxupip's peasants that agrarian reform would avenge Carrillo Puerto's death by "taking everything from him and screwing [Felipe G. Cantón] good because I know he is one of those who paid to have poor Felipe killed."[75]

For his part, Cantón, probably the state's wealthiest landowner, galvanized the owners of the estates around Muxupip. When their haciendas were threatened with partial expropriation, Cantón and lesser landowners fired workers and cut wages in order to turn popular opinion against the federal Agrarian Bank.[76] They underwrote a local organization of the CGT (the Union of Peasants and Ejidatarios) in Muxupip and three neighboring haciendas, using as their front man a charismatic peasant turned peddler, Santos A. "El Gallo" Chalé. Followers of "El Gallo" (The Cock) turned out to CGT meetings to enjoy a chocolomo (festive barbecue) probably washed down with free alcohol, adopting his macho nickname and styling themselves Gallistas.[77]

The economic situation in Muxupip worked in favor of the hacendados and the CGT. Peons, some 30 percent of Muxupip county's population, could not join the ejido of Muxupip and would thus lose their livelihood if agrarian reform were carried out.[78] Hacendados also upped wages and offered more jobs on their other haciendas to make ejido membership less attractive. As another material incentive, hacendados offered some peons free shoots of henequen so that they could cultivate their own plots.[79] Felipe G. Cantón wielded the power to hire and fire as a political weapon: when the ejido of a neighboring pueblo threatened to take land from another of his haciendas, Kancabchén, he replaced peasants from that town with Gallistas from Muxupip.[80] CGT organizer Santos A. Chalé pointed out that, unlike the Agrarian Bank, the landlords paid the minimum wage and gave workers a paid seventh day of rest (as required by federal law).[81]

As in other areas of the state, the CGT of Muxupip appealed to peasants' preference to control their own means of support and avoid dependence on either federal bureaucrats or hacendados. Writing on behalf of the peasants of Muxupip, Santos A. Chalé told President Cárdenas: "They ask to receive parcels as they are due under the Agrarian Code, to support themselves and not to turn over their products to the agrarian engineer under the pretext of collective work in the guise of false cooperatives that force them to work for them [the agrarian engineers]."[82]

Landowners coupled their efforts to attract popular support through the CGT with the co-optation of local institutions. They bribed Muxupip's mayor and town secretary, the president of the Socialist Party league, and even the first president of the ejido into joining the Gallistas and opposing the Agrarian Bank.[83] Reyes wrote Governor Alayola in mid-July 1935 that agrarian reform in Muxupip had effectively been blocked by "difficulties due to the influence of the hacendados over the dissidents [opponents of the ejido] and over the actions of the town council and the local Socialist Party." Indeed, the agrarian Cardenistas of Muxupip found themselves in the minority by mid-1935.[84]

To try to resolve the problems of Muxupip, the district chief of the Agrarian Bank recommended that the "dissidents" of Muxupip be integrated into the ejido.[85] Despite the Agrarian Bank's orders, the leader of the agrarian Cardenistas, Diego Domínguez Tacú, refused to give the Gallistas work or share scarce resources with people they considered to be enemies of the Revolution. The Gallista mayor and Santos A. Chalé insisted the people wanted "free labor" on the haciendas, not the low pay of the ejido.[86]

As haciendas locked more workers out and the date for the distribution of estate lands (13 August 1935) approached, tensions between Muxupip's agrarian Cardenistas and Santos A. Chalé's self-styled "free workers" escalated. On the last day of July 1935, the Gallistas and their foes clashed violently.[87] Although a detachment of state police restored calm, the agrarian Cardenistas held a secret meeting and then armed themselves with the help of sympathetic officials of the Agrarian Bank. On the eve of the scheduled transfer of much of the hacendados' land to Muxupip's ejido, the community remained deeply divided between a majority who resisted the ejido and an embattled minority backed by the Agrarian Bank. Agrarian Cardenistas admitted that Gallistas outnumbered them some 180 to 120, but they felt that their opponents were dupes of the landlords.[88]

Even after the Agrarian Bank declared that land from four haciendas belonged to the ejido, landowners flagrantly ignored the decree and refused to negotiate with federal officials or the agrarian Cardenistas of Muxupip. The antiagrarian mayor had to be forced to sign the act bringing the local credit chapter of the Agrarian Bank—the economic base of the ejido—into legal existence.[89] At the invitation of Cantón, Gallistas continued to cut henequen from the fields of his hacienda, San Juan Koop, claimed by Muxupip's ejido.[90] Hacendados eagerly bought this poached sisal, thus draining the ejido's future income and encouraging ejidatarios to desert. At this critical moment, Santos A. Chalé announced that hacendados would pay wages 33 percent higher than advances on the ejido, creating another incentive for people to oppose it. Santos Chalé also played on widespread suspicion of the agrarian engineers, saying that the ejido's profits would go to the bureaucrats, not to the people. After nearly a month of widespread popular resistance by the Gallistas, the Agrarian Bank had to send in a small detachment of federal troops to occupy the fields claimed by the ejido.[91]

A few weeks later, the Agrarian Bank worked out a less coercive solution: Muxupip's agrarian Cardenistas grudgingly agreed to admit their enemies into the ejido, although the status of peons remained unclear.[92] This second truce soon fell apart in part because the ejido could not give enough work and in part because neighboring ejidos expanded onto land claimed originally by Muxupip.[93] The future looked equally grim: a year after its founding, only one field of Muxupip's ejidos had been seeded with the young sprouts needed to sustain production and make up for the lack of productive land.[94]

In January 1936, the agrarian engineers had helped agrarian Cardenistas file petitions for more land, but opponents of the ejido still refused to join, leaving only eighty petitioners.[95] The community remained deeply polarized through all 1936. Tiring of "El Gallo," Candelario Reyes hauled him before the governor in Mérida and threatened him with imprisonment should he not desist immediately.[96] The Agrarian Bank remained so unpopular that in mid-1936 its chief in Muxupip's zone was stoned by residents while touring its ejidos.[97]

Widespread popular opposition continued to thwart the functioning of Muxupip's ejido until 1937, when the Gallistas finally abandoned the CGT and joined the agrarian faction. The union was personally sealed with a visit by President Cárdenas in August 1937. The consolidation of the ejido and its acceptance of peons under a presidential mandate led to the migration of peons from neighboring hacienda communities to Muxupip.[98] Some three years after its founding, the ejido finally triumphed—not because agrarian reform won opponents over, but because, after years of struggle, resisting peons and peasants and the hacendados that backed them realized that further opposition was hopeless in the face of Cárdenas's determination to redistribute land. The residents of Muxupip did receive some economic relief in September 1937, during Cárdenas's visit, when the president gave the pueblo an additional 856 mecates of henequen.[99]

The ejido in Muxupip clearly failed to achieve the Cardenista goals of economic improvement and broad popular mobilization. Candelario Reyes's invocation of the mythic figure of Carrillo Puerto and the promise of economic self-sufficiency failed to inspire most peasants, while the landlords' economic incentives and the CGT's discourse of independence for "free workers" swayed peasants and local leaders alike. Of course, the ejido was plagued, not just by insufficient land and capital, but by the landlords' sabotage and punitive layoffs and the corruption of local officials. In contrast to its actions in other localities, the Agrarian Bank's attitude toward peasants in Muxupip was far from autocratic. Reyes never backed an ejidal cacique to squelch opposition. Instead, he and bank officials tried to smooth over local divisions by counseling reconciliation. In the end, the majority of Muxupip's residents reluctantly joined the ejido, but the Cardenista reform was popularly perceived as intervention, not liberation. Agrarian reform failed to forge popular support for Cárdenas among most residents of Muxupip; instead, it hardened attitudes of suspicion and apathy toward the national state.

Popular Antiagrarianism in Tixkokob and Beyond

If Cantón and other hacendados were to halt agrarian reform, they would have to follow the example of Muxupip and unify peon and peasant discontent into a single, statewide organization. Urban labor would need to be brought into the fold and a united urban-rural coalition against land reform created under the banner of the CGT's anarchosyndicalism. On 1 September 1935, the CGT took the bold step of organizing a local federation of CGT unions in the provincial town of Tixkokob, located in the center of the henequen zone to the east of Mérida. The headquarters of the federation, the Casa del Campesino (House of the Peasant), would provide a focus for local activities of the CGT and a counterbalance to the PSS-controlled town hall of Tixkokob. Workers from allied urban anarchist unions in Mérida helped organize the Tixkokob peasant and peon federation in order to cement an urban-rural coalition.[100] The CGT also invited several federal bureaucrats to the ceremonies, including the chief of the federal troops in the state, General Rafael Cházaro Pérez — a young, charismatic native Yucatecan with political ambitions and close ties to Cárdenas — and delegates of the national Departments of Health and Agriculture. Their presence countered charges that the CGT was just a front for the hacendados and suggested that the Cardenista regime actually endorsed it.

The public ceremony opening the Tixkokob headquarters also gave the CGT the chance to restate and publicly affirm its doctrine. The CGT was determined to set the record straight on its ties to hacendados. An unidentified speaker at the Tixkokob rally complained that the CGT had been slandered as anti-Cárdenas by malicious "official elements" for asking for fair agrarian reform.[101] To justify its advocacy of the continued existence of haciendas, the CGT compared them favorably to state-run ejidos as the lesser of two evils.[102] And, as it always had, the CGT endorsed the idea of "independent" small plots free from the poor management and onerous supervision of the federal engineers. The CGT charged the latter with "not giving them [the peasants] their own land and imposing political *capataces* [overseers] more voracious than their old *amos* [lords]."[103] Singled out for special criticism was Estanislao Chim, who had controlled politics in Tixkokob for over thirteen years already and was now exploiting the ejido to continue his rule.[104]

A local PSS official in Tixkokob reacted by sending in pro-Socialist peasants to invade and vandalize the recently opened CGT headquarters. Sensitive to the fact that high-ranking federal officials had just attended the building's opening, Tixkokob officials were quick to point out to Cárdenas that hacendados' overseers led the CGT in Tixkokob.[105] Although the CGT's hammer-and-coa alliance of peasants and workers against agrarian reform was thwarted, the experience of organizing at Tixkokob would be tried on a larger scale in the fall of 1935. This time, the results would be much more to the CGT's liking.

The Fall of Governor Alayola

The aborted CGT offensive in Tixkokob was part of a larger strategy designed to mobilize peons in the countryside against agrarian reform and unite them with independent, urban labor unions upset with Alayola's conservative labor policies. Hacendados, anarchosyndicalist workers in Mérida and Progreso, and the CGT peon unions all shared a common foe in Alayola. Working together, peons and hacendados sought to overthrow him as a way to stall land reform, while independent labor wanted to end harassment by state officials. They moved against the embattled governor at a propitious time, when the national struggle raging since June 1935 between President Cárdenas and his former mentor, Plutarco Elías Calles, led to the overthrow of governors like Alayola associated with the former maximum chief's regime.

Alayola's number one enemy in Mexico City was General Francisco Mújica. At the time, Mújica was minister of communications and public workers, but he had previously served as federal military zone commander in Yucatán, where he developed a low opinion of Alayola for his lack of radicalism.[106] The beleaguered governor also felt undercut by the growing power of Agrarian Bank chief Candelario Reyes, who hounded the governor to move more quickly on the agrarian reform front.[107] When the governor flew to Mexico City to confer with Cárdenas in September 1935, the president dismissed Alayola's protests against Reyes and sent him back with strict orders to counter "disruptive forces."[108] Alayola was increasingly preoccupied with these "disruptive forces" — the CGT and independent labor — because they threatened to make Yucatán ungovernable, a key concept in relations between the national government and state governments.

Since the Porfiriato, governors of Mexican states ruled at the pleasure of the president. Should a state become ungovernable, the president removed the governor. All political actors understood the rules of the game, and, consequently, opponents of governors historically have schemed to plunge their states into chaotic situations to force the president to remove governors. As president, Cárdenas continued to hold state governors responsible for maintaining the governability of their states.

But, after the Cárdenas-Calles break in June 1935, with the new emphasis on agrarian reform and the opening of politics to the masses, Cárdenas gave workers and peasants a role in deciding when a governor should be ousted. If popular forces convinced Cárdenas that a governor was unpopular and opposed to the interests of workers and peasants, then by "right of the majority" they could demand his removal.[109]

Alayola had good reason to fear workers' invoking this right. In spite of attempts at suppression by the state government and the PSS, several strong independent labor organizations had emerged in 1933. By September 1935, Alayola was on a collision course with the most potent independent (non-

PSS) labor organization in Yucatán: the Union of Peninsular Railroad Workers (Sindicato de Ferrocarrilleros Peninsular, or SFP). For years, corruption and mismanagement had plagued the government-run railroad cooperative. By 1935, it faced bankruptcy owing to a 17 million peso debt, it had no way to make good back pay owed employees, and its monthly income was dropping steadily.[110] Encouraged by national Secretary of Communications Mújica, the SFP threatened a strike to demand a worker takeover of the state railroads.[111] On 14 September, the SFP formed a united front with the other independent labor organizations in Yucatán: the Communist Independent Syndical Front (Frente Sindical Independiente, or FSI); the Regional Federation of Workers and Peasants (Federación Regional de Obreros y Campesinos, or FROC), which represented most artisans and service workers in Mérida and was linked to national, radical labor leader Vicente Lombardo Toledano; the CGT; the Unión de Trabajadores de Enseñanza de Yucatán (UTEY), a Communist-influenced union of federal teachers; the Workers' Federation of Progreso (Federación Obrera de Progreso, or FOP); and the cordage factory workers (Sindicato de Cordeleros de Yucatán, or SCY). Together, the SFP and its allies called for a general strike to remove Alayola on the grounds of his Callismo and anti-labor policies and in the name of Cardenista democracy.[112]

Alayola's fate was sealed by the fact that Mérida and Yucatán as a whole were ungovernable after days of massive demonstrations. The governor failed to convince Cárdenas that hacendados would benefit and agrarian reform suffer with his removal because of the CGT's role in the strike. Just as importantly, the Cardenista arbiter of Yucatecan politics, federal military zone commander General Cházaro Pérez, ordered his troops not to disperse the strikers or allow Alayola to use state police or the remaining PSS stalwarts to contest the demonstrators' control of the streets. Unable to use force to end the strike, and with no help or mediation forthcoming from Mexico City, an exhausted Alayola accepted the inevitable and resigned on the evening of 5 October. Alayola nominated his close friend and secretary of government, Fernando López Cárdenas, as interim governor.[113]

The choice of López Cárdenas raised more than a few eyebrows. First, he was close not only to Alayola, but also to the Bartolista camarilla around Callista-era governor Bartolomé García Correa (1930–33). Second, his actions during the strike seemed opportunistic. López Cárdenas had handled the negotiations with the SFP that had failed to head off the strike, but now, with Alayola out of the picture, he quickly resolved the dispute by turning the railroads over to the workers. Not only did the energetic new governor quickly end festering labor disputes, but he could also count on his friendship with Francisco Mújica and the support of General Rafael Cházaro Pérez to smooth his acceptance in Mexico City.[114]

Such support was widely rumored to have been bought: it was whispered that López Cárdenas had greased his rapid rise to power and purchased the support of General Cházaro with money supplied by the landowner Francisco Vega y Loyo, whom the new governor soon appointed as mayor of Mérida.[115] Because Cházaro was the president's privileged intermediary in Yucatán, and because the federal military had traditionally served to remove and install governors on orders from Mexico City, his support for López Cárdenas (purchased or not) and his report to Cárdenas that Yucatán was now free of Callismo allowed López Cárdenas to retain power. Consequently, the strikers, most of whom backed hacendado front man Alfredo J. Pérez, failed to convince Cárdenas to name their man governor.[116]

López Cárdenas clearly understood both the national situation and the national Cardenista agenda. He supported his claim to the governorship on the "classist" ideals of the president, which required politicians to identify their interests with those of workers and peasants.[117] The new interim governor also promised Cárdenas that, under his administration, agrarian reform would be carried out to "free the peons from the old slave prisons of the decrepit capitalist system."[118]

Behind the radical rhetoric, López Cárdenas crafted a political deal that split apart the independent labor groups that had participated in the general strike. He buried the hatchet with the Communist FSI and the independent labor unions of the FROC as well as with two small student groups.[119] The addition of the FSI and the FROC to the PSS and Reyes's agrarian Cardenistas finally gave López Cárdenas a coalition that allowed him to claim a popular mandate and beat back the CGT. Coupled with General Cházaro's endorsement, the battle for regional power was over, at least for the moment.

On 14 October, President Cárdenas telegraphed General Cházaro his full support for López Cárdenas.[120] Moreover, Cárdenas condemned attacks on Reyes and the Agrarian Bank, singling out the CGT and some federal teachers as "agitators" who were "attacking the agrarian program of the Revolution and defending the great landowners."[121]

After the Fall of Alayola: Whither Cardenismo?

At first glance, the strike that toppled Alayola seemed a clear-cut Cardenista victory. The alliance of teachers, workers, peons, and peasants that protested against the conservative governor suggested that there was a tremendous political force in the workshops of Mérida and on the haciendas of the henequen zone that the Cardenistas could mobilize. The young independent labor movements organizing workers and peons all pledged their support for Cardenismo. If labor could be united with the peasant beneficiaries of agrarian reform, a grassroots Cardenista coalition would be created. Candelario Reyes and Rafael Cházaro Pérez wielded national power effectively in the state, demonstrating the ability of the national Cardenista government to intervene in regional politics despite recalcitrant regional interests.

However, the fall of Alayola also demonstrated the weakness of Cardenismo. As we have seen, agrarian reform, the keystone of Cardenista state formation, suffered from serious problems, and the political power of the agrarian Cardenistas created a strong backlash. Hacendados adeptly exploited contradictions within the Cardenista alliance, mobilizing peons for their own political ends. Vertical ties connecting labor and peasant leaders to regional camarillas had yet to be replaced by horizontal, class-based political allegiances.

Even after the resolution of the strikes, the future of Cardenismo in Yucatán remained unclear. The removal of Alayola satisfied just about everyone, but Cárdenas's decision to recognize López Cárdenas as governor and keep Candelario Reyes as head of the federal Agrarian Bank in Yucatán prolonged other serious conflicts. Powerful hacendados, the CGT, and independent labor unions opposed the new interim governor and would continue to attack federal agrarian reform.

A profusion of radical labor and peasant groups had promised to mobilize popular forces, flush out the remains of the corrupt Callista regime, and end the stranglehold of the hacendados over the henequen economy. However, the wave of popular support for Cárdenas never crested into a unified popular front. Although independent labor overthrew the sitting governor, it failed to unify popular forces behind Cárdenas. The ejido's shortcomings and its exclusion of peons allowed the CGT to mobilize thousands of rural workers against Cardenista agrarian reform. Urban workers in Yucatán, too, remained largely outside the Cardenista camp.

On the local level as well, there were signs of trouble for Cardenismo. Federal labor regulations and land reform paradoxically empowered a new generation of ejidal bosses that sapped popular support for Cárdenas. All too often, popular leaders allied themselves with regional camarillas and opposed each other in bitter political struggles that stalled land reform and threw the region into political chaos: a complex, at times contradictory process that I will examine in the next chapter.

2

Left-Cardenismo and the López Cárdenas
Administration, 1935–1936

THE FALL OF ALAYOLA BARRERA represented a watershed for Cardenismo in Yucatán. Before it took place, two groups claimed to represent popular Cardenismo in the state. The first we can term *agrarian Cardenismo* — the peasants who made up the henequen collectives under the direction of Candelario Reyes and the federal Agrarian Bank. The second was known as *independent labor* — railroad (SFP) and cordage factory (SCY) workers, anarchosyndicalist peons of the CGT, and Communist (FSI) and non-Communist (FROC) labor federations. But neither agrarian Cardenismo nor independent labor could truly be considered a strong popular Cardenista movement.

As we have seen in the case of Muxupip discussed in chapter 1, agrarian Cardenistas were usually the minority factions in their communities, and they suffered from the economic and political blunders of the federal agrarian bureaucracy. While the independent labor faction, on the other hand, had much broader support among workers, peons, and some peasants, it generally opposed agrarian reform and in several cases aligned with elements of the old landowning class. In short, the agraristas were Cardenista but not broadly popular, while independent labor was more popular but not truly Cardenista.

The strike of October 1935, however, created an environment in which Cardenismo at last found a broad popular base in Yucatán. This is not to say that grassroots Cardenismo was created from above. Rather, federal and state governments worked alongside emerging popular groups to forward the national Cardenista agenda. The newly installed interim governor, Fernando López Cárdenas, expanded on the coalition that he had assembled during the strike of October 1935. He adopted much more radical policies and pacted with the Mexican Communist Party (Partido Comunista Mexicano, or PCM) in Yucatán.[1] This Left-state alliance created the political opening for thousands of peons, young people, and women to mobilize and would finally give Cardenismo its popular grounding in the state.

In this chapter, I will consider how Left-Cardenistas in many areas not only fought for local political power, but also challenged traditional gender, generation, and class boundaries. Local Left-Cardenista movements took different trajectories in various parts of Yucatán: the unionization of peon communities and successful strikes on haciendas in the western and southern henequen zone; the difficult task of organizing in less socially stratified and more Mayan communities in the far south and east; and the rejuvenation of the old Partido Socialista del Sureste (PSS) in the eastern henequen zone by a Communist cadre led by Rogerio Chalé. Finally, the chapter examines the continuing inability of the Cardenista agrarian bureaucracy to overcome the often violent, intracommunity struggles between pro- and antiagrarian factions that continued to hinder the formation of a broader popular Cardenista base in Yucatán.

Left-Cardenismo in Yucatán

The roots of the Left-state alliance lie, not in ideological common ground between López Cárdenas and the PCM, but in political self-interest. To keep his hold on power in Yucatán and maintain the support of the president, López Cárdenas tried to create a "united front" of workers and peasants committed to Cardenismo but firmly under his own control. He also tried to garner the support of the key national Cardenistas in Yucatán — the federal military commander in the state and Candelario Reyes, head of the Agrarian Bank. At the same time, López Cárdenas hoped to win over some hacendados to divide and neutralize the landowning class of Yucatán and fund his own camarilla.

In order to achieve his goal of mobilizing worker-peasant support, López Cárdenas reached out to four popular groups. First, he courted independent labor. Second, true to his Bartolista past (he was a federal congressman under Governor Bartolomé García Correa), he relied on old Bartolista caciques in several rural communities. Third, he tried to win over Reyes and incorporate the ejidatarios into his political base. Fourth, as we will see, he allied with the strong PCM in Yucatán.

Co-opting independent labor proved extremely difficult. Attempts to court labor politically through material concessions also fell short.[2] The governor's political outreach, however, had more success in the campo. López Cárdenas backed a generation of older, Bartolista-era caciques against town councils elected under the former governor, César Alayola Barrera. As a result, many towns in the maize-producing east and south became battlegrounds between Bartolista bosses championing the poor and municipal authorities linked to the provincial petite bourgeoisie, or vecinos.[3]

Consider events in the town of Tizimín. Merchants and landowners involved in the cattle, corn, and lumber economy of eastern Yucatán dominated its town council under Governor Alayola. To oust Tizimín's upper class from town hall, López Cárdenas dispatched a veteran Bartolista boss, José I. Villafaña (known by his foes as the "Hyena of the East"), to head the PSS league in the town. Tizimín's town council charged that Villafaña stirred up the populace against it with "numerous and constant appeals signed supposedly by workers, who on the whole can neither read nor write."[4] Under López Cárdenas, the old bosses were effective in some areas of the countryside, although their Callista-era origins, questionable ideology, and propensity for graft and violence made them unreliable allies at best.

In order to build a broader popular base, López Cárdenas aligned himself with the PCM in Yucatán. The governor, a former teacher, turned to an ex-student of his, Antonio Betancourt Pérez, a graduate of Moscow's Lenin Institute and recent head of federal schools in Yucatán, to serve as the nexus in this Left-state alliance. To seal the deal, López Cárdenas appointed Betancourt Pérez to head the state education system.

The Left saw this alliance with the state government as an opportunity to infiltrate its official party, the PSS, and parts of the state government with Communist cells. The young trucker and Communist Rogerio Chalé joined the PSS directorate in late 1935 and assumed its presidency in June 1936, another indication of the Left's growing power in the state government.[5] For his part, López Cárdenas believed that the Communists would replenish the leadership and popular base of the moribund PSS and thus strengthen his government.

Although there were definite tensions in the Left-state alliance over corrupt labor arbitration and some Communists' desires to avoid an entangling involvement with the state, that alliance strengthened both the governor and the PCM in Yucatán. Even before the pact with the state government, the PCM scored several successes in building grassroots support. Yucatecan Communism's core had been teachers, students, government employees, and a handful of radicalized workers. The rapid expansion in the Yucatecan Left came in October 1934, when it founded the labor federation known as the FSI to unionize peons and, to a much lesser extent, urban labor. Like other independent labor federations, the FSI bypassed hostile Yucatecan state authorities during the Alayola administration to register unions directly in Mexico City.[6] Direction of the FSI was shared between Betancourt Pérez, director of federal education in the state in early 1935, and Diego Mongiote Rosado, who had been fired in 1925 from his job working in a bakery when caught eating a piece of bread.[7] Rosado brought to the PCM years of experience organizing urban workers in Mérida as well as a fluency in Maya and a rural background that would greatly aid him in the countryside.[8]

It was on the large henequen haciendas south and west of Mérida that the FSI found its grassroots base. It focused on peons, the rural proletariat who lived and worked on henequen haciendas. Given their insularity, social conservatism, and clientelistic links with landowners, peons would seem to be an unlikely group for the PCM to organize. However, the Great Depression undermined paternalistic relations on estates, and the federal agrarian reform that began in 1935 further worsened peons' economic situation. The Left focused its recruiting efforts on the larger haciendas in the southwest part of the henequen zone, where peons often experienced more strained relationships with owners.[9]

Although urban workers often served as FSI organizers, federal teachers in Article 123 schools proved to be the key link between the PCM and peons.[10] At a time when the Great Depression continued to weigh heavily on workers, the FSI's teacher-delegates assisted peons to bargain collectively.[11] They set up consumer cooperatives on haciendas where peons had previously been at the mercy of one storekeeper and forced landowners to respect peons' right to grow corn.[12] The FSI intervened to help peons in numerous other ways, such as ejecting from their communities those who spied for owners and aiding peons unjustly fired by a hacendado for participating in the scholastic census.[13]

From the start, Communist teachers' outreach to peons coupled material improvement with a cultural campaign: in place of religious festivals and men's recreational drinking, the FSI tried to build a new communal life through basketball and baseball (for girls as well as for boys), patriotic festivals, and adult literacy campaigns. In place of the crucifix and *jaranas* (traditional folk dances), the FSI spread new symbols (the red hammer and sickle painted on schoolhouse walls) and songs of the international Left. All these activities, especially night schools for adults, were intended both to create new foci of social life and, less obviously, to serve as forums to raise class consciousness.[14]

As director of federal education in Yucatán in 1935, Betancourt Pérez had stocked hacienda and rural schools with young leftists. He used his new position as head of state education under López Cárdenas to make the state school system a second transmission zone for the PCM. The PSS-affiliated League of (State) Teachers dissolved at the end of 1935, replaced by the new Union of Revolutionary Teachers (Unión de Maestros Revoluciona-rios, or UMR), which, like the FSI, was covertly controlled by the PCM. Betancourt Pérez's shake-up of the state education system also resulted in promising experiments with bilingual instruction, a normal school to train rural teachers, and the creation of ninety-eight night schools for adults where leftist instructors schooled thousands of men and women.[15]

Under Betancourt Pérez, the Cardenista-PCM project implemented in the rural schoolhouse stressed self-improvement, vocational education, and the dangers of alcohol as well as the need for land reform, unionization, and a more inclusive government. The teachers' message, then, blended Marxist ideas of class struggle with a generic Mexican revolutionary and patriotic agenda that espoused modernization, science, and a strong nation.[16]

The FSI's peon unionization drive began in early 1935 but accelerated in late 1935 and early 1936, when López Cárdenas's state government worked with leftist state teachers to aid the FSI's campaign. The Left-state alliance threatened hacendados with higher labor costs, strikes, and, in a few cases, land reform. In response, landowners co-opted state labor officials, police-men, members of the federal military, even leaders of the PSS and rival labor federations, to try to halt the FSI.[17] Hacienda Temozón, in the municipality of Abala, was the site of the longest and bloodiest struggles between the Left and its foes.

In early 1936, federal rural teachers and FSI workers from Mérida's beer factory began to organize the peons on Temozón. The FSI's devotion of considerable resources to Temozón reflected its strategic location as gate-way to the southern henequen zone and the formidable reputation of its owner, Humberto Peón Suárez (son of a prerevolutionary governor and peninsular Brahmin). For almost a year, the state FSI and the sympathetic state labor inspector José María Bolio Méndez supported Temozón's work-ers in a long strike to try to force Humberto Peón to accept a collective contract. Before the strike ended, the battle between the FSI and Peón would become a symbolic test of wills between Cardenistas and their foes that attracted national attention. After months of escalating threats on both sides and repeated, and failed, attempts to break the strike through replace-ment workers and the corruption of state and local officials, the FSI filed an agrarian claim to seize most of the estate. Shortly thereafter, on 19 January 1937, estate employees shot and killed two peons active in the FSI. In the resulting firestorm of national publicity, Peón could no longer count on sympathetic officials to aid him. It would take direct presidential intervention, however, to finally end the strike on Temozón.[18]

The FSI's peon unionization resulted in several long strikes and occasional violent confrontations with hacendados and white unions across the southern and western henequen zone and around Mérida. To make matters even more difficult for the Left, after the death of Cardenista general Rafael Cházaro Pérez the new federal military commander in Yucatán, General Ignacio Otero Pablos, took a much dimmer view of peon unionization — perhaps influenced by close contacts between his general staff and some hacendados. He began to order his troops to harass the FSI, reportedly in return for financial considerations.[19]

Even intimidation by federal troops could not slow the growth of the FSI in the henequen zone. But, in the corn-growing south and east, the Left encountered a new set of challenges.[20] In a few towns, the Left gained a strong foothold.

In Maní, a typical town in the maize-producing southern half of Yucatán, the FSI aided peasants in their struggle against a handful of families who had long controlled commerce and political power. From 1936 until at least the early 1940s, leftist federal teachers helped peasant leaders in Maní brave attacks by the municipal police in order to organize land invasions, file agrarian reform petitions, and remove abusive local officials. Maní's FSI even demanded that the parsonage abandoned by an expelled Spanish priest be turned over to serve as the ejido's office. Not only did the Left give Maní peasants legal and political support in their fight against provincial burghers, but it also gave them a critical discourse with which to challenge historical inequities in the distribution of land and power. A petition signed by some 120 peasants on 1 March 1938, demanding the removal of a corrupt president of the ejido, characterized their enemies as "prochurch and reactionary"; "[they are] always against the workers and have always lived through extortion."[21] But the Left's success in Maní was exceptional, as most attempts to create FSI peasant unions in the maize zone of the south and east proved ephemeral.

The economic and social structure of these areas posed difficult obstacles for the Left. Communities outside the henequen zone tended to be smaller and more autonomous than henequen towns; class differences existed but were less extreme than on plantations, making class-based organizing more difficult. The persistence of Mayan culture in the south and east presented another challenge for the Left. Although in 1932 the PCM called for special attention to the "indigenous problem" of Mexico, education remained predominantly monolingual (Spanish only), and the Left's leaders failed to build on pueblos' collective traditions. Leftist organizers—usually teachers from the city—often saw peasants as dependent on them for leadership and incapable of acting without considerable guidance from them.[22] In areas where homegrown leaders were not nurtured, the Left failed to put down deep roots.

Left-Cardenismo as Social Revolution: Young People and Women

Failures in the south and east were offset by the Left's remarkable success in organizing women and young people. In early 1936, the Communist professor Hernán Morales Medina founded a Yucatecan chapter of the Young Socialists (Juventud Socialista Unida de México, or JSUM). The Young Socialists established chapters in provincial towns as well as Mérida's mushrooming suburbs and older, working-class neighborhoods.[23] Its Instituto Cultural Obrera (Institute for Workers' Culture) in Mérida offered almost fifty classes nightly. Instruction in the school aimed at spreading the PCM's doctrine; among the social sciences offered were history of the world workers' movement (beginning with the French Revolution), theory and practice of workers' rights, and history of socialist thought. The economics class included the building blocks of Marxist economics. Geography boasted several classes on the Soviet Union and only one on the United States.[24] Despite its frankly political orientation (classes stuck close to the party line), its vocational curriculum (commercial correspondence, accounting) and enrichment activities (appreciation of classical music, movies, expeditions to the museum and library) had a distinctly bourgeois ring to them. The Young Socialists' focus on drawing young people away from delinquency and unemployment with sports, bringing dropouts back to the classroom, and campaigning against young adult illiteracy dovetailed with the social goals of Cardenismo. The Young Socialists' compromise between consciousness-raising and social betterment was summed up in the institute's mission statement, which called for spreading "revolutionary theory" as well as "useful technical skills for the daily struggle."[25]

The Young Socialists gained a remarkable following, not only because of the PCM's political outreach, but also because its social assemblies—with a strong dose of sports and recreation — responded to the needs and aspirations of young people in a traditional society in transition. It appealed to young men and women increasingly aware of political ideas that promised both social and individual liberation in the form of freedom from the restraints of the patriarchal family. There were strong similarities with Chile in the 1960s and early 1970s, when the Communist Youth transformed neighborhood sports clubs into cradles of the popular Left.[26]

At its peak, the Young Socialists claimed some sixteen thousand members in Mérida and the countryside — an inflated figure perhaps, but even half that number would have been impressive. Like the FSI, the Young Socialists set up municipal committees that campaigned in town council and ejidal elections.[27]

If the outreach to young people represented one case of Left-Cardenista cooperation, the mobilization of women represented another successful joint attempt to organize an even more marginalized sector of society. On 15 January 1936, Communist federal *profesoras* headed by Dolores Uribe de Peraza (wife of Communist teachers' leader Gaudencio Peraza) created a Yucatecan affiliate of the national United Front for Women's Rights (Frente Unica Pro-Derechos de Mujeres, or FUPDM). As they did other leftist popular organizations, teachers dominated the regional FUPDM leadership, although some local directorates boasted a strong *campesina* presence.[28] Moreover, although the FSI's urban presence remained generally weak, the FUPDM did unionize the only group of urban women workers organized in the 1930s: those laboring in Mérida's cigarette factory.[29]

The strength of the FUPDM was especially impressive considering that the official feminism of the Left was often tepid at best. A prominent male Yucatecan Communist teacher wrote a primer for adult literacy that also served as a political dictionary of the Left. In it, he specified that support for women's demands was not the same as feminism, characterized negatively as women's struggle against men.[30] Nevertheless, the FUPDM supported the Cardenista goals of improving wages and working conditions for women as guaranteed under the Federal Labor Code and of bettering the lives of women through libraries, night schools, health centers, and cooperatives. It also aimed to incorporate women — especially peasant and indigenous women — into the "larger culture" of Mexico. At times, the FUPDM challenged the economic subordination of women by founding cooperatives and in at least one case offered legal aid to a woman abandoned by her husband.[31]

Much of the Left's success in Yucatán must be attributed to the fact that it gave women a role (albeit a subordinate one) in organizing students, teachers, and peons—this at a time when women were virtually excluded from politics and labor unions. In the western village of Kinchil, young campesina Felipa Poot led a popular leftist movement that included both women and men, a striking development in Mexican politics. With the aid of federal teacher Bartolomé Cervera, Poot and other peasants founded a charcoal cooperative, built a strong adult literacy program, and liberated Kinchil from the grip of hated caciques.[32]

Efforts like those in Kinchil called into question the social status quo of conservative, rural Yucatán. The Young Socialists upset traditional carnival festivities in Tizimín by organizing well-to-do young women as well as workers and peasants into a social club that crossed class and ethnic lines.[33] The conservative *Diario de Yucatán* noted with disdain that thirty Communist students ran through the streets of Motul screaming insults offensive to families with children and then publicly confronted hacendado Miguel Ceballos in a park.[34] The sight of rowdy young people challenging an older member of the dominant class in a public space shocked the provincial elite of Motul—and probably older peasants as well. Taken together, all these events suggest that the Left encouraged a genuinely radical spirit among the young, the poor, and women in many areas of the campo.

Still, agitation often outpaced local organizing. Mobilization along lines of gender, generation, and class was often abandoned in favor of politicking and the search for bureaucratic posts.[35] Reflecting on the Yucatecan Left over fifty years later, Betancourt Pérez said that although the PCM organized many cells in the countryside, it used "exaggeration and provocation" to magnify its strength.[36] Painting the hammer and sickle on schoolhouse walls was easier than building a party organization from the ground up, and both time and resources were always limited. Leftist organizers' agitprop and bluff whipped up support, but, at times, such tactics threatened to overshadow their program.[37] Moreover, the Right seized on attacks on patriarchy and traditional social mores to denounce the allegedly antifamily values of Cárdenas's program.[38]

The FSI's project provoked strong resistance in other ways: old Socialist bosses resented its political potential, landlords opposed peon unionization and land reform, and merchants and artisans feared consumer and producer cooperatives. The backlash against the Left was widespread and often violent. On many estates, peons were fired (and in at least one case had their huts burned) for joining the FSI, and teachers constantly faced threats and physical attacks when they presented peon demands. In Kinchil, political enemies assassinated Poot in March 1936 during the senatorial campaign (see chap. 3).[39]

In trying to create a new consciousness among peasants and peons, federal teachers had to face other, less obvious obstacles. They had to win over a rural populace generally suspicious of outsiders and state representatives in particular.[40] Reading between the lines of FSI bulletins and archival correspondence, we find a picture of the Left's relationship with peasants and peons somewhat at odds with its representation of its agents as selfless guides of the downtrodden. The hierarchical structure of the FSI and its subordination to secretive Communist cells meant that control of local organizations remained mainly in the hands of outsiders — teachers and occasional worker-delegates from Mérida — with locals often excluded from decision making. This encouraged suspicions and misconceptions about Communism — something that opponents of the party were quick to exploit.[41]

The FSI's growing involvement with electoral politics was another contested issue in many communities. Its *compromisos* (political obligations) to support unpopular candidates and FSI secretary general Diego Rosado's political horse-trading alienated grassroots support. Rosado reportedly used the FSI to elect a merchant with a reputation for violence as mayor of the town of Peto in exchange for money and appointed another merchant turned boss, Sóstenes Carrillo, as head of the FSI in Ticul.[42] The growing preoccupation of Communist teachers with politics contributed to *chambismo,* the search for bureaucratic sinecures, which created more strains within the FSI.[43]

In spite of the frequent tensions between the Left and agrarian factions of Cardenismo and the conflicting demands on leftist teachers from educational and political commitments, the Left-Cardenista alliance produced important gains for both the Cardenista project and the PCM in 1935 and 1936. The FSI's hard-fought unionizing campaigns on many haciendas and the Young Socialists' and the FUPDM's outreach to young people and women created the first mass Cardenista movement in Yucatán. Among the foci of Left-Cardenismo, the provincial town of Motul figured prominently.

The Motul of Rogerio Chalé: Bulwark of Left-Cardenismo

In his day, no Cardenista leader commanded more popular support than Rogerio Chalé, a young truck driver turned peasant leader.[44] During the hotly contested and often violent gubernatorial campaign of 1933, Chalé supported opposition candidate Gualberto Carrillo Puerto.[45] The campaign was Chalé's political baptism, and his clashes with oppressive local authorities made a name for him in Motul as a valiant political fighter willing to stand up to intimidation.

After the campaign, however, Chalé left the opposition camp and made peace with then-governor Alayola, becoming head of the Socialist Party in Motul and a vocal supporter of Cárdenas. In making the potentially dangerous switch, Chalé publicly denounced the hacendados. He accused them of corrupting Gualberto Carrillo Puerto's partisans with money and quoted the words of Lázaro Cárdenas: "To know the will of the people, money is not necessary."[46]

The charismatic presence of Chalé and his position as a Cardenista working-class leader possibly contributed to the Agrarian Bank's selection of Motul as one of the first two pueblos to receive grants of henequen. Chalé's physical resemblance to Felipe Carrillo Puerto (he was rumored to be his illegitimate son) reinforced the association of Cardenismo with Carrillo Puerto in the minds of Motul's peasants. By emphasizing popular political empowerment, Socialist education, and agrarian reform, Chalé revived Yucatecan Socialism and fused it with Cardenismo. But there was an important third ideological source on which Chalé drew: Communism. At some point, probably in late 1934, Chalé joined a secret PCM cell in Motul.[47]

Chalé's mobilization of Motul's peasants and peons—uniting the Left, Cardenismo, and a revived Yucatecan Socialism—did not go unchallenged. Landowners around Motul tried to elect clients to the town council in order to frustrate agrarian reform and the unionization of peons. Their candidate denied Chalé the mayorship in 1934 through fraud.[48] Chalé supporters took to the streets to protest and suffered harassment from the municipal police throughout early 1935. Alayola finally bowed to popular pressure and dumped the unpopular mayor of Motul.[49] The experience of successfully battling the landowners for town hall gave the popular Left-Cardenista movement in Motul a class-based unity relatively rare in other communities.

Much of the success of the Left-Cardenista alliance in Motul was due to the character of Chalé's leadership. Exceptional charisma, physical courage, a command of Maya, and what one old Chalista would recall as *cariño*—genuine concern and sympathy for the common folk—allowed Chalé to realize legal mandates for social change in Motul while they remained dead letters in many areas where the hacendados or the old caciques retained political power. Under Chalé's leadership, the local PCM and a revived PSS made inroads into peon communities where Chalé personally enforced the Federal Labor Code over the objections of corrupt state officials.[50]

Chalé's Motul branch of the Socialist Party and leftist teachers worked not only to better the lives of peasants and peons economically, but also to break their mentality of deference. Thanks to Chalé's energetic encouragement, hundreds of Motuleño peasants and peons visited the "Workers and Peasants" school for adult literacy classes at night and frequented its small library. Motul's baseball team, "the Socialist School," represented both a newly found pride among the lower classes and the importance of radical education.[51]

While popular education succeeded, other aspects of the cultural campaign—prohibition and "defanaticization"—fizzled. Still, the ambition and longevity of the attempts to reform provincial society in Motul were exceptional. For instance, Chalé, his collaborators among the local PSS, and leftist teachers put on evening socials (*veladas*) with poetry readings and musical performances interspersed with consciousness-raising sessions—a lecture on feminism, a speech on the benefits of socialist education, and a dramatized appeal for peasant support for land reform, "The Day of the Ejido." Other theatrical acts like "The Priest's Daughter" and presentations like "Religions and the Revolution" tried to disseminate anticlerical ideas. Chalé also hoped that these cultural meetings would bridge social boundaries, heal old factional wounds, and help unify Motul's lower classes against the hacendados.[52]

Chalé's efforts would be tested, not only by landowner resistance, but also by the federal agrarian bureaucracy. Motul had been chosen to be a model ejido, receiving one of the first two grants of henequen land. But the fledgling peasant collective lacked sufficient land and access to rasping machinery, in part because of hacendados' sabotage, but also because of the federal government's failure to deliver promised financial support. Managerial errors by federal officials and skyrocketing operating costs harmed Motul's ejido. Many Motul peasants refused to join the local ejidal credit chapter because of these problems, making the Agrarian Bank's operation of the henequen collective virtually impossible.[53] These internal problems, and the resulting tension between peasant ejidatarios and federal agrarian engineers, drew Chalé into a dispute with the Agrarian Bank. In reprisal for contesting their authority, federal authorities suspended Chalé's allies from the Motul ejido council and sent an army detachment to Motul to intimidate his supporters.[54] The federal Agrarian Bank's fumblings and subsequent attempts to punish rather than negotiate with protesters poisoned attitudes toward federal agrarian reform in Motul. Even as he fought with agrarian officials, Chalé often had to defend the bank against its enemies, like the hacendado-funded CGT, because of his Cardenista commitment.[55]

Although he was one of the few loyal supporters of Governor Alayola, Chalé survived Alayola's fall in the October strike unscathed, and the new governor quickly named Chalé director of the labor department of the PSS. By bringing in the popular young leader with sterling Communist credentials, López Cárdenas hoped to repeat the successful mobilization of Motul's peasants and peons in other communities across the central and eastern henequen zone.[56] Chalé balanced the difficult tasks of supporting peons' demands for the minimum wage and building support for agrarian reform.[57] He personally intervened in labor disputes on haciendas and heard peasant complaints against unresponsive local authorities. Although resistance by landlords and corruption of state officials and army officers blocked worker demands for the minimum wage in many areas, Chalé's presence in the PSS directorate, along with the PCM presence within the PSS in the central and eastern areas of the henequen zone, revived the largely moribund Socialist Party.[58]

The strategy developed by López Cárdenas and Chalé of fusing the remnants of the PSS with the leftist cadre of the PCM bore fruit in the eastern half of the henequen zone. Significantly, a strong cadre of Left-Cardenista leaders survived the ouster of López Cárdenas and the death of Chalé in July and September 1936, respectively. For instance, FSI peon unions merged with the declining PSS leagues in the large town of Izamal in 1937, helping revive the Socialist base there.[59] The case of the eastern henequen town of Temax provides another example of how the Left revived Yucatecan Socialism.

Aging popular leader Pedro Crespo, a hero of the armed phase of the Revolution in Temax, was losing his grip, and the town was increasingly under the sway of landowners, who successfully kept the Agrarian Bank out of their fief.[60] The Left in Temax was energized in 1937 by the arrival of Professor Bartolomé Cervera, an effective Communist organizer who had already helped turn the western village of Kinchil into a Left-Cardenista bulwark. He recruited Luciano Kú and Melchor Zozaya Ruz, younger men of humble origins, to lead the FSI and the Young Socialists, respectively. Kú drew such strong support that he was elected head of the Socialist league, where he remained until 1939 — another case of the PCM rebuilding a hollow Socialist league. The strength of the Young Socialists under Zozaya Ruz prompted the governor to grant the group a medium-size farm, "Santa

Rita," to run as a cooperative. The group's success prompted a violent backlash from threatened local interests, who forced Kú off the winning slate for town council. Hacendados Manuel and José Monsreal Castellanos almost killed Melchor Zozaya and teacher-activist Cervera.[61]

In Temax, the Left unified with the PSS to challenge large landowners by mobilizing broad popular support along horizontal class lines against hacendados. But the Left faced tougher going when it challenged caciques who, over the years, had built up large clienteles among peasants and peons. In Cansahcab, a coalition of Communist teachers, an FSI union, and Young Socialists challenged cacique Antonio Aranda, who had long monopolized local political power and Cansahcab's ejido. Aranda proved too tough for the Left to dislodge because of his large number of supporters and the many favors that governors owed him.[62]

The case of Ixil, near Motul in the heart of the henequen zone, presents another example of the difficulties that the Left faced in going up against entrenched bosses. The FSI organized peasants to challenge the dominant Quijano and Escobedo clans. These extended families of landowners, cantina owners, and merchants had run Ixil as their own bailiwick for over two decades with the acquiescence of the Socialist Party. With the help of a female Communist teacher, Carlota Baeza, and male teachers, the FSI organized a union of peasants to seize local political power. But the Quijano-Escobedo faction used its political connections in Mérida and with Socialist Party barons to beat back the Left's challenge.[63]

The many local variations in the Left's strategy and its varying degrees of success in mobilizing a Left-Cardenista popular base defy easy generalization. Undoubtedly, the peons of Temozón, who won a long strike with the help of the PCM and Cardenista politicians, strongly identified with Cardenismo. The Left-Cardenista popular base was weaker in places like Motul, where the federal Agrarian Bank alienated many peasants and peons, and in Cansahcab, where bosses dampened popular mobilization. Across the henequen zone in general, the Agrarian Bank hampered the Left's operations. In many villages in the southern maize zone, the Left's class-based appeals failed to resonate, in spite of some successes like the mobilizations in Maní. And the limited resources and time of the Left meant that federal teacher and worker delegates never reached dozens of villages and hundreds of smaller hamlets. Still, it is clear that, in many locales, the Left created vibrant popular organizations. Just as importantly, the PCM in Yucatán looked beyond the vaunted urban worker–rural peasant alliance to find the true base of Left-Cardenismo: young people, women, and peons.

With the support of the FSI, the Young Socialists, and a revived PSS under Rogerio Chalé, López Cárdenas stood a chance of both holding on to power and gaining the trust of President Cárdenas. But, given the president's determination to carry out agrarian reform, López Cárdenas would have to win the support of Agrarian Bank chief Candelario Reyes.

The Agrarian Dilemma, 1935–36

Having promised the president to carry out land reform in Yucatán, López Cárdenas's future depended on its successful execution. In his first few months in office, he reversed Alayola's policy of passively resisting agrarian reform and executed several new grants in the henequen zone. By mid-January 1936, López Cárdenas had reduced ten more haciendas to their legal maximum of two hundred hectares.[64] Moreover, the governor's relationship with Candelario Reyes was, for the time being, quite good, and together the two resolved to deal with the plight of the peon.[65]

The new agrarian reform offensive launched by López Cárdenas and Reyes targeted the peons of the central region of the henequen zone around Tixkokob and Motul. In Motul, the Agrarian Bank granted more henequen fields to peasants and worked with Rogerio Chalé to try to bring peons into the ejidos.[66] Reyes and the bank had more success in Tixkokob. Despite accusations of stalling reform in the past, Tixkokob's authorities cooperated with the Agrarian Bank to expropriate land specifically for peons, both to lower widespread unemployment and to counter CGT organizing. In nearby Ixil, a hotbed of Left-Cardenismo, López Cárdenas found that the 1928 land grant to the pueblo was insufficient because ninety-seven (male) heads of families and young men under sixteen had been left without work, a violation of the Federal Labor Code that justified more land grants.[67]

Even though the agrarian reform processes initially went smoothly and apparently succeeded in winning over peons on haciendas around Tixkokob, several problems soon emerged. The governor and Reyes differed over how to deal with landowners. To ease tensions between peons and ejidatarios, who were up until now disproportionately peasants, López Cárdenas's administration tried to mediate arrangements between ejidatarios and hacendados that gave the ejidos and the peons still working on haciendas shared access to rasping machinery.[68] This kept the hacendados from sabotaging their equipment and gave many peons a chance to keep working. However, López Cárdenas's willingness to compromise with hacendados was not matched by that of Reyes, whose hard-line position against concessions to hacendados alienated peons.[69]

Other problems cropped up between the PSS and the Agrarian Bank. Despite attempts by López Cárdenas and the PSS leadership to raise flagging popular support for agrarian reform, the rivalry between PSS leaders and federal agrarian engineers only increased. On 15 February 1936, at a huge assembly convened by the PSS to convince peasants that the ejido would solve their economic problems, peasants demanded that the Agrarian Bank pay the minimum wage and criticized the "fabulous salaries" paid to engineers and "excess personnel." Ejidatarios of Motul complained of a lack of work and demanded more land—a difficult task considering that Motul's ejido was already fenced in by ejidos of neighboring villages and towns.[70] The day after the Motul rally, the state government's official newspaper, the *Diario del Sureste,* published a letter from the Socialists of Izamal pointing out that the bank paid an ejidatario 20 percent less in "advances" than what hacendados paid.[71] Growing resentment among members of the Socialist Party toward federal agrarian reform threatened to pull apart López Cárdenas's fragile alliance with Reyes.

Even as López Cárdenas and Reyes tried to push ahead with land reform, conflicts among peasants, peons, and the Agrarian Bank grew and often turned violent. Hacienda Xcanatún, just north of Mérida, had its processing machinery expropriated in May 1935 to service henequen produced by fifteen hundred ejidatarios of nearby villages. Fearing the loss of their jobs, many of the three hundred resident peons of Xcanatún joined the anarchist CGT. Xcanatún's CGT demonstrated against the Agrarian Bank in the general strike of October 1935 and repeatedly complained to government authorities that the expropriation of their hacienda's machinery and the loss of many of Xcanatún's fields to neighboring ejidos had unfairly put them out of work. The crisis was seemingly averted on 29 October 1935 when Xcanatún's owner received an amparo, or legal stay, against the occupation of the machinery by the pueblos.[72]

But before the court formally halted the expropriation of machinery, the peons of Xcanatún, organized by the female federal teacher of its school, Antonia Febles, and armed by delegates sent in by the CGT, struck to block the rasper's occupation. José Brito, the federal engineer supervising agrarian reform in the district around Mérida, reportedly armed ejidatarios and ordered them to break the peon strike and to take the machinery by force on the night of the twenty-ninth. He and the ejidatarios probably hoped that a quick show of force would convince the judge to drop the amparo and cow peons into backing down. However, when the armed ejidatarios of Chuburná, led by Brito and the peasant leader (and alleged ejidal cacique) Marcos Pox, entered the hacienda grounds, a shoot-out ensued. Some seventy peons forced some fifty invading ejidatarios to surrender, disarmed them, and proceeded to beat several of them. Brito escaped the fighting (federal engineers proved themselves to be skilled escape artists) and went back to summon federal troops, who soon arrived to punish the peons. The federal troops suffered two casualties before they could subdue and disarm the peons and free the captive agrarian Cardenista fighters of Chuburná.[73]

Enraged by the resistance, the *federales* carted off three Xcanatún peons without bothering to arrest them and briefly took the federal teacher who had aided the peons into custody. After the federal troops were accused of raping the teacher, the incident became a national embarrassment for the army and the Agrarian Bank.[74]

Although no one was ever prosecuted for the violence — the de facto impunity enjoyed by all sides tended to encourage more violence — the Agrarian Bank negotiated an agreement between the peons and the ejidatarios to share access to the rasping machinery of Xcanatún.[75] The agreement proved problematic since the machinery was shared among four ejidos and the Agrarian Bank gave each of the four ejidos eight hours of daily access to the machinery. Only a month later, the rasper broke down (perhaps overly stressed by running thirty-two-hour days), and the ejidatarios lost eight thousand pesos daily as the unprocessed harvest spoiled.[76] Violence by government agents like the army and the lack of basic logistic support for henequen ejidos conspired to undermine peasant faith in agrarian reform.

The day after the gunfight on Xcanatún, violence flared to the east in Motul between Chalé's Cardenistas and the CGT. Miraculously, only one of over a thousand rioters was killed. At the victim's wake on 3 November, some six hundred supporters of the CGT (predominantly women) blamed the local PSS, Rogerio Chalé, Motul's police, and Candelario Reyes for his death.[77]

The violence on Xcanatún and Motul was, unfortunately, a recurring problem. In Tepakan, the agrarian Cardenista mayor led peasant ejidatarios in an attack on peons of neighboring hacienda Kantirix to punish them for complaining about federal engineers.[78] In other towns in the henequen zone such as Tixkokob and the nearby village of Euán, ejidatarios organized and armed by the Agrarian Bank clashed with Socialist town councils often connected to landlords and merchants.[79]

Elsewhere, violence erupted, not between supporters of the ejido and its opponents, but between ejidatarios and federal agents. On 3 January 1936, the Agrarian Department's chief in the district of Acancéh arrived in the town to review the ejidos' books for the year that had just ended. The meeting was far from businesslike: the ejidatarios demanded a full review of all financial accounts and the resignation of the responsible official, the engineer Alberto Castillo. The federal government's failure to fund ejidos caused ejidatarios to suspect that Agrarian Bank officials had pocketed missing subsidies. To make matters worse, the poor soil around Acancéh diminished henequen yields, a fact that federal planners failed to take into account when allocating credit. Unconvinced by Castillo's reply that he was not accountable to them, several in the crowd began to physically threaten him. While the town council tried to calm the situation by moving the discussion indoors, a panicked Castillo shot off his pistol and then leapt several garden walls to escape the angry crowd at his heels. Denied a final accounting with Castillo, the crowd cut the telegraph lines to Mérida in protest.[80]

The Agrarian Bank had met with peasant protesters to discuss poor wages and interference in communal matters since the beginning of the reform, but as the number of ejidos grew, a new problem cropped up: peasants eligible for land refused henequen fields. Chapab's potential ejidatarios rejected cooperation with the Agrarian Bank because they wanted vacant plots to raise beans and corn, not fields planted with henequen.[81] Similarly, agrarian reform stalled in Conkal as some ejidatarios asked for land to grow corn, beans, and squash instead of fields already planted with henequen.[82] Did the ejidatarios refuse henequen land on the prompting of the CGT or hacendados? Or did they know of the poor economic outcome of agrarian reform in other pueblos? Both motives were probably behind peasant refusal to participate in the ejidos.

The poor yields in Acancéh and the resistance in Chapab and Conkal underscore another daunting problem faced by the Agrarian Bank: the wide variations in age and quality of the henequen fields, which made planning ejidos extremely difficult. Resistance to agrarian reform was strongest in the south and west (especially around the towns of Acancéh, Ticul, Hunucmá, and Sotuta), precisely the part of the henequen zone where yields were the poorest.[83] The often-confused plan of land divisions and the high start-up costs of collective cultivation worsened the already poor economic situation of ejidatarios.

The west had yet another structural barrier to reform: estates located in this area tended to have larger resident peon populations, which meant that the hacendados had influence over a larger share of each municipality's population. Consequently, hacendados in the west could influence town councils through their patron-client ties to peons. In the western town of Umán, four hundred hectares were legally transferred from a hacienda to

Umán's ejido in December 1935, yet, eight months later, the ejido was still waiting for the land. The transfer had been stalled by Umán's town council, which Reyes believed to be under the influence of the powerful Palomeque hacendado clan.[84] Landowners in many other southern towns, such as Sotuta, Hocaba, and Tekit, could count on friendly local authorities to oppose the Agrarian Bank.[85]

The fact that haciendas were not evenly distributed among municipalities, leaving some towns and villages with few estates within their municipal boundaries, created more headaches for federal engineers. Other towns, like Sanahcat, actually had too small a population to farm the land granted to its ejido from nearby haciendas.[86] To make up for the uneven distribution of haciendas across counties, the Agrarian Bank often created ejidos that crossed county boundaries. But this practice was often seen by villagers as taking work and land away from them and giving them to outsiders.[87]

While the Agrarian Bank encountered many problems in the southern and western parts of the henequen zone, agrarian reform also stalled on its eastern edge, around Dzidzantún and Temax. Because, as in the south and west, haciendas in the far east were generally larger, there were proportionally more peons. More peons usually meant more resistance to land reform.[88] For instance, when federal engineers divided the hacienda San Francisco for assignment to two nearby pueblos, they put its peons in the difficult position of dealing with distant, unfriendly peasant communities like neighboring Dzidzantún in order to make a living on the new ejidos.[89]

In spite of all these complex problems, Reyes dismissed peasant and peon complaints as landlord "deception" and moved ahead full speed.[90] The new head of the Agrarian Department (the sibling agency of the Agrarian Bank charged with technical support) in Yucatán, Florencio Palomo Valencia, pushed ahead with four new ejidal grants in early 1936, not even waiting for the paperwork to clear the state's Agrarian Commission.[91] But amparos kept many more pending ejidal grants mired in legal disputes. Endless political squabbles among federal engineers, ejidatarios, peons, and local politicos made matters worse. Reyes created a Yucatecan branch of the federal Agrarian Militia, but the arming of several platoons of ejidatarios resulted, not in the intimidation of the landowners, but in a spate of local clashes between armed peasants and their foes, often peons on nearby hacendados.[92]

While sharing a commitment to agrarian reform, Governor López Cárdenas and the head of the Agrarian Bank deeply mistrusted each other. Because López Cárdenas was an in-law of the landowning Palomeque clan and appointed politicians with close ties to certain hacendados to key state posts, Reyes accused him of covertly aiding hacendados.[93] In fact, the rivalry between Reyes and López Cárdenas resulted from the struggle for control of state politics between the governor's camarilla (state congressmen, PSS leaders, Left-Cardenistas, and most town councils) and the agrarian Cardenistas (the Agrarian Bank's network of supporters made up of federal agrarian engineers, the peasants who served on the ejidal councils, and the notorious Agrarian Militia). Reyes accused Socialist state congressmen and town councils of trying to regain "political control, which [they] believe they have lost owing solely to our work of organizing ejidos in the pueblos," by plotting to "incite a group of malcontents in the ejidos" against federal engineers.[94] Rather than admit that peasants or peons could act on their own, Reyes blamed all problems on corrupt state officials or hacendados.[95] López Cárdenas, for his part, said that he had repeatedly ordered local officials to support agrarian reform and blamed problems with reform on the fact that federal engineers often arbitrarily intervened in local disputes, which resulted in their unpopularity.[96]

The dispute between Reyes and the governor came to a head in April and May 1936. Cárdenas convened a conference in Mexico City to consider the future of agrarian reform. After several delays, the junta of hacendados, López Cárdenas, and the head of the national Agrarian Department, Gabino Vázquez, met. The Agrarian Bank received permission to go ahead with its aggressive plan, which called for reducing all haciendas to two hundred hectares of land and stripping much of their processing equipment. But Cárdenas also removed Candelario Reyes, who was increasingly antagonistic toward the governor, from the head of the state delegation of the Agrarian Department. Reyes retained the less powerful position of head of the Agrarian Bank in Yucatán.[97] The governor, in exchange, ordered all PSS leaders and elected officials in the state to support federal engineers in disputes with ejidatarios.[98]

Cárdenas's attempts to reconcile Reyes's agrarian Cardenistas and governor López Cárdenas's camarilla, however, failed to address two key issues: the lack of adequate federal financial support for the henequen ejidos and the question of which group truly represented Cárdenas in Yucatán. By mid-1936, the henequen ejidos were broke, and Cardenismo in Yucatán was again internally divided and facing an uncertain future.

Conclusion: Many Cardenismos, More Problems

After national Cardenista agents Mújica, Cházaro Pérez, and Reyes ousted Alayola, Cárdenas recognized the interim governor, López Cárdenas, in return for his pledge to form a worker-peasant coalition and back agrarian reform. López Cárdenas sought to mobilize popular forces by supporting leftist teachers, by backing the revived Chalista pss in Motul, and by reaching out to Candelario Reyes's agrarian Cardenistas. Yet López Cárdenas also brought back old Bartolista caciques and left untouched the old Mérida monopolies and corrupt labor arbitration boards that so antagonized urban workers. While independent labor remained outside López Cárdenas's tent in Yucatán, the power struggle pitting Left-Cardenismo against agrarian Cardenismo threatened to bring his tent down entirely.

For the architect of the Cardenista agrarian reform in the state, Candelario Reyes, political infighting was only half the problem. The exclusion of peons, planning gaffes, hacendado resistance, and, above all, lack of federal funding remained daunting obstacles in the path of agrarian reform. Instead of resolving the ejidos' problems, speeding up the pace of agrarian reform multiplied them.

Even with all its flaws and contradictions, Cardenismo made notable progress in Yucatán in late 1935 and 1936. It is fair to say that this period marked the high-water mark of popular Cardenismo in Yucatán. From Tizimín in the east, where the Young Socialists challenged the provincial elite, to Motul, where Rogelio Chalé and Communist teachers battled the cgt and landowners, to Temozón near Mérida, where peon communities dramatically confronted hacendados, the pcm mobilized thousands for Cárdenas. If Left-Cardenista bulwarks scattered across the state could be unified into an effective political force, agrarian reform rescued, and urban labor tamed, then Cardenismo in Yucatán might still triumph.

3

Cardenismo in Crisis: Gualbertismo,
the Fall of López Cárdenas, and
the Rise of the Official Camarilla

GRARIAN REFORM AND the rise of Left-Cardenismo provoked a
powerful reaction. Although Governor Fernando López Cárdenas
was far from radical, he supported the growth of the PCM in Yucatán and backed land reform. For opponents of both, the governor represented a much easier target than either the federal agents in Yucatán or
leftist organizers. Consequently, most great hacendados plotted to remove
him from power, just as Alayola had been toppled in October 1935.

Landowners realized, however, that they would have to tread carefully.
In order to strike at López Cárdenas, they renewed alliances with independent urban labor and bought the help of Gualberto Carrillo Puerto, heir to
the Socialist political dynasty founded by his brother Felipe. In the senatorial campaign in April 1936, hacendados weakened López Cárdenas by
backing the candidacy of Gualberto Carrillo Puerto; via strikes in May and
June, they removed him. In the process, the hacendados and their allies
threw Cardenismo in Yucatán into a crisis from which it never recovered.

*The Senatorial Campaign of 1936 and
the Rise of Gualbertismo*

Scholars often assume that elections in Mexico after the Revolution were
meaningless because of impositions from above and fraud. At times, however, opposition candidates running against the official (government-backed) nominees did stand a chance of winning — if they lined up powerful allies in Mexico City and strong popular support. The senatorial election
of 1936 took place at a time when Mexico City had established no clear
preferences in Yucatán, meaning that an opposition candidate had a much
better shot at snatching victory from the governor's group. At the time, the
national Cardenista state was still consolidating its hold over power after
the battle with Calles. Moreover, Cárdenas's inner circle was deeply divided

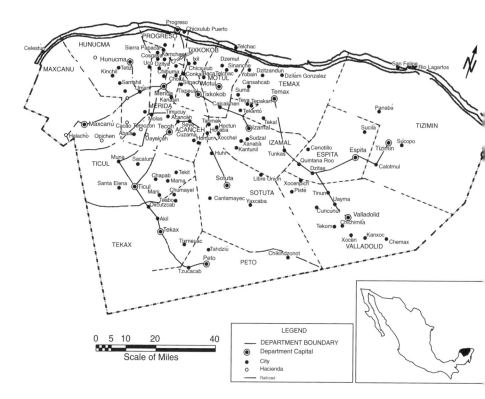

over intervention in regional politics because of internal strife between moderate PNR president Emilio Portes Gil and the more radical wing of Cardenismo, led by Secretary of Communication Francisco Mújica.[1] The senatorial election of 1936 in Yucatán was also clouded by uncertainty because Cárdenas had ousted many governors elected during Calles's reign — something that López Cárdenas, with his ties to Callista governor García Correa, feared.

With no clear preference in Mexico City on the senatorial election, Governor López Cárdenas believed that he could simply impose an official candidate of his choosing. But he blundered with his first choice: his own brother Mauro, a doctor with a long bureaucratic career but absolutely none of the requisite populist credentials. Realizing his error, the governor withdrew his brother's nomination and tapped cousin Gonzalo López Manzanero, leader of a Socialist truckers' cooperative since the Callista era. Not only did this decision again raise the issue of nepotism, but it also allowed opponents of the governor to charge him with Callismo and rouse Portes Gil into action against him. Sensing the chance to steal the senate seat away from the governor's camarilla and thus isolate him from the president, opposition forces led by several leading hacendados coalesced around Gualberto Carrillo Puerto.

Their support for Carrillo Puerto seemed counterintuitive; Gualberto's brother Felipe personified the Revolution in Yucatán by distributing land, founding schools, and mobilizing peasant communities.[2] After rebellious federal troops executed him during the abortive de la Huerta coup on 3 January 1924, the national postrevolutionary regime joined with the PSS to deify Felipe Carrillo as a revolutionary hero. As Ilene O'Malley has shown, the national postrevolutionary regime legitimized itself through the use of martyred machos Emiliano Zapata and Pancho Villa. By claiming that the revolutionary heroes died fighting for the workers and peasants, the state mobilized popular support while promising to fulfill their agenda.[3] Just as the national state used Villa and Zapata as symbols, so too did the regional politicos of the PSS use Felipe Carrillo Puerto.[4] The official discourse of the Felipe Carrillo Puerto cult, like that of Zapata, suggested that his sacrifice helped win land for the masses and that the state would redeem them and thus complete the martyr's mission of ethnic and class justice.

Gualberto Carrillo was both a promoter and a beneficiary of the hero cult of his brother, using it to position himself as the head of a reformist wing of the PSS and angle for political posts.[5] Undoubtedly, the boldest move that he made to establish his claim to be the heir to his brother's radical legacy came in June 1930, when he confronted national strongman Plutarco Elías Calles over the question of agrarian reform. When Calles publicly stated that continued land reform in Yucatán would be an economic disaster for the nation, Gualberto Carrillo Puerto took the potentially risky step of writing to Calles to rebuke him for his proclamation.[6] Three years later, Gualberto Carrillo made the fortuitous decision to endorse Lázaro Cárdenas for president before virtually any other Yucatecan politician. Even though Cárdenas's clout did not allow Gualberto Carrillo to win the governorship in 1933, it greatly raised his stature in regional politics.

For his part, Lázaro Cárdenas apparently believed Gualberto to be a legitimate heir to Felipe Carrillo Puerto, one of Cárdenas's idols, and a supporter of agrarian reform, the key item on Cárdenas's agenda.[7] After Cárdenas assumed the presidency, Gualberto Carrillo cultivated his friendship with the president through a series of letters in which he sharply criticized the governors of Yucatán, repeatedly pledged his absolute loyalty to the president, and constantly reminded him of his own popularity and knowledge of agrarian conditions and the Maya.[8] The president's confidence in Gualberto Carrillo continued to rise, and he soon became a key agent of Cardenismo in Yucatán.

Gualbertismo as Cardenismo: Ideology and Social Base of a Camarilla

The support of the national Cardenistas made Gualberto Carrillo a key player in Yucatecan politics as a perennial gubernatorial candidate and, in 1936, a strong challenger to the official nominee for the senate. On the local level, Gualbertismo — Gualberto Carrillo Puerto's regional political movement — was superficially the sum of Carrillismo and Cardenismo, the old and the new revolutionary traditions. But Gualbertismo was also an expression of regional political culture that valued the violent defense of manly honor. All these factors affected Gualbertista political discourse and shaped the social base of Gualbertismo.

On the campaign trail, Gualberto Carrillo used the populist style perfected by his brother Felipe. Despite his years in business and bureaucratic service, he presented himself as a humble man of the people — speaking fluent Maya, riding and hunting, and recalling the heady days of brother Felipe's administration. A typical Gualbertista tract claimed that the candidate had lived in "direct contact for many years with the working class of Yucatán" and had "defended the interests of the indigenous people." Gualberto Carrillo's political discourse also conflated Cardenista and Felipe Carrillo Puerto's agrarianism; one widely circulated poster trumpeted that "Carrillismo is Synonymous with Agrarismo."[9] Gualbertismo claimed to be revolutionary, but, like the Mexican Revolution itself, it lacked a clear ideological doctrine. Gualberto Carrillo's use of the term *revolution* was fundamentally nostalgic; it revered the heroic figure Felipe Carrillo Puerto, but it interpreted the meaning of Felipe's life just as the state did, as a paternalistic symbol subordinating the masses to their leader.

As Gualberto Carrillo's star rose, and as his status as a key representative of Cárdenas in Yucatán became apparent, criticism mounted that he was manipulating the hero cult of his brother. To many, Gualberto continued a long, if not honorable, tradition of the *hermano incomodo* (annoying brother) of the successful revolutionary. Notable hermanos incomodos included the ineffective playboy Hipólito Villa, who was called the Rockefeller of the Revolution, and the hard-drinking and cruel Eufemio Zapata.

Lázaro Cárdenas might not have been surprised by Gualberto Carrillo's shady conduct, given the fact that his own brother Dámaso enriched himself and ran part of their home state of Michoacán as his own fief.[10]

Still, even in the often cynical world of Mexican politics, many regarded Don Gualberto as exceptionally corrupt. Opponents mocked his reliance on his last name by calling him "Gualpellido," as *apellido* means "last name," and charged that he was a weak and easily managed man willing to sell his cause out if the price was right.[11]

Certainly, Gualberto's image as an outsider fighting to restore his brother's legacy and fulfill Cárdenas's dream of agrarian reform was often at odds with his actions. He regularly accepted questionable electoral losses in return for the promise of other posts in the future. Of course, the national postrevolutionary state demanded that losing candidates accept party discipline in order to centralize power in Mexico City more effectively. But this questionable behavior undermined the faith of his own followers. The phrase "better to jump ship in time than to stick with Gualberto" became a political truism in Yucatán.[12]

More serious were the charges that Gualberto Carrillo's camarilla represented members of the conservative landowning class who opposed and perhaps assassinated his brother and were now battling Cárdenas. Gualberto Carrillo reportedly attracted financial support from wealthy hacendados, businessmen, and the hacendados's organization lobbying against Cárdenas's agrarian reform, the Association to Defend the Henequen Industry (Associación de Defensa de la Industria Henequenera, or ADIH). Even observers who did not believe Gualberto to be personally corrupt felt that he was under the sway of conservative upper-class advisers. In another biting example of Yucatecan political humor, Gualberto Carrillo was nicknamed "the horsefly" because he was said to follow mules.[13]

The substantial sums that flowed from conservative landowners into Carrillo's coffers were undoubtedly aimed at purchasing his influence in stopping agrarian reform. Despite his ardent public Cardenismo and pious veneration of his brother, Gualberto Carrillo maintained a calculatingly vague attitude toward land reform that allowed him to curry favor with Cárdenas while at the same time encouraging contributions from (if not out-and-out shaking down) wealthy landowners. For instance, in October 1935 he wrote to Cárdenas that the hacendados were deceiving peasants into opposing land reform and advocated a "radical agrarianism." But, only a few months earlier, when the state congress authorized the expropriation of rasping machinery from haciendas, he walked out rather than hurt "the

Indians of the haciendas" and help only peasants in the village. For good measure, he added that "hacendados and merchants are justifiably alarmed" by land reform. Similarly, he praised agrarian reform in the henequen zone in principle but privately urged Cárdenas to adopt an alternative plan more favorable to hacendados' interests.[14]

Gualberto Carrillo Puerto's ambiguous position on agrarian reform suggested collusion with hacendados. Many contemporaries as well as more than a few historians have dismissed Gualbertismo as a counterrevolutionary movement.[15] However, that begs the question of how Gualbertismo enjoyed genuine, broadly based popular support throughout the 1930s.

In order to capture the complexities of Gualbertismo, it is necessary to understand what the movement meant to his many supporters. The historian and anthropologist Claudio Lomnitz-Adler developed the concept of *intimate culture* to explain how class and ethnic inequality in Mexico is expressed through symbolic systems unique to each region.[16] After applying this concept to Yucatán, it would seem that much of the political power of the Carrillo Puerto clan was derived, not only from Socialist ideology, but also from the ability to combine violence and access to political, economic, and social resources with a knowledge of the Maya language and folk ways. Both Gualberto and Felipe shared a keen understanding of this intimate culture of rural Yucatán and used it — albeit for quite different ends — to their advantage.

Gualberto Carrillo's willingness to confront enemies in defense of his honor gave him a reputation as *fuerte* (strong) and even *grosero* (lit., gross, one willing to shame and embarrass enemies publicly) and was often contrasted to Felipe's mythical role as the sacrificial lamb by Gualberto's enemies. Both Gualberto Carrillo and his supporters were involved in several riots and firefights as well as the assassinations of political enemies. But had the Gualbertistas simply become *pistoleros* for hacendados, as their enemies charged?

A careful reading of rural politics and culture suggests otherwise. Gualberto Carrillo was blamed when the Gualbertista faction in the town of Dzitas murdered Rogerio Chalé, who was the president of the Socialist Party and a former follower of Gualberto Carrillo. Investigation of the murder suggests that Chalé was targeted because he had betrayed the "Carrillista party." He was a Gualbertista in 1933 but abandoned the Gualbertistas in 1934 and, as president of the PSS, ruled against them in a disputed town council election in Dzitas. Seen from this perspective, the murder of Chalé was not a hit for the landowners, but simply the enforcement of codes of political conduct.[17]

Gualberto Carrillo's intimidating presence and bloody reputation led enemies to label him a *cabrón,* literally a "big he-goat," but figuratively "one mean son of a bitch." His reputation for violence alienated some but also earned him respect and in some cases even admiration. Recently, scholars have rightly subjected the notion of Mexican hypermasculinity or machismo to careful scrutiny, questioning its supposed pervasiveness in Mexican society. Even if machismo did not saturate all Mexican society, political power in Cardenista-era Mexico was often expressed and enhanced through stereotypical macho behavior like predatory sexual conquests and killing in defense of masculine honor. Granted, not all people admired such conduct, and some might in fact have been repelled by it.[18] Yet Friedrich Katz has argued that part of Pancho Villa's popularity was due to the fact that he personified the macho — an image that included his well-documented cruel streak.[19] Similarly, it seems likely that Gualberto Carrillo's willingness to defend perceived challenges to his honor publicly contributed to his appeal.

Seen in this context, the violence that marked Gualbertismo indicates, not pro-landowner pistolerismo, but an expression of prevailing political norms and expectations. The circumstances of Gualberto Carrillo's life also seem to have conditioned his attitudes toward violence. Three of his brothers were executed by a firing squad on 3 January 1924, and he himself had at least one serious brush with death during his 1933 gubernatorial campaign, when agents of the governor occupied his campaign train and only intervention by federal troops saved his life.[20] His supporters, moreover, routinely faced violent reprisals from state agents.[21] A political leader who could not protect the members of his camarilla from violence would find his popular support slipping; Gualberto Carrillo's ability physically to confront enemies would be necessary to embolden his followers in the face of violent intimidation.

If Gualberto Carrillo was in many ways a typical politician of his era, he was exceptional in his ability to keep a sizable popular base together year after year without a political machine. Although Gualbertismo was socially, ethnically, and geographically heterogeneous, its backbone was its organizations in dozens of pueblos led by peasants and the lower middle strata of rural Yucatán — smallholders, merchants, artisans — folk very similar to the Carrillo Puerto clan's own origins. Available data on Gualbertista upper-level leadership, however, reflect a strong middle- and upper-middle-class presence.[22]

Gualbertismo, however, continued to draw strong support from the lowest rung of rural society. The hero cult of Felipe Carrillo Puerto and Cardenismo gave the Gualbertista camarilla powerful propaganda tools.[23] Just as importantly, the Gualbertista leadership was drawn from the middle-class vecinos, not the great landowners. These provincial merchants and smallholders shared the Maya language and a rural way of life with the peasants. Like the smallholding "peasant bourgeoisie" who dominated politics in central Mexico, they bridged class differences with peasants by drawing on a common intimate culture.[24]

Petty burghers were quite adept at using the populist rhetoric of Gualbertismo to rally peasants. Consider the letter to President Cárdenas written by merchants of Dzitas supporting Gualberto Carrillo's claims to have the senatorial election of 1936 overturned. They called Gualberto Carrillo Puerto a "man of clean conscience, an old Cardenista partisan, and a defender of the workers." The Cenotillo town committee backing Gualberto Carrillo Puerto's state congressional campaign was named "[Gualberto] Carrillo Puerto, Friend of the Peasants." Gualbertista discourse stressed the candidate's cariño for the campesinos.[25]

At the same time, Gualbertismo also gained strong popular support in many localities because it represented a way of opposing Cardenista agrarian reform and Left-Cardenismo without opposing Cárdenas himself. Artisans, craftsmen, and smallholders threatened socially by the rise of the Left and its youth and women's wings and economically by agrarian reform and cooperatives found in local Gualbertista organizations a way to defend their interests without rejecting the Revolution, from which they had benefited. The provincial middling strata clearly dominated Gualbertismo's many local chapters. For instance, Gualberto Carrillo Puerto's gubernatorial campaign in Xocchel in 1937 was headed by artisans with both Spanish and Maya surnames—the carpenter José E. Espadas Leal, the former mayor Raymundo Barrera Pinzón, the mason Gregorio Canché, and the *cohetero* (artisan who makes fireworks) Miguel Puc.[26] In Yaxcaba, another henequen town, carpenter Lorenzo Díaz and barber Moises Santos recruited among the poor for Don Gualberto; they denounced voter fraud by corrupt officials and the Communist teachers, who misused the schoolhouse for political rallies, at which they "insult[ed] Don Gualberto Carrillo Puerto, saying that he is lower than a trash can."[27] Although many of these families from the middle stratum were, like Gualberto Carrillo's own, bound by ties of marriage, godparentage, political alliance, and business arrangement to the large hacendados, they still shared the intimate culture of the Yucatecan campo with the peasants.

Finally, a generational factor explains Gualbertismo's base. Since the early 1930s, Gualberto Carrillo had championed the older generation of Socialist Party leaders, men who lost power under Governors García Correa (1930–33), Alayola, and López Cárdenas. Old Socialists pushed from power often turned to Gualbertismo to regain town hall. These *viejos socialistas* included both peasants and middle-class vecinos, and they often still had much political pull in their communities.

Seen from below, Gualbertismo was an eclectic, at times self-contradictory political movement. It enjoyed widespread popular support from the peasantry in many municipalities but was far from an agrarian movement. The core of its local and regional leadership remained in the hands of provincial burghers and small landowners. While calling for state attention to the problems of the rural poor and championing the cause of local democracy, Gualbertismo also gave both large landowners and the provincial petite bourgeoisie a means of blocking agrarian reform and regaining local power. Gualbertismo claimed to advance Cardenismo by opposing the regional bloc headed by Callista-era governors while quietly working to block land reform and protect local interests.

Gualbertismo on the Campaign Trail

In the 1936 senatorial campaign, Gualberto Carrillo and the governor's choice, Gonzalo López Manzanero, followed identical strategies: mobilize strong enough popular support to convince national authorities that your opponent is a Callista and that you yourself have a Cardenista worker-peasant popular base.[28] Although both had links to camarillas of politically connected operatives and wealthy men (the former especially close to landowners, the latter to groups that had used government posts for financial gain during the Callista era), each portrayed himself as the candidate of the workers and peasants and denounced his opponent as an enemy of the Mexican Revolution and a crypto-Callista. The Gualbertistas accused López Manzanero of being a mere tool of the Communists, while supporters of López Manzanero cited Gualberto Carrillo Puerto's ties to landlords and right-wing groups with fascist leanings like Avanzada Cívica.[29]

These charges meant relatively little on the local level, where the senatorial campaign would be won or lost. The bases of the two candidates varied substantially from locale to locale, at times following class and ethnic lines, at other times crossing them.

In the small western village of Kinchil, for instance, the Gualbertistas were a small minority dominated by ranchers, merchants, and older Socialists, while the vast majority of peasants and peons were mobilized for López Manzanero by the FSI.[30] In Tekax, on the other hand, the political situation reflected not class conflict, but intraelite rivalry.

The Gualbertistas of the large southern town of Tekax followed rancher

Pedro Romero Solís, who had been boss since Felipe Carrillo Puerto's day. Romero's clients and supporters opposed the López Manzanero campaign headed locally by Ricardo Marín, a rival sugar landowner with ties to the Molina hacendado clan. Both factions counted teachers and peasant leaders among their supporters as well as peasant unions (Romero Solís through the CTM, Marín via federal teachers). In Tekax, then, political factionalism, not social divisions, defined the Gualbertistas and their opponents. The senatorial campaign there was just another battle in a partisan war between two groups, both very similar in socioeconomic terms, for control of the sugar industry and the local government.[31]

In the henequen town of Izamal, however, both the factions and the stakes were quite different. There, the Gualbertista ejidatarios, led by the Agrarian Bank engineer Adán Cárdenas, squared off against peons led by the veteran Socialist leader Eustaquio Avila Sosa, who backed López Manzanero. The two factions in this henequen town were divided over control of Izamal's ejido and access to work: the ex-peons in the Socialist Party complained of being denied work on the peasant collective; ejidatarios, who were all from town, replied that there was too little work to go around.[32]

On the regional level, the directorate of Gualberto Carrillo Puerto's campaign contained a mix of landowners, merchants, officials, teachers, and peasants, as did that of his opponent. The major ideological difference was the presence of the Yucatecan PCM in López Manzanero's camp. Ironically, the Gualbertista camarilla drew more support from both the great hacendado families trying to stave off land reform and the federal agrarian bureaucracy that detested the clique of Governor López Cárdenas and resented the Left-Cardenista support of peons. The political cohabitation of Reyes and hacendados in the Gualbertista camp was yet another indication of how political calculation often overrode class interests in Cardenista Mexico.

After two months of statewide campaigning, lobbying in Mexico City, and occasional ambushes, the voting took place. Both sides explained the low voter turnout with charges of fraud, and it was soon apparent that PNR president Emilio Portes Gil would impose Gualberto Carrillo even though the official tallies favored López Manzanero. Portes Gil was a moderate and fierce anti-Communist, and the strong Left-Cardenista presence in Yucatán would grow stronger if López Manzanero won.[33] Moreover, the head of the agrarian Cardenista camarilla in Yucatán, Candelario Reyes, was a native of Portes Gil's home state, Tamaulipas. And both wanted to organize

Yucatecan ejidatarios into the national peasant federation affiliated with the national PNR, a task that would be facilitated by weakening López Cárdenas and his group.[34] With the election's outcome decided in Mexico City, national institutions moved to implement Portes Gil's decision and install Gualberto Carrillo.[35]

An unintended consequence of Portes Gil's imposition of Carrillo Puerto, however, was that it fortified the opponents of agrarian reform. When the election's outcome was in doubt, hacendados staged a massive demonstration in Mérida to try to convince Mexico City of the popular support that Gualberto Carrillo Puerto enjoyed. They assembled the same coalition of popular forces as was involved in the October 1935 strike — peons and urban labor — to denounce the regional political machine (now headed by López Cárdenas) and its candidate, López Manzanero. But they also attacked land reform and the actions of Agrarian Bank chief Candelario Reyes, who ironically also supported Gualberto Carrillo Puerto. The demonstrators favoring Gualberto Carrillo Puerto carried banners echoing the CGT and hacendado critique of agrarian reform: "We do not want more deceptions with the division of land in Yucatán" and "For the ejidatarios there is no paid seventh day because the ejidatarios are just slaves of the [Agrarian] Bank."[36] Nevertheless, the Gualbertistas received more help from national Cardenistas when Candelario Reyes and Benjamin Tobón, delegate of the CTM (Confederación de Trabajadores de México, a national labor federation), announced their support for Gualberto Carrillo and Reyes called Carillo Puerto a supporter of agrarian reform to cover his links to hacendados.[37] López Manzanero briefly considered running as an independent candidate, but, on 25 June, he accepted the PNR's discipline in spite of his claimed "massive majority" of twenty-four thousand to eight thousand votes.[38]

López Manzanero could hope for future rewards for obeying the national PNR, but the future of his cousin the governor was less bright. Portes Gil and a host of powerful figures around Cárdenas had challenged his control of the state by imposing Gualberto Carrillo. And the same coalition of hacendados, urban labor, and the CGT that had helped topple Alayola in the October strikes had once again proved its strength.

The July 1936 Strike and the Overthrow of López Cárdenas

The election of Gualberto Carrillo Puerto to the senate over Gonzalo López Manzanero represented only the first step in a larger strategy aimed at overthrowing López Cárdenas and stalling agrarian reform.[39] Enrique Aznar Mendoza, a distinguished lawyer from a prominent family and bitter foe of the PSS since the beginning of the Revolution, directed the efforts of a coalition of landowning-mercantile family groups by channeling funds to the anarchosyndicalist CGT, the railroad workers' SFP, and other labor groups.[40]

To remove López Cárdenas, Aznar Mendoza realized that he would need the acquiescence of the federal military commander in the state. Fortunately for him, General Rafael Cházaro Pérez had died in an aviation accident in January 1936, and the new federal military commander in Yucatán, General Ignacio Otero Pablos, had expensive ambitions to be governor of Sonora, his home state. Consequently, he gladly accepted sizable contributions to his campaign chest from Yucatecan hacendados.

To incorporate military and labor leaders in their camarilla, hacendado families intermarried with and granted land to their new clients. General Otero Pablos's assistant chief of staff became engaged to the daughter of the owner of hacienda Temozón, Humberto Peón; the railroad union leader Mamerto González Inurreta married the daughter of another hacendado, receiving a dowry of two hundred hectares of henequen. In another of the internal alliances cementing Aznar's camarilla, González's cousin received an appointment to Otero Pablos's staff.[41] Wealth and family ties bound the anti–López Cárdenas alliance together.

The operations of Aznar's hacendado camarilla were, like those of most others, cloaked in secrecy because, since the Revolution, landowners had been forced to cover their tracks carefully when interfering in politics. Traditionally, the greatest landowning clans viewed each other as rivals, not as allies, making collective action by the upper class difficult. It was no small feat to unite fractious hacendado families who, historically, had been separated by ideological and personal differences as well as old economic grudges. However, the threat of agrarian reform brought together such rivals as the Molina family and the Peón family as well as Governor López Cárdenas's in-laws the Palomeque family.[42] During a few crucial months in the middle of 1936, the great landowners of Yucatán displayed a rare degree of unity of purpose, pouring considerable financial resources into an effort to topple López Cárdenas and thus end agrarian reform in the henequen zone.

Aznar Mendoza marshaled the hacendados' financial and political resources and acted as matchmaker in the triple political marriage of hacendados, independent labor, and the military. He also used his legal talent and connections in Mexico City (his brother was on the federal supreme court) to get the SFP (Mamerto González's railroad workers' union) the right to form a tax-exempt trucking cooperative and a lucrative electric trolley route linking Mérida and Progreso.[43]

The plan to oust López Cárdenas involved a series of calculating alliances between hacendados and labor groups like the SFP, yet, rather than being a case of simple corruption of labor leaders, the hacendado-labor coalition was actually an opportunistic union of groups that shared a common enemy. And if the leaders of the SFP enjoyed personal gain, the rank and file also derived important benefits, namely, the chance to preserve their jobs against competition from trucking.

It was a sign of Aznar Mendoza's political dexterity that, even as he supported railroad workers against trucking competition, he also made common cause with taxi drivers and the drivers of Mérida's busing cooperative, who resented their poor pay and denial of legal benefits under a Socialist-run cooperative. Encouraged by Aznar Mendoza (who acted as their legal representative and reportedly funneled four hundred pesos a day from hacendados to the cooperatives) and SFP leader César González Inurreta, the eight hundred–some workers formed the independent Frente Unico de Trabajadores de Volante (United Front of Rapid Transportation Workers, or FUTV). The FUTV demanded the legal status necessary to run its own routes in addition to an end to the twenty-five-cent toll on the Mérida–Progreso road. Like other independent labor organizations, it also denounced state government harassment.[44] Aznar and his operatives would use the FUTV's strike as the catalyst for a larger popular mobilization to overthrow López Cárdenas.

While the SFP, the FUTV, and the cordage factory workers of the anarcho-syndicalist SCY represented the urban wing of Aznar Mendoza's camarilla, peon unions of the CGT made up the rural component.[45] The anarchosyndicalist CGT had already organized dozens of peons and a few peasant unions with help from hacendados. Landowners once again provided *aguardiente,* meat, and money for CGT members to come to Mérida to support the FUTV by protesting against the governor. Macario Aké, a peon on Felipe G. Cantón's hacienda San José Grande located near Muxupip, recalled decades later how the hacendados told the peons to support striking taxi drivers in Mérida because they, too, were victims of the government.[46]

By mobilizing the CGT to support the FUTV strike, the hacendados could inject attacks on agrarian reform into the drivers' labor conflict.[47] In trying to attack Reyes and the Agrarian Bank in the state without openly rejecting

President Cárdenas, the strikers often contrasted the reality of agrarian reform with the promise of the Revolution. For instance, around the time of the July strike, the CGT of Huhí accused Reyes of using land reform as a pretext to seize power in Yucatán and replace old bosses with new ones. It pointedly complained to Cárdenas that the Revolution occurred "to take us out of the slavery in which our parents lived, but sadly twenty-six years after the Revolution we realize that [it] has all been nothing but words." Further pursuit of the current agrarian reform, warned the CGT, would ruin Yucatán's economy.[48]

To challenge the regional power of López Cárdenas's clique, Aznar Mendoza needed approval from Mexico City as well. Having rented the support of the federal military in Yucatán, Aznar's allies worked to gain the support of Vicente Lombardo Toledano, Cárdenas's national labor czar and head of the CTM. SFP leader César González Inurreta and the leader of anti-Communist teachers, Arturo Albertos, assembled an umbrella group for unions linked to the Aznar camarilla known as the Independent Unions or Sindicatos Independientes. They convinced Lombardo Toledano to recognize the Independent Unions as the sole CTM affiliate in Yucatán and pledged to destroy the "Callista" PSS, which had been keeping the CTM out of Yucatán.[49] This helped drive a wedge between President Cárdenas and the embattled governor, bringing Aznar Mendoza one step closer to success.[50]

The national CTM's support for the Independent Unions encouraged workers of the port of Progreso, butchers of Mérida, and brick masons to join Aznar's coalition. Allied unions formed among sugarcane cutters and chicle gatherers as well.[51] Socialist peasant leagues in three large provincial towns—Oxkutzcab, Tekax, and Halachó—disassociated from the PSS and affiliated themselves with the Independent Unions movement to boot.

While elite politicking created the conditions for the rise of the Independent Unions, the movement also represented genuine popular grievances. In Halachó, camarilla politics alone cannot explain popular support for the FUTV strike. There, backing for the Independent Unions strike in support of the FUTV grew out of frustration over the deteriorating henequen economy and a series of unpopular mayors imposed from Mérida.[52] In Cansahcab, peasants and alienated vecinos—several of them Gualbertistas as well—formed an independent union to challenge longtime boss Antonio Aranda, Cansahcab's "dictator" for over a decade. But Cansahcab's independent union and Gualbertista faction also had strong ties to several hacendados as well as Catholics resentful of Aranda's hard line on anticlerical laws—not exactly a grassroots Cardenista mobilization.[53]

Throughout the months of May and June, the Independent Unions movement repeatedly called for a general strike in support of the FUTV against López Cárdenas. At the same time, the CGT began organizing mass protests against agrarian reform. This threat in late June led López Cárdenas to turn loose armed state police to clear the streets of demonstrating workers.[54] On 30 June, the FUTV and the Independent Unions began their general strike.

The sequence of events that unfolded on that day strongly suggests a prearranged plan coordinated by Aznar Mendoza. At 11:00 A.M., the strike began. CGT peons brought in by truck, by train, and on foot soon joined the FUTV in the downtown area. The number of strikers swelled as urban workers of the Independent Unions bolstered their ranks. Meanwhile, FUTV drivers blocked the major downtown intersections in Mérida with their cabs. Within a few hours, the urban labor–rural peon alliance brokered by Aznar Mendoza had effectively shut down the state capitol, bringing Yucatán precariously close to anarchy.[55]

As in the October 1935 strike, removing a governor required the complicity of the federal army commander in Yucatán. If General Otero Pablos should order his troops to disperse the strikers or simply pull his troops back and allow the state police with their carbines and submachine guns to clear the streets, the threat to the governor would be ended. On the other hand, if the general were to order the federal troops to surround the strikers and prevent the state police or the governor's partisans from taking action, the strike could paralyze the capital indefinitely. Aware of the close ties linking General Otero Pablos to Aznar Mendoza and the hacendados, Governor López Cárdenas had reportedly tried to secure the general's loyalty by giving him a new car and three thousand pesos. But when the federal troops stood by as the demonstrations grew in size, it became clear that General Otero Pablos would let the strike topple the governor. Realizing that he had been outbid by Aznar Mendoza, López Cárdenas desperately telegraphed President Cárdenas to order Otero Pablos to move against the strikers. He never saw the president's affirmative reply, reportedly pocketed by an aide in cahoots with Aznar's clique.[56]

With the federal troops still protecting the strikers, a second day of demonstrations began on 1 July with a march from the SFP headquarters down Sixty-first Street to the main plaza, accompanied by chants of "Viva Cárdenas!" and "Death to the Governor!" Once in the main plaza, speakers called for the demonstrators to "wipe out the caste of Judases and Cains" holding power in Yucatán. A crowd of some five hundred striking FUTV drivers, accompanied by around two hundred railroad workers, cordage workers, and over a thousand CGT peons, gathered in front of the state capitol building launching fruit, garbage, rocks, and, reportedly, a few homemade explosives against its walls. The tension between demonstrators and the state police was broken when a rocket arched across the main square and exploded over the governor's palace. Scattered gunfire and scuffles quickly broke out. Twenty state police armed with Thompson submachine guns stationed on the roof of the state capitol opened fire on the packed crowds below. By the time the shooting stopped, the bodies of seventeen dead and many wounded protesters littered the central plaza. Most had been shot in the back of the head while trying to flee.[57] With the state police responsible for such widespread bloodshed, Governor López Cárdenas could no longer hope to remain in office.

The Plot within a Plot:
Florencio Palomo Valencia, Governor

In the wake of the massacre, the FUTV, the SFP, and the CGT called on Cárdenas to replace the governor with Aznar Mendoza.[58] The architect of the anti–López Cárdenas movement and would-be governor assumed that General Otero Pablos and other complicit federal agents would support his nomination. A plot within the plot, however, would rob Aznar Mendoza of the governorship.

Unbeknownst to him, members of Aznar Mendoza's own camarilla—namely, hacendado Hernán Ancona Ancona, the alleged treasurer of the group, as well as General Otero Pablos—had conspired with a second group inside the governor's clique, which consisted of state congressman Pedro Castro Aguilar, veteran Socialist Party leader Agustín Franco Aguilar, and his son Agustín Franco Villanueva, Governor López Cárdenas's personal secretary. Together, they plotted to use their influence in Mexico City to install their own man as governor: Florencio Palomo Valencia, the agrarian expert who, at the time, headed the federal Agrarian Department's delegation in Yucatán. Working through Franco Villanueva, this eclectic group backing Palomo Valencia convinced López Cárdenas to name Palomo Valencia as interim governor while López Cárdenas went to Mexico City to clear his name after the massacre of 1 July, thus depriving Aznar Mendoza of the post. With enemies in Mexico City and General Otero Pablos blocking his return, López Cárdenas's departure became permanent, and Palomo Valencia had the governorship.[59]

The fall of López Cárdenas and the naming of Palomo Valencia as governor refutes the common assumption that changes of governors in the period 1935–36 followed presidential orders to purge Callistas. In fact, President Cárdenas had not endorsed the removal of López Cárdenas, and he quickly named him to the national supreme court to restore his reputation.[60] The shadowy ring that launched the coup within a coup showed remarkable political acumen both in convincing López Cárdenas to resign and in orchestrating the naming of the virtually unknown Palomo Valencia as governor. The state deputy Pedro Castro Aguilar, the only member of congress who knew Palomo Valencia, lied to congress by informing them that Cárdenas wanted Palomo Valencia to be governor. Just as importantly, General Otero Pablos as well as General Francisco Mújica, the latter a friend of Palomo's who believed him to be a radical agrarista, leaned on the state deputies to appoint Palomo Valencia quickly, which they promptly did.[61]

The Palomo Valencia Regime: The Rise of the Official Camarilla and the Independent Ejido Plan

While a combination of money, political networking, and careful plotting vaulted Palomo Valencia into the governorship without Cárdenas's consent, staying in office required gaining the president's confidence as well as building a strong political base in the state. Fortunately for Palomo Valencia, his long career in a string of academic and federal bureaucratic posts brought him to the attention of several high national figures who helped him win over Cárdenas. His membership in the YMCA, ties to the PCM, and contacts in Masonic circles allowed him to draw on a diverse network of connections in the nation's capital.[62] But even with support in Mexico City, Palomo Valencia had few contacts in Yucatán.

Palomo Valencia quickly established a strong base of support, commonly known as *the official camarilla* (because of its control over state offices), which dominated state politics until the 1950s. Moreover, he achieved this at a time when the national government's power waxed, Yucatán's powerful hacendados forcefully reasserted their power, and the countryside and the city were frequently plunged into political turmoil. Palomo Valencia and his close collaborators mastered the art of camarilla politics, assembling a strong and diverse collection of alliances, patron-client ties, and covert understandings to anchor their hold over Yucatán and maintain the president's favor.

At the core of this camarilla was the enigmatic figure of Palomo Valencia himself. A technical expert on agrarian reform, he had already used his connections in Mexico City with progressive Cardenistas to be named head of the Agrarian Department in Yucatán on 29 April 1936.[63] Palomo's grasp of realpolitik helped him assemble a broad coalition without being troubled by ideological inconsistencies.[64] One of his most important assets was his political pragmatism, which allowed him to forge pacts with three mutually hostile groups, cementing his hold on power: some powerful hacendados, the federal military commander in the state, and Left-Cardenismo.

His channel to landowners was Hernán Ancona, who reportedly acted as the bagman, distributing payoffs in the plot within a plot. As a reward, Palomo Valencia named Ancona to head the state-run henequen-exporting monopoly, Henequeneros de Yucatán, and for good measure granted Ancona and other cordage factory owners tax breaks and subsidized henequen. To win over the Manzanilla family, historically one of the most stubborn opponents of the Revolution, Palomo Valencia nullified land grants that threatened one of their estates.[65] Although enemies of Palomo would characterize these moves as signs of his subservience to the landowners, such a careful cultivation of some hacendados helped divide them as a class and thus break apart the unified front of large landowners that Aznar Mendoza had carefully assembled. While the governor coddled some hacendados, his state labor prosecutor, José María Bolio Méndez, backed FSI peon unions striking against other landowners, like Temozón's owner Humberto Peón (see chap. 2).

The second leg of Palomo Valencia's camarilla was General Ignacio Otero Pablos. His tacit support for Palomo Valencia made both the overthrow of López Cárdenas and the freezing out of Aznar Mendoza possible. Not only had Otero Pablos allegedly received substantial sums of money for his actions and inactions, but important members of Otero Pablos's staff also assumed key law enforcement positions in the state administration.[66]

The third leg of Palomo Valencia's group was the Left. The new governor used his old friendship with Hernán Laborde, secretary general of the national PCM, and a covert understanding with Hernán Escalante Mendoza, secretary general of the PCM in Yucatán, to oust Betancourt Pérez. By removing the key ally of López Cárdenas in the party, Labordé and Escalante brought the Left into Palomo Valencia's political umbrella group, the Popular Alliance of Yucatán (Alianza Popular Yucateca, or APY). In this renewed alliance with the state government, the Left gained an even larger share of influence in the state bureaucracy and the state education system.[67] In return, the Left's peon (FSI), youth (Young Socialist), and women's (FUPDM) organizations provided the key popular base for Palomo Valencia's official camarilla.

The final element supporting the official camarilla was the PSS. Since its origin in 1915 (under another name), the PSS had been linked continuously to the state government and in effect served as an official party. After the assassination of its charismatic young president Rogerio Chalé in September 1936, the PSS's radical revival abruptly ended. The party largely returned to its pre-Chalé role as an electoral machine with limited interest in social reform or labor arbitration. Still, it retained some support among government employees and peasants in the southern and eastern areas of the state.[68]

While the bedrock of Palomo Valencia's popular front (the APY) remained the PSS and the FSI, Palomo also reached out to the CGT. Although supposedly heir to the anarchosyndicalist tradition of Yucatecan labor, CGT leaders had become dependent on hacendados for funding; Palomo Valencia extended subsidies to some of them at a time when hacendados were probably cutting payments, thus bringing the CGT under his control.[69] With the addition of the CGT to the FSI, the Young Socialists, and the PSS, the official camarilla controlled most major popular organizations in Yucatán. Only the FROC and the major independent trade unions, such as the SCY, the SFP, and the FUTV, remained beyond its reach in Mérida. In the countryside, Palomo Valencia allowed the Gualbertista faction to retake several town halls, such as Cansahcab's, and to keep power in certain locales, like Halachó, but denied the Gualbertista camarilla a share of regional power, sapping its grassroots base.[70]

The new governor was shrewd enough to know that, as long as the federal Agrarian Bank ran ejidos in the henequen zone and the agrarian Cardenista faction controlled many municipalities, the official camarilla could not control rural politics. To weaken the Agrarian Bank, Palomo Valencia launched the Independent Ejido Plan. It granted credit, henequen shoots, and vacant fields to peasants and peons in the form of so-called independent ejidos outside the federal reform program. In addition, the state government bought four haciendas and turned them over to peons as cooperatives to run under state as opposed to federal supervision and promised to purchase additional rasping machinery for ejidatarios. The Independent Ejido Plan implicitly spared most haciendas and provided the governor political cover to halt further expropriation of land. Palomo Valencia thus weakened the agrarian Cardenista faction while at the same time promising peasants and peons more work and land without federal supervision via state patronage.[71]

The Independent Ejido Plan served two important political purposes. First, it reassured hacendados that Palomo Valencia would stop federal agrarian reform by advancing the Independent Ejidal Plan as an alternative. Second, popular organizations linked to the official camarilla, like the Communist FSI, the PSS, and the CGT, could offer loans and land to members by means of Palomo Valencia's plan, thus bypassing the federal Agrarian Bank.[72]

Popular support for the Independent Ejido Plan fed on serious problems in the federal agrarian reform process. These problems worsened with Palomo Valencia's halt of new land grants.[73] From the end of 1936 to July 1937, the Agrarian Bank failed to substantially increase the number of peasants receiving land via federal ejidos in the henequen zone, and only 50 percent of those who had petitioned for land had so far been granted it.[74]

In trying to get the Independent Ejido Plan adopted and the Agrarian Bank to withdraw from Yucatán, Governor Palomo Valencia also used the contacts that he had built up during years of service in Mexico City to isolate and weaken the embattled head of the Agrarian Bank in Yucatán, Candelario Reyes. He had the national Agricultural Department send five brigades of engineers and advisers into the henequen zone so that peasants could avoid using the technical skills of the pro-bank Agrarian Department. Palomo Valencia also invited the head of the federal Agricultural Department, Saturnino Cedillo, to visit the state in person to endorse the governor's independent ejido scheme. Meanwhile, Palomo worked to divide the ranks of the Agrarian Bank by co-opting one of Reyes's most important subordinates, Hernán Pérez Uribe. Pérez headed the zone of Tixkokob, and the official camarilla endorsed him for mayor of Mérida for the 1937–38 term in return for breaking with his chief, Reyes.[75]

The official camarilla's oblique attacks on the Agrarian Bank represented but one front in a war being waged across Mexico by governors against national Cardenistas for regional dominance. National Cardenistas hoped to increase their influence on the state level by organizing affiliates of the national labor (CTM) and peasant (CCM [Confederación Campesina Mexicana], later CNC [Confederación Nacional Campesina]) federations in each state. Even before Palomo Valencia's rise to power, regional organizations such as the PSS and the FSI resolutely resisted joining the CTM, and attempts to establish the CCM in Yucatán failed miserably in July and August 1936. During his administration, Palomo Valencia worked hard to keep the CTM and the CNC out by using groups affiliated with the official camarilla to organize popular groups of their own like the APY.[76] The governor's success in stalling agrarian reform and reversing attempts to extend Mexico City's power in the state put the future of the Cardenista project in jeopardy.

Conclusion: Cardenismo at the Crossroads

López Cárdenas tried to forge a united Cardenista popular front out of the agrarian Cardenistas, Left-Cardenismo, and independent labor. Aznar Mendoza exploited the fault lines in this coalition, taking advantage of the clash between agrarian Cardenismo and the governor, peon and peasant resentment of agrarian reform, and urban labor's alienation from the governor. Using these conflicts to his advantage, he assembled a strong base to oppose López Cárdenas. Gualberto Carrillo Puerto mobilized another regional bloc against Governor López Cárdenas, drawing on peasant resentment of unpopular local officials as well as the provincial bourgeoisie's fear of the Left and agrarian reform. Aznar Mendoza's camarilla aligned with the Gualbertistas to defeat the governor's clique in the senatorial campaign, then overthrew López Cárdenas in the 1 July strike. Although Aznar Mendoza's camarilla mobilized peasants, peons, and urban workers against López Cárdenas by denouncing bossism, economic problems, and violations of federal labor law in the name of Cárdenas, its goal remained seizing power in Mérida and stalling agrarian reform. Because independent unions and local Gualbertista factions depended on Aznar Mendoza and in some cases were aligned with conservative provincial vecinos, their Cardenista agenda of popular empowerment and worker and peasant rights would prove difficult to realize. Failing to seize regional power and lacking the internal cohesion of the Left or the strong national support of the agrarian Cardenistas, Gualbertismo and the Independent Unions would slowly decline as regional powers after the dramatic mobilizations of the spring of 1936.

Aznar Mendoza himself was also unable to control the outcome of the popular mobilizations. Palomo Valencia thwarted Aznar Mendoza's political ambitions by staging a coup within a coup and seizing the governorship himself. It would be elements of the clique of state officials later known as the official camarilla that would eventually prevail. By late 1936, Palomo Valencia and his official camarilla had stabilized the political situation in the state and either co-opted or neutralized almost all potential rival camarillas. Outmaneuvered on the regional level and undercut in many locales, the Gualbertistas and the agrarian Cardenistas looked to Mexico City to counter Palomo and resolve the agrarian impasse. Cárdenas's reaction and his dramatic solution of the state's "agrarian problem" would be revealed in August 1937.

4

The Crusade of the Mayab:

Cardenismo from Above

B Y MID-1937, Yucatán's agrarian problem had become a crisis for
Cárdenas. The popular Cardenista mobilizations of 1935 and 1936
had diminished, dulled by the economic problems of the ejidos,
divisions between peons and peasants, resurgent cacique power, and the
violent deaths and co-optation of a generation of young Cardenista leaders.
The national state had no unified popular base in Yucatán, and recalcitrant
regional politicos of the official camarilla seemingly had regained control
over the state's destiny and stalled agrarian reform. By the fall of 1937,
Cárdenas's patience had run out. If Yucatán could not be brought under the
control of the central government, the central government would have to
go to Yucatán.

During his term, Cárdenas had increased his popularity and power
by making forays into the provinces in response to grassroots mobilizations. He journeyed to the Laguna region in 1936 to divide the cotton haciendas after a massive peon strike broke out. Widespread labor disturbances
prompted visits to Puebla and Monterrey. However, in Yucatán, there was
no single, unified mass movement among workers or peasants on which
Cárdenas could build.

Long the hope of Cardenistas, agrarian reform in the henequen zone in
Yucatán faced a host of problems in mid-1937. In Hoctun, for instance,
henequen grants proved insufficient for the community, forcing peasants to
complain that the Revolution had yet to reach their town.[1] In Kanasín, on
the other hand, some peasants refused to accept henequen land from the
Agrarian Bank, demanding vacant land to plant with corn without federal
supervision or credit — prompting an acrimonious intracommunal dispute
in which each faction charged the other with corruption, fraud, and collusion with hacendados.[2] The division between agrarian supporters of the
bank and their opponents cropped up again and again across the henequen
zone, preventing a horizontal, class-based, pro-Cárdenas mobilization in
the countryside.

Cárdenas desperately needed to consolidate embattled Cardenista popular forces in Yucatán to provide a mandate to rescue agrarian reform, and he had to mobilize a strong base before the gubernatorial election scheduled for September 1937. By personally going to Yucatán, and by bringing the full brunt of federal power to bear on the state, Cárdenas hoped in one stroke to overcome the legal, political, and economic barriers to completing agrarian reform and in the process mobilize Yucatán's peasantry and workers. Luis Cabrera, a prominent former Maderista now an intellectual condottiere in the service of Yucatecan hacendados, mocked the president's audacious mission as "the Crusade of the Mayab" (land of the Maya), a name to which the Cardenistas took with pride.[3]

The Agrarian Crusade: Yucatán Redeemed?

Cárdenas planned to overcome resistance and bottlenecks in the agrarian reform process by increasing the speed and scale of land reform in the henequen zone rather than dealing with specific planning problems or answering popular grievances. On 3 August, Cárdenas announced his Solución Salvadora (Redeeming Solution): nothing less than rapid execution of all pending land grants in the henequen zone. Five days later, the president fleshed out his solution in further proclamations that amended the Federal Agrarian Code and greatly expanded the scope of federal activity in the henequen zone.[4] Cárdenas proclaimed by fiat the "immediate and total resolution" of all pending acts of land reform, including restitution (return of lands illegally seized from communities before the Revolution), donation (new ejidal grants to meet peasant and peon needs), and enlargement of existing ejidos whose lands were insufficient for its members. The number of new henequen ejidos to be created virtually overnight — a staggering 94 — would raise the total to 272 and would supposedly reduce all haciendas to *pequeñas propiedades* (small properties) of a uniform 150 hectares.

The new grants ensured that every pueblo in the henequen zone received a grant, whether it wanted one or not. More importantly, Cárdenas's accord explicitly gave henequen fields to fifty-six communities of hacienda-dwelling peons, "the most oppressed group, whose living conditions are the most difficult out of all the working peasants of the Republic."[5] This inclusion of peons, who had for the most part been excluded from agrarian reform before August 1937, aimed to calm social tensions by demobilizing the CGT.

At the same time, Cárdenas promised to aid existing ejidos with enough federal support to purchase sufficient rasping machinery.[6] Carrying out the surveys, legal transfers, and administrative tasks that Cárdenas mandated was a mammoth task. Nevertheless, in August and September 1937, the federal technical support staff created fifty-six new ejidos manned (women could not receive land according to law) by 8,091 new ejidatarios.[7] Over the next several months, state and federal officials executed many more grants as well. On paper at least, presidential word became deed.

But in spite of the herculean efforts of federal authorities, the Crusade of the Mayab failed to save agrarian reform, and, in many ways, it only expanded existing problems. Even after engineers reduced most haciendas to just 150 hectares and dropped the per capita average of land grants from 9 hectares in 1934 to 4, many eligible peasants and peons never received land. Some thirteen thousand peasants and peons with a right to henequen land — perhaps one of every four or five — still had none after the crusade, and many that had received henequen land complained that they did not have enough.[8] An estimated 125 of the 272 henequen ejidos never received all the land to which they were entitled, while 71 got more than their legal allotment.[9] Only 10 of 272 ejidos received an appropriate balance of idle land to fields in production, hindering future plantings.[10]

Although the crusade left Motul's ejido with a fairly good ratio of planted to vacant land, much of the land that it received was fourteen kilometers away. An estimated forty-five ejidos faced the same problem. Ejidos created for ex-peons were especially prone to receive land grants far away from their communities, perhaps because the Agrarian Bank had already allocated the nearby land to villagers.[11]

Other problems loomed on the horizon. Some hacendados claimed that they had been left with fewer than 150 hectares and threatened legal action. Staffing the expanded number of ejidos created other complications. Seeking technical and management expertise, the Agrarian Bank turned to former hacienda employees, with the result that new ejidatarios at times found themselves taking orders from the same hated foremen. Ejidatarios charged that the Agrarian Bank's personnel new and old skimmed from the budget and conspired with hacendados to charge for access to rasping machinery, robbing ejidos of their thin profit margins.[12]

Rasping and cultivation problems, bureaucratic mismanagement and corruption, and dropping global sisal prices forced the Agrarian Bank to lower already paltry advances (wages paid to ejidatarios against future earnings) in December 1937, barely three months after the triumphant culmination of reform. A year and a half later, at the end of July 1939, 197 of the 272 henequen ejidos still needed subsidies, and 65 of these languished in a critical financial situation.[13]

The land grants of the crusade finally achieved the transfer of a huge amount of land from the hands of hacendados to the ejidos. Sustaining collective units of production would require an even greater financial commitment from the national government as well as the cooperation of state authorities — both dubious propositions.[14]

Even while Cárdenas and his national collaborators scrambled to fund the commitments created by the crusade, the president was trying to accommodate the state government of Yucatán. Implementing the creation of so many ejidal grants so quickly required the economic support, legal help, bureaucratic assistance, and general cooperation of Yucatecan authorities. Cárdenas's personal presence forced Governor Palomo Valencia to reverse his earlier position and wholeheartedly embrace radical land reform.[15] Behind the scenes, however, Palomo Valencia and his official camarilla wrung a key concession from Cárdenas in return for their support. Cárdenas granted individual ejidos the right to declare their independence from the federal agrarian bureaucracy, fatally weakening the Agrarian Bank in the state.[16] Not surprisingly, Agrarian Bank chief Candelario Reyes strongly protested Cárdenas's decision. He accused the governor and (unnamed) hacendados of using the FSI and associated Communist professors to convince no fewer than 15 percent of ejidatarios to declare their independence in a thinly disguised attempt to "eliminate" the Agrarian Bank.[17]

The Crusade of the Mayab's agrarian blitzkrieg vastly expanded the number and size of henequen ejidos. But the political equation was much more complex than a simple triumph of Cárdenas and the national government over all. In terms of the center-region dynamic, this key concession to the official camarilla headed by Governor Palomo Valencia had strengthened the state administration and weakened the federal Agrarian Bank. But it had not resolved the dispute between agrarian Cardenismo and its enemies, which would continue. This conflict would play out on the local level, where ejidatarios affiliated with the Agrarian Bank would clash with so-called independent ejidatarios linked to the official camarilla for control of local power and resources.[18]

Another key factor in the regional political situation was the hacendados. The Crusade of the Mayab had earned Cárdenas and the postrevolutionary state in general the lasting hatred of the vast majority of landholders. Not only had Cárdenas pointedly ignored their entreaties to spare their haciendas, but, in a private presidential audience, he also reportedly told the Yucatecan hacendados that he would "take the last screw they had hidden up their asses." And some families felt unfairly singled out, having lost much more land than others.[19]

Yet, despite their lamentations that Cárdenas had ruined them, Cárdenas had also liberated hacendados from the threat of strikes and the legal obligations to house and provide education and medical attention to most peons, who were now wards of the federal government.[20] The slow economic decline that many had been experiencing long before Cárdenas because of poor henequen markets and the failure to diversify investments was now blamed on the president. More importantly, virtually every hacendado kept at least 150 hectares of land and by far the most valuable part of any hacienda, the processing machinery.[21] As a result, the hacendados survived the Crusade of the Mayab with more of their wealth intact than usually thought.

We know less about the group that supposedly benefited the most from the crusade: the ejidatarios. Because there were 272 henequen ejidos made up of thousands of former peasants and peons, and because the economic and social conditions of the individual ejidos varied widely, it is difficult to generalize about their situation. Cárdenas's personal presence and sweeping promises probably raised hopes, but without resolution of political conflicts and the ejidos' financial problems, optimism could not become strong, pro-Cárdenas sentiment.

Still, in many locales in the henequen zone, the immediate effect of the Cardenista agrarian offensive seemed to be positive. Where pro-agrarian support existed — around Tixkokob and north of Mérida, for instance — additional land grants and promises of further financial support raised the spirits of agrarian Cardenistas.[22] The ejido of the pueblo Chablekal, north of the state capital, had already been operating for over a year and a half and running a profit. It was doing so well that it could hire peons from neighboring haciendas to process henequen and invest in new plantings.[23] But, among peons and where the crusade had to create ejidos hastily, resistance to agrarian reform remained strong. On hacienda Xteppen, near Umán, peons were afraid to accept land and had to be told by the overseers and the owner himself to take possession of it.[24]

Because the historical record of Cardenista Yucatán is mainly made up of either sympathetic accounts that celebrated agrarian reform or denunciations of corruption and accounts of resistance in the opposition press or in complaints to federal officials, it is very difficult to discern how peasants viewed Cárdenas's crusade. One public assembly of ejidatarios held during the crusade provides a brief, although somewhat filtered, glimpse into the popular reaction to the Cardenista land grants.

The First Ejidal Congress and the
Balance of Agrarian Reform

The best measure of the short-term results of Cárdenas's attempts to mobilize popular support came at the First Ejidal Congress, held in Mérida on 16–17 August 1937, a few days after Cárdenas's climactic proclamation. Federal and state officials invited delegates from every ejido in the henequen zone to the congress, with the aim of giving peasants the opportunity to air grievances and respond to the presidential initiative. This kind of meeting reflected the democratic impulse of Cárdenas at its best, a chance for the president to engage in dialogue directly with the common folk, bypassing bureaucrats, technical advisers, and politicians.

The pro-Cárdenas, propagandistic accounts of the convention suggest that peasants responded warmly to the crusade in a suspiciously uniform manner. The participation of the ejidatario delegates was summarized as follows in the official transcript: "They expressed, clearly, bravely, and concretely, their needs and problems, inspired by the very positive attitude and wishes of the president, General Lázaro Cárdenas, who reaches out to solve in a satisfactory manner all their needs and problems."[25] Delegate after delegate rose to the podium and presented a list of pressing needs of his ejido and his community. Requests ranged from dynamite and pumps for wells to mules and tools. Many delegates voiced precisely the same demands that Cárdenas had already pledged to meet: more land for the ejidos, access to rasping machinery, schools, sports and medical facilities, roads, and consumer cooperatives. Of course, the tributes to Cárdenas might well have come from the agrarian Cardenistas who were with him all along; Cárdenas might have been preaching to the choir. On the other hand, many ejidatarios speaking at the convention were members of local credit societies that had racked up large debts to the Agrarian Bank, amounts that would require years to repay. Their calls for extended repayment periods figured prominently at the assembly—but Cárdenas and federal officials sidestepped them.[26]

Even when taken at face value, the petitions raised questions about the dynamic of agrarian and social reform. Marcos Tzek, the delegate from Opichén, echoed Cárdenas's justification of land reform when he said that peasants had bought the land with their blood. While following the state discourse in this respect, he went on to challenge the authority of federal teachers by accusing (unnamed) educators of corruption and of giving classes while drunk. Other delegates complained of federal, state, and local officials interfering with their ejidos.[27]

It could be argued, of course, that merely by creating a dialogue between state officials and popular representatives, the Cardenista state legitimized itself. However, building popular support required not only efforts on the part of the state, but active, positive participation by communal representatives, who in turn had to be convinced that the ejidos could be sustained.

Had Cárdenas finally instilled that confidence among ejidatarios? In spite of the litany of praise for Cárdenas entered in the official written record of the convention, one pro-Cárdenas visitor concluded from the behavior and actions of peasant delegates that there was little actual enthusiasm for Cardenismo. Aldo Baroni described it as "a spectacle lacking emotion and interest." Despite Cárdenas's personal inauguration of the convention and the energetic hectoring of a federal official who implored delegates to speak freely, the peasants dutifully took the podium and spoke (at times barely audibly) from notes taken out of the pockets of their guayaberas. They read in monotonous voices lists of demands with what Baroni called the enthusiasm of a notary. Baroni also speculated that officials vetted the lists beforehand, as they all were apparently typed on the same typewriter on the same paper.[28] Clearly, a few delegates — like Opichén's — departed from the official script, but, on the whole, the event seemed stale and perfunctory, not a real outpouring of popular opinion.

The account of the convention in the opposition newspaper *Diario de Yucatán* confirmed Baroni's skeptical view. The paper's reporter noted with delight that peasant delegate Názaro Pisté's prolonged reading of a lengthy list of requests was cut short when peasants waiting in line to speak shouted him down. The next speaker said, in Maya, that he would just as soon enter his petition by hand so that he could go home and return to work sooner — and was warmly applauded.[29]

Other glimmers of humor enlivened the assembly and suggests that many participants had been dragooned into coming and wisecracked to express their resentment. Marcos Tzek, the feisty delegate from Opichén, bragged that he would welcome visitors to his hometown by giving them everything "except anise, because there are no dens of vice, or milk, because we don't have cows." His triple pun played on the fact that Opichén had been dry since the early 1920s, that the slang word for bootleg rum was *milk,* and that Opichén was too poor to have many cattle.[30] The ovation that he received suggests that his humor was a welcome relief to the endless series of rote recitals and canned messages. A few moments of levity aside, the accounts of both Baroni and the *Diario de Yucatán* suggest that the convention was a staged attempt to manufacture popular Cardenismo, an attempt that largely fell flat.

If the official convention revealed the cautious or apathetic response of peasants toward Cardenista land reform, Candelario Reyes's address to the convention sheds some light on the condition of the ejidos at the end of the crusade. Reyes boasted that the federal Agrarian Bank had made progress in providing medical care to replace hacendados' services as well as beginning an ambitious infrastructure project including telephone lines and rural electrification.[31] Reyes promised to transform the henequen zone in the future but also hinted at how much the Agrarian Bank had yet to do: only half the communities eligible for land had received it, and a shocking three-quarters (his figures, not his critics') of those eligible had refused to join. Reyes blamed the lack of peasant enthusiasm on the fact that the federal government had turned its back on agrarian reform in Yucatán from 1924 until 1935, undermining peasant confidence, and on "professional politicians and the teachers responsible for the schools of the haciendas"—in other words, the official camarilla and Communist teachers now aligned with it.[32]

Reyes was too loyal a Cardenista to mention that the federal government simply had not advanced enough credit to meet the needs of the ejidos, making peasants suspicious of the plan. And, with the stroke of a pen, Cárdenas had greatly increased the bank's responsibilities. Indeed, Eduardo Suárez, Cárdenas's financial guru who was at the First Ejidal Congress, undoubtedly left Yucatán worried about how to fund the tremendous commitment that the federal government had now assumed.[33] The number of henequen ejidos had gone from around fifty or sixty to close to three hundred, and with that increase came more infrastructure and service needs. Cárdenas's crusade had been predicated on the assumption that accelerating the process and expanding federal intervention would improve the situation by building up peasant confidence in the federal Agrarian Bank and thus denying the antiagrarian forces a popular base. The expected groundswell of popular support had yet to take place, and Cárdenas still had to meet the greatly expanded financial commitments of the federal government in the henequen zone.

Even as Cárdenas and his retinue tried hastily to draw up a comprehensive blueprint to see the new henequen ejidos through, the president executed other elements of his project, cultural and social reforms.

The Cultural and Social Crusade: Reform from
Above, Response from Below

At the time the crusade took place, the underlying economic problems of agrarian reform were largely overshadowed by the drama of Cárdenas's personal presence in Yucatán. Through the pro-government press, Cárdenas made Yucatán the focus of national attention during his visit. Accompanied by technocrats, diplomats, and writers (Dr. Atl, Martín Luis Guzmán, Aldo Baroni), Cárdenas set up his traveling capital on the western outskirts of Mérida. During his three-week stay in Yucatán, Cárdenas and his coterie presided over several massive public ceremonies and visited dozens of towns and villages across Yucatán.[34] Denied use of the Presidential Olive Train because of Yucatán's isolation from the national rail network (the swamps of Tabasco and southern Campeche rendered the Yucatán peninsula an island in all but name), Cárdenas had to travel in the old 1915 vintage *fordtingos* (Model Ts) of the PSS.

Another head of state might have been aggrieved to be chauffeured about in the weather-beaten, big-tired cars lovingly named "Jesús de Mucho Poder" and "The Four Winds," jalopies whose shock absorbers and body paint were long gone. But Cárdenas took to them. Like the transportation, meals were bare-bones: canned sausages, salmon, and sardines.[35] Yet, despite the unimposing nature of Cárdenas's travels, or perhaps because of the absence of pomp and ceremony, the presidential tour of the Yucatecan campo took on a kind of quiet dignity.

Aldo Baroni described a visit to the small settlement of Yotholín. A single trumpet announced Cárdenas's arrival in the middle of the night. Like almost all villages, Yotholín had no electric lighting, but moonlight lent the caravan of fordtingos, followed by the "Orquestra Típica" of the Agrarian Department stuffed in a larger truck, "a natural majesty" that suggested to the usually hard-edged Baroni "a trembling in the human spirit, a sincere desire for redemption, an intimate confession of human fraternity."[36]

Public ceremonies staged by state and federal officials provide insight into the Cardenista project for Yucatán—not just the agrarian aspect, but social and cultural reforms as well. After the proclamation of agrarian reform in Mérida, Cárdenas and his entourage moved south to the hacienda Temozón on 8 August to stage the ceremonial kickoff of land reform.[37]

Ceremony and Cardenista organs proclaimed the FSI leaders slain at Temozón in January 1937, Ignacio Mena and Adalberto Sosa, agrarian martyrs, in hopes that the hero cult of the Yucatecan Castor and Pollux would draw support for agrarian reform.[38] The symbolically charged signing of the first land grant of the crusade at Temozón was prefaced by peasant speakers and an elaborately choreographed agrarian tableaux that lasted several hours under the blazing August sun.[39] Orators representing the recipients of the hacienda's land took the podium to thank their secular messiah.[40] One unidentified Maya speaker at Temozón was photographed addressing the president; the caption in *Menzay* (a Left-Cardenista mouthpiece — the Mayan *menzay* translates as "labor") read, "The Mayas have not opened their mouths to explain their situation in a long time," implying that Cárdenas's presence opened up a genuine dialogue between the people and their government.[41]

Peasants receiving land then acted out the numerous stages in the cultivation and processing of henequen that began with clearing the land and ended with packing the fiber. Such a presentation not only displayed the disciplined skills of Yucatán's rural workers but also answered landowners' doubts that peasants would be able to cultivate henequen without their guidance. Later, members of the newly created ejidos of Temozón and surrounding areas paraded along with federal soldiers and their uniformed wives. Hundreds of bused-in peasants waved small red pennants emblazoned with the phrase *Agrario* (land reform) and a scythe (a symbolic reference to the peasants taken from Communist iconography — a tool completely unknown as wheat was not grown in the state). Cárdenas also granted Temozón a federal school commemorating the agrarian martyrs Mena and Sosa. Sports, another important part of the Cardenista social reform agenda, were prominent in the form of baseball and basketball games between teams of ejidatarios and the federal Agrarian Department. Like the parade, these athletic events represented a sharing of public space in which peasants and federal agents were, for the moment at least, equals.[42]

Public ceremonies exemplified the new order of rural society envisioned by the Cardenistas. But ritual was not always the same as practice: the dialogue between Cárdenas and peasants and the ball games and marches uniting bureaucrats, the army, and ejidatarios suggested egalitarianism; the day-to-day operations of the collective ejidos demonstrated to the ejidatarios that federal officials were definitely in charge. Still, public events marking Cárdenas's arrival and the division of hacienda land served a didactic purpose. Ceremonies, translated into Maya and accompanied by many symbolic displays, conveyed to Cárdenas's Maya-speaking audience the national Cardenista blueprint for an idealized rural society, one in which the nature of the state, class and ethnic divisions, even the structure of the family and gender roles, would be transformed. In sharp contrast to Calles, Cárdenas downplayed anticlericalism and emphasized new aspects of social reform.[43] Education was a key part of both Calles's and Cárdenas's social projects of rural modernization and has rightfully drawn scholarly attention.[44] But other important components of Cardenismo's cultural and social agenda have largely been overlooked. The dedication of the sports stadium of Izamal that took place on Mexican Independence Day (16 September) 1937 during the crusade displayed its other aspects, like sports, a new family structure, and the racial "revitalization" of the Maya.

Because Cárdenas had already returned to the capital, Agrarian Secretary Gabino Vázquez presided over the elaborate ceremonies christening the stadium. Vázquez's remarks summarized the new, Cardenista policy on religion: the state respected the freedom of choice of the people of Mexico because "it is not the believers who are responsible but bad governments who have neglected popular education."[45] Thus, he implied, the abandonment of religious values—which were still seen as backward or harmful in the eyes of the Cardenistas—would come only by giving the people a positive alternative, education, not through suppression of religion as in Calles's day. Even though previous anticlerical legislation had not provoked armed resistance in Yucatán as it had in some parts of the country, the abandonment of punitive attacks against the church was undoubtedly well received by almost every social stratum.

Among the positive cultural alternatives, sports figured prominently. National Cardenistas like Vázquez hoped that sports would promote a more sober, productive ideal of manhood. They saw athletic games as a healthy alternative to men's recreational drinking. Moreover, the discipline of physical education promised to instill valued characteristics such as self-control, teamwork, and goal orientation. National Cardenistas thus continued the old Socialist tradition of handing out baseball gloves and building baseball diamonds in the countryside but took sports to a new, monumental level with Izamal's athletic stadium. By Cárdenas's day, sports had come to take on an even greater importance, associated with agrarian reform, ethnic revindication, and a new vision of masculinity.

All were prominent in the Sports-Agrarian Festival inaugurating the stadium of Izamal. The building's architecture, the public spectacle of the celebration, and the associated public discourse all reinforced the Cardenista belief that sports would help redeem and modernize the male Maya campesino. Izamal's agrarian Cardenista town council was strongly identified with the ejido, and the stadium straddled Maya ruins, coupling it with the glorious pre-Columbian Maya past. A plaque above the entry spelled out the connection: "Above these ruins that were the grand constructions of our ancestors, we raise this ejidal stadium where strong men and future generations of ejidatarios will be forged." Slogans emblazoned on the walls of the stadium stressed related themes, such as popular support for Cardenismo ("All for Cárdenas . . . to victory or death"), the link between sports, masculinity, and citizenship ("Clean bodies, strong men"), and the importance of agrarian reform to the nation's economic health ("The mass of peasants will rise again and increase the economy of Yucatán"). Spectacle and ceremony dramatized the idea that the state would uplift the peasantry through sports.[46] After a procession of soldiers, ejidatarios, and students from the federal high school bearing the national and the agrarian flags, a flame symbolizing the liberation of the peasants was lit. Ceremony and architecture together broadcast Cardenista social doctrine: sports, like the ejido, redeemed "the Maya."

Just as Heidi Tinsman has perceptively suggested in the case of agrarian reform in Chile in the 1960s and early 1970s, the Cardenista agrarian reform in Mexico reinforced men's supposed prerogatives as heads of families (only men could receive land on the ejidos) and emphasized a more asser-tive masculinity. In Yucatán, as in Chile, the national state hoped to use land reform to remove peasants from a childlike dependence on hacendados and transform them into independent men possessing "masculine agency and pride."[47]

The dedication of the stadium of Izamal revealed the Cardenista blue-print for a new gender and family structure. While sports would strengthen men, technology and socialization would transform women and, given the privileged place that women were assumed to have in the private sphere, the family as well. At Izamal, Gabino Vázquez replicated a strategy that he had first used in Torreón (in the northern Laguna region) the year before. Vázquez rewarded Cardenista women's groups in both areas with a mecha-nized corn-grinding *nixtamal* mill, a technological innovation that each day saved women laborious hours of pulverizing corn by working the tradi-tional *metate* on their hands and knees. But to Vázquez, not only did the nixtamal emancipate women from the hard labor of grinding corn, it also freed up their consciousness from the traditional mind-set, reorienting them toward the state and modern ideas by getting them out of the house and exposed to new ideas and new economic activities.[48]

The location of the nixtamal mill also spoke to Cardenista gender and family norms. It was housed in the arsenal of Izamal's Agrarian Militia, which in turn bordered a park.[49] The arrangement of the arsenal, the mill, and the playground suggested an idealized family structure that the Car-denistas hoped to achieve: men would be improved by sports and rifles; women would be emancipated from the drudgery of grinding on the metate to take on new roles; and the new mill, the arsenal, as well as children's recreational space would all come under the national state's benevolent supervision. The Cardenistas used the stadium and the arsenal/mill/park in Izamal to instill social behavior considered desirable and progressive for men/ejidatarios, women, and children.

The Crusade against Alcohol

National Cardenistas believed that the spread of sports not only modernized society and forged a new masculinity, but also promoted abstinence. In trying to limit drinking, the Cardenistas had an uphill fight. While eliminating alcohol had been a key part of the Cardenista social agenda since 1935, federal prohibition efforts had made little headway in Yucatán before the crusade. Although the federal solicitor for indigenous affairs in Yucatán made a few perfunctory attempts to prevent illegal alcohol sales in 1936 and 1937, his support for the Gualbertistas in regional political feuds largely diverted his attention.[50]

During the Crusade of the Mayab, federal agencies redoubled their efforts to wipe out drinking as part of a larger attempt to reform rural society and culture. Undaunted by resistance, Cárdenas himself lent a hand in the prohibition effort. During the moonlight visit to Yotholín that so impressed Baroni, Cárdenas granted the small but relatively prosperous village a water pump, a radio, sporting equipment, and school supplies to encourage their industry and virtue (ironically, one result was diversification into tobacco cultivation) and because "they had opposed the opening of cantinas and the vice of gambling."[51]

The Cardenista prohibition campaign was not limited to weaning drinkers away from the bottle with healthy alternatives like sports. During the crusade, Dr. Mario Villamil, representative in Yucatán of the federal Public Health Ministry, enforced the provisions of the Federal Labor Code of 1931 that legally barred cantinas from operating close to schools or places of employment. In an unzoned city like Mérida, the scattering of small factories and workshops meant that most taverns would be effectively put out of business.[52] But, just as the hacendados used legal delays to frustrate agrarian reform, so too did the tavern owners of Mérida and Progreso. By obtaining the Mexican legal stay known as the amparo, they effectively ended the short experiment in drying out urban Yucatán through state action.[53]

Although defeated in the city, the Cardenista prohibition campaign enjoyed more success in the countryside. Rural prohibition efforts were usually led by people within the communities, as opposed to the top-down effort in Mérida. Popular prohibition movements in the countryside, however, often provoked conflicts that divided communities along lines of gender and age. Although federal teachers of both sexes and younger men affiliated with leftist groups like the Young Socialists often led grassroots antialcohol efforts, most support came from women. And opposition invariably came from older men who patronized cantinas, often backed by the cronies of the caciques who ran them.[54]

In the large western town of Hunucmá, the leftist women's group known as the FUPDM asked Cárdenas to close the "baneful centers of vice" where "husbands and sons spend their money." Although the FUPDM was a Communist organization, it framed its request in the language of traditional notions of women as wives and mothers responsible for guarding the purity of their homes and their community. And, in another example of Cardenismo's reach exceeding its grasp, Cárdenas never answered the appeal from the Hunucmá FUPDM, probably because of his limited time and resources and the prioritization of agrarian reform ahead of other reforms. Not surprisingly, local officials took no action in spite of the women's entreaties.[55]

If Hunucmá typified the battle of the sexes over alcohol, Izamal was something of an exception. Fernando Acosta Navarrete declared a "war without quarter" against Izamal's cantinas. Like male federal officials (and unlike the women of Hunucmá), he invoked the federal legal code that supplemented Cárdenas's "Plan of Social Health" to try and close cantinas.[56] Prohibition campaigns at times united men and women in the same movement, but distinct rationales continued to reflect gendered divisions in society between men, who controlled the public sphere, and women, limited to protecting the family.

As was often the case, Acosta's movement was linked closely to the federal schools. He used this base to reach out to the Mexican PTA, the "Parents of the Family."[57] As in many other locales, a generational division emerged in the prohibition campaign. Its appeal was strongest among those boys not yet old enough to be "poisoned" by older men in the taverns; the Young Agrarian Vanguard and the Exploradores (Boy Scouts) handed out the "ABCs of Antialcohol." As was often the case, Izamal's mayor (in spite of being a dedicated agrarian Cardenista) tolerated widespread evasion of alcohol regulations.[58]

Another unusual feature of Izamal's prohibition campaign was its leader. Acosta became an ardent foe of cantinas only after he lost three of his own—La Guardia, El Nido, and Los Tres Chiles—and was arrested for continuing to sell liquor out the back door. Such a sudden conversion from cantina owner to prohibition crusader seemed suspicious to the publicans whom he hounded.[59] Whether his actions amounted to revenge against former competitors who might well have convinced authorities to put him out of business or whether, as he claimed, his motives were purely altruistic, it seems that Acosta had a great deal of credibility among his fellow Izamaleños.

The unusual success of Acosta's movement can be gauged from the strong and violent counterattacks that it provoked. During a parent-teacher-student rally against drinking, two cantina patrons stormed the proceedings and cruelly dismembered a piñata, scattering the crowd.[60] A few months later, foes believed to be *cantineros* (tavern owners) waylaid and beat Acosta in the streets.[61] Resistance did not always take such violent forms; when ordered to remove advertising for an alleged illegal bar, Juan Herrera painted over the sign out front to read "Ask for a nip."[62]

The Cardenista campaign against alcohol certainly succeeded in mobilizing grassroots opposition in Izamal, but Acosta's campaign was not a singular event. Women, children, and teachers of both sexes spearheaded prohibition efforts in several other localities. However, three local prohibition movements—those in the large town of Tizimín far to the east of the henequen zone, the comparably sized henequen town of Acancéh, and the small town of Ucú just west of Mérida—resembled popular reform movements less than struggles for local power. Because politicos in Tizimín, Acancéh, and Ucú customarily received kickbacks from, or directly owned, local watering holes, charges of violating alcohol regulations provided a handy weapon for factions "on the outs" to use against elected officials.

Take the case of Tizimín's Antialcohol Committee. It began operations the day before Labor Day (1 May) in 1936, adopting the nationalistic motto "Temperance for the Country and the Race." Tizimín's teetotalers soon joined forces with the local Sports Association (founded by elites on the outs with the current town council) to encourage residents to sell popsicles as a substitute for beer on Sundays.[63] In 1937, the Sports Association and its allies on the Antialcohol Committee built political support to overthrow the town council, using the Cardenista social agenda to hound local rivals.[64] A similar political struggle in Acancéh also generated a prohibition campaign. Ejidatarios of the Union of Workers and Peasants called for the closing of a *salón cerveza* because they opposed the mayor who owned it.[65]

Another struggle pitting "outs" against "ins" in Ucú led to charges of violations of the Dry Laws. In this small western town, the local Socialist Party organization charged the mayor, who was affiliated with the CGT, with selling aguardiente. These charges were but the latest skirmish in an ongoing war between PSS and CGT factions in Ucú. Unlike other similar denunciations, charges in Ucú resulted in an investigation and apparently a conviction of the accused in June 1937 on charges made by the state Department of the Treasury. Although no punishment was recorded, the mayor resigned nine months later.[66] It seems likely that the influence of the PSS over state government, not a newfound puritanism among Mérida's bureaucracy, resulted in the mayor's removal.

Significantly, men who were not teachers dominated the prohibition movements in Tizimín, Acancéh, and Ucú; women and children played minor roles. Their involvement in local struggles for power subsumed prohibition into politics, suggesting that, when men controlled these movements instead of the more usual coalition of teachers, women, and children, they tended to be less dedicated to social reform and more oriented to political competition.

The often intimate relation between local bosses and cantinas, on the one hand, and the tendency of male-dominated opposition factions to use prohibition opportunistically as a weapon for political ends, on the other, blunted the Cardenista prohibition campaign. Given that Cárdenas needed the support of Yucatecan politicos for agrarian reform, he was unwilling to spend too much political capital trying to close cantinas when he needed to build support for agrarian reform in the henequen zone.

The Crusade of the Mayab: Cardenismo Triumphant?

The sweeping land grants overseen by President Cárdenas in late 1937 finally fulfilled his "solemn promise" to carry out land reform in Yucatán's henequen zone. Although some of the henequen ejidos thrived, most had serious problems, and the effect of the crusade on the agrarian situation would not be fully apparent for years to come. Even more so than in the case of agrarian reform, the effect of the crusade's social and cultural project is hard to judge. Pro-sports campaigns seem to have been the most successful, probably because state agents coordinated their efforts with some popular campaigns.[67] Prohibition ran up against strong resistance, and the Cardenista national state had little stomach for a protracted fight against alcohol. Attempts to transform gender roles involved such a complex number of factors that any short-term effort from above was almost certainly doomed to failure. More active cooperation with the FUPDM might have produced more changes. Still, social and cultural reform was always secondary for Cárdenas, as he believed that agrarian reform had to precede other changes in rural society in Yucatán. Just as importantly, Cárdenas had to husband scarce resources to push through agrarian reform, and he was willing to jettison social and culture reform in order to do so.

Along with renewed attention to social and cultural reform, the Cardenistas hoped that the president's "redeeming solution" would end the problems that had plagued Yucatán during the first half of Cárdenas's term. There is no question that Cárdenas's whirlwind tour captivated the nation's attention and convincingly demonstrated the president's willingness to help the common people. Yet serious problems still faced the new henequen ejidos, social and cultural reform would take years to change rural Yucatán, and the strong popular support that Cárdenas believed his crusade would create failed to coalesce. Only a few weeks after his departure from Yucatán, Cardenismo from above would be put to the test in the gubernatorial election of 1937.

5

Alliance Failed: Cárdenas, Urban Labor, and the Open Door Election of 1937

CÁRDENAS TIMED THE Crusade of the Mayab to precede the gubernatorial election of October 1937. Completion of agrarian reform would, he hoped, calm popular ferment in the henequen zone and create a strong Cardenista base to elect a progressive, loyal governor. To that end, the national Cardenista regime reformed the electoral process to increase popular participation. Its Open Door Plan invited worker and peasant groups to vote in PNR primaries by automatically registering all members of federally recognized unions and ejidos. The national PNR further pledged to completely take over the balloting process from state governments to ensure that Cardenista workers, peasants, and soldiers, instead of front groups controlled by local bureaucrats and regional cliques, would select PNR candidates.[1]

The national ruling party believed that the Open Door Plan would also reverse the rising rate of voter abstention. In the 1933 gubernatorial election in Yucatán, some 57,639 votes were cast, a number probably inflated by multiple voting, but still almost twice the 28,000–30,000 figure for the 1936 senatorial election.[2] Still, the national Cardenistas originally believed that they could increase popular participation and at the same time guarantee that a loyal, pro-Cárdenas governor would be elected. But, for a Cardenista candidate to win, the Open Door Plan would need to deliver thousands of union members and ejidatarios to the polls.

The first part of this chapter examines the process of the Open Door gubernatorial election of 1937 to judge the success of Cardenismo in mobilizing popular support and dismantling the electoral machine of the regional official camarilla. In other states where Cardenismo thrived, workers formed its vanguard. Given the problems of agrarian reform in Yucatán, the success of the Open Door Plan would hinge on Cárdenas's ability to put together an urban worker base. Consequently, the second part of this chapter focuses on relations between Cárdenas and urban labor.

The Open Door Election of 1937

Cárdenas's visit to Yucatán and the promise of a more open electoral process lured prospective gubernatorial candidates out of the woodwork in the fall of 1937. Aspirants ranged from such political heavyweights as perennial candidate Senator Gualberto Carrillo Puerto to an ambitious physical education teacher. Even after some attrition, no fewer than twenty-seven candidates remained in the race during the crusade; most besieged the president's temporary residence on the west side of Mérida to ask for his endorsement. Popular excitement never matched the enthusiasm among the political class for the election: the Mexico City journalist Aldo Baroni wryly noted that "the number of candidates was sufficient to form their own union; but, from what I saw, there were more candidates than there were those who wanted to vote for them."[3]

The absence of popular mobilizations for the election can be traced back to the electoral process itself. Although Open Door reform promised a bottom-up selection process to determine the PNR candidate, the party president, Silvano Barba González, allowed the PNR primary to be decided in the traditional, top-down manner. Instead of canvassing peasant and worker groups to select a candidate, he consulted with the governor and the federal military commander in the state as well as with Senator Gualberto Carrillo Puerto and other self-proclaimed "heads of opposition groups." Privately, Barba González frankly admitted to Cárdenas that the numerous candidates "lacked the necessary qualities to be governor," but he worried that a genuinely open campaign might unleash "a strong political agitation" that would in turn undermine land reform. Barba González's actions ensured that the official camarilla and rival cliques, not workers and peasants, would control the outcome.[4] The fear of a popular backlash against the shortcomings of agrarian reform and the need to maintain the support of regional politicos outweighed the desire to democratize the gubernatorial nomination process.

Consequently, while the national PNR initially said that only federally registered groups could vote, it later allowed 646 organizations registered by the state government to participate, dwarfing the 72 federally registered ones.[5] This concession allowed the governor's group to fill the electoral rolls with the PSS and FSI affiliates that it controlled, shutting the door on independent groups.

Because of the exclusion of popular input into the PNR primary process, the race attracted a host of apparatchiks, also-rans, and dark-horse candidates. All vied to proclaim their blind adherence to Cardenismo, especially in the matter of agrarian reform; one candidate's manifesto characteristically pledged to "consolidate in Yucatán the revolutionary principles sustained by our great president Lázaro Cárdenas."[6] But, behind the stock Cardenista slogans, the aspirants for governor were linked to interests who shared few of the president's ideals; most ran campaigns that relied on frustrated bureaucrats and office seekers or organizers linked to either pro-state government or pro-hacendado political fronts.

Behind the Open Door: The Official Camarilla

From the outset of the Open Door gubernatorial campaign, the official camarilla, headed by sitting governor Palomo Valencia, enjoyed substantial influence over the PNR's selection process. Palomo Valencia could draw on many resources to support the candidacy of his chosen successor, none other than his own secretary of communication and public works, Humberto Canto Echeverría, an engineer with no political base of his own. The official camarilla's campaign followed, not the Open Door's blueprint for grassroots participation, but the familiar pattern of imposition by the outgoing governor. On 12 September, the leaders of the PSS assembled a carefully selected group of delegates in its headquarters, the Casa del Pueblo, to choreograph the nomination of Canto Echeverría. Members of the state congress then visited town councils across the state, ordering them to turn out the vote for the official candidate and suppress opposition campaigning or face dismissal. In order to garner votes for a virtually unknown candidate, the official camarilla reportedly diverted some 300,000 pesos from the state treasury and state-run Henequen Cooperative to purchase propaganda murals, favorable press coverage, electric signs, and, of course, liters of aguardiente. In another sign of the national government's weakness, Palomo Valencia took the mandatory deductions from the checks of state employees destined for the national PNR and gave them to the PSS.[7] The national PNR regulations that bound the governor and its regional affiliate, the PSS, specifically banned all these examples of machine politics (indeed, since 1935, the PSS was supposed to be prohibited from all electoral activity), but Palomo Valencia practiced them with impunity.

The impotence of the national PNR virtually guaranteed that the candidate tapped by Palomo Valencia would be the next governor. Humberto Canto Echeverría faced some opposition, but, ironically, most of it came from within the closed circle of the official camarilla.

Outside the official camarilla, Miguel Alonso Romero, the former leader of an old hacendado-linked party that dated back to the early 1920s, announced his intentions but then withdrew. He would later run with official camarilla support for federal congress, suggesting a quid pro quo. The political neophyte Emilio Guerra Leal never picked up much support despite spending freely on propaganda. Although the old Socialist baron Rafael Cebada Tenreiro threw his hat in the ring, there remained only one candidate with a chance to deny Canto Echeverría victory: Gualberto Carrillo Puerto.

Gualberto Carrillo Puerto, Perpetual Candidate

As we have seen, Carrillo Puerto had already won a seat in the senate because of his strong ties to President Cárdenas and prominent national Cardenistas as well as the mythic stature of his brother Felipe. As in his successful senatorial campaign, he could also rely on a broad network of local supporters in virtually every pueblo in the state as well as organizations on many haciendas and in most neighborhoods in the state's capital.[8] A public proclamation featuring endorsements from national luminaries included agrarista Marte R. Gómez's message to Don Gualberto; he stated that Gualberto Carrillo would "put into practice the socialist doctrine of Felipe," revealing the success that he enjoyed in trafficking on the national prominence of his brother's hero cult.[9] In spite of his own ambiguous position on agrarian reform in the past, Gualberto Carrillo now styled himself as the champion of land reform in the state during the crusade. The president had frequently used Don Gualberto as his personal interpreter during the Crusade of the Mayab, allowing Carrillo Puerto to hitch his gubernatorial campaign to Cárdenas's wagon. Carrillo's frequent appearances with Cárdenas bestowed on him immeasurable prestige among rural audiences. The closeness of the two led opponents to charge Carrillo Puerto with publicly claiming that the president had promised him the governorship. Indeed, numerous joint appearances did amount to a virtual endorsement by Cárdenas.[10]

The conflict between state and federal officials over agrarian reform gave Gualberto Carrillo another advantage. To strike at Palomo Valencia, federal Agrarian Bank chief Candelario Reyes covertly backed Gualberto Carrillo and supported his dubious claim to be a champion of agrarian reform. The federal agrarian bureaucracy used its control over access to land and work to turn out the vote for the candidate. Opichén's town council accused the ejido's president of threatening those who did not support Gualberto Carrillo Puerto with exclusion from the pending ejidal grant. Attempting to block the spread of Gualbertismo among local agrarian Cardenista leaders, the official camarilla illegally overthrew ejidal commissaries and accused the Agrarian Bank of meddling. Protests by the official camarilla eventually forced Candelario Reyes to leave the state until the end of the election, but there is little doubt that federal patronage helped mobilize support for the Gualbertistas.[11]

Gualberto Carrillo Puerto garnered more peasant support from the disintegration of the PSS under Palomo Valencia. Many older Socialist leaders resented not having been consulted in the choice of Canto Echeverría (who reportedly was not even a PSS member) and defected to the Gualbertistas. As in past Gualbertista campaigns, many older peasants fondly recalled Gualberto's martyred brother Felipe, and the Gualbertistas strengthened these recollections through the free use of traditional symbols of the Socialist Party. Campaign rallies featured the old red triangular banner of the PSS with a photograph of Gualberto imposed on its center. Many low-level politicos risked reprisals from the governor and openly declared for Carrillo Puerto. At least twenty town councils (of ninety-five) openly backed Gualberto Carrillo in 1937, including those of such large provincial towns as Acancéh, Izamal, Maxcanú, and Halachó.[12]

Carrillo Puerto diversified his constituency by bringing in marginalized groups, namely, women and recently urbanized residents of Mérida. To the inhabitants of Mérida's growing suburbs, Carrillo Puerto promised basic urban services, like sporting fields, schools, parks, public lighting, and cheap electricity. In recruiting women, Gualberto could call on the services of his sister Elvia, a nationally prominent feminist leader whose radical beliefs and mobilization of women under their brother Felipe earned her the nickname of "the Red Nun." Elvia organized local chapters of women into the Gualbertista Central Agrarian Communities for Females, committed to Cárdenas's agenda for the economic, social, and political liberation of women.[13]

Although women and suburban voters were a sizable percentage of the state's population, their effect was limited by the Open Door Plan, which favored established worker and peasant unions. Consequently, Gualbertista hopes lay in encouraging the existing labor and campesino groups to defect from the official camarilla, in courting independent labor, and in using Carrillo Puerto's ties to the federal government to found new popular organizations. The Gualbertistas did pick up many renegade local affiliates of pro-official federations like the PSS, the CGT, the FSI, and the FROC. As in the 1936 senatorial election, they garnered the support of the Independent Unions confederation, made up of truckers and artisans, Arturo Albertos Betancourt's anti-Communist teacher faction, and other unions of Mérida. And, with the help of the federal Agrarian Bank and the sympathetic national Department of Indigenous Affairs, the Gualbertistas founded their own network of peasant organizations, known as the League of Agrarian Communities. Although Candelario Reyes and the Agrarian Bank could not legally participate in politics, they helped Gualbertista peasant leaders form so-called agrarian communities and gain voting rights under the Open Door Plan. The key role of federal agents was clear in Cansahcab, where cacique Antonio Aranda ejected the peasants who supported the Gualbertista campaign from the ejido (the bank quickly rehired them). The alliance between Gualbertismo and the agrarian Cardenista camarilla was also evident in Espita, where peasants saluted candidate Gualberto Carrillo with chants of "Viva Carrillo Puerto, Viva the Agrarian Bank!" and "The ejidatarios are with Gualberto!"[14] But, for the most part, outside of a few communities with long histories of support for the Carrillo Puerto family, like Opichén and Muxupip, Gualbertismo was on the decline.

To impose Canto Echeverría, the official camarilla tried to counter the Gualbertistas' appropriation of the agrarian issue. It produced a poster featuring a picture from the 1910s of Canto Echeverría presiding over a transfer of land to a peasant village during his previous career as a state agrarian engineer. The text of the poster reminded peasants that while Canto Echeverría was giving out land, Gualberto Carrillo was selling chocolate. The official camarilla also attacked Gualberto Carrillo's financial ties to some hacendados and his refusal as a senator to defend agrarian reform in the federal supreme court.[15]

As we have seen in chapter 4, beneath its Cardenista-populist veneer, Gualbertismo was led by a coalition of disparate groups, mainly political "outs" seeking to get back in power on the local and state level. Similarly, like the official camarilla, the Gualbertista gubernatorial campaign selected its slate of congressional candidates, not through consultation with worker and peasant groups (as required under the Open Door Plan), but by cutting deals with rural caciques and urban bosses. While the Gualbertistas mobilized a wide base of popular support in the city and the countryside, the inner circle of the Gualbertista campaign directorate was composed of the burgeoning bureaucracy and Mérida's upper middle class, groups that neither benefited from nor supported agrarian reform or Cardenismo.

Machine Politics and the Official Camarilla's Victory

If Gualberto Carrillo Puerto and the other gubernatorial candidates failed to excite much popular fervor, government employees (especially teachers) as well as veteran ward heelers and provincial power brokers did show a great deal of interest in the race. But careerism, not Cardenismo, motivated them. Gualberto Carrillo Puerto picked up the lion's share of caciques and civil servants who defected from the official camarilla, but his appeal in the campo dimmed.[16]

Competition for political middlemen was especially fierce given the lack of genuine popular mobilizations in the campaign. Confidential federal observers confirmed the failure of the Open Door Plan to overcome peasant apathy toward the gubernatorial election. An investigator from the Secretary of the Interior visiting southern Yucatán found the peasants apolitical and voting only out of disciplined loyalty to the governor's machine.[17]

One barometer signaling the lack of popular interest was the low level of bloodshed. Dozens had died violently during the last gubernatorial election in 1933, and the bitterly contested 1936 senatorial contest between Gualberto Carrillo and the official candidate, Gonzalo López Manzanero, had provoked several riots and a few deaths. The 1937 gubernatorial election, by contrast, was relatively peaceful.

In terms of political violence, there was only one spectacular assassination during the campaign — the murder of the Gualbertista mayor of Kanasín by agents of the official camarilla — and a few isolated violent clashes.[18] The bloodiest incident during the campaign occurred in Chacsinkin, a small village near the southernmost town of Peto. On 1 November, Peto policemen, led by its new strongman, the Left-Cardenista operative Antonio Teyer Horta, shotgunned and macheted followers of Elías Rivero, the old Socialist boss, killing five and wounding several others. The brutal attack punished Rivero for his support of opposition candidate (and veteran Socialist) Rafael Cebada Tenreiro.[19] Nevertheless, violence was confined to a handful of localities, suggesting that the opposition candidates posed little threat to the official imposition.

In spite of Cardenista attempts to promote cleaner and more inclusive elections, the political culture and practices of the 1937 campaign resembled the gubernatorial election of 1933 and the senatorial campaign of 1936 — albeit with lower levels of public participation and violence. Campaigners still shot off fireworks and distributed raw cane rum to lure potential voters to polling places, in spite of the national PNR ruling that ballots cast at conventions where people were drinking would not be counted. The official camarilla denied opposition candidates the right to hold fiestas and dole out rum to their supporters, indicating that political culture as usual continued in spite of Cardenista prohibition efforts.[20]

Other familiar practices of machine politics sustained Canto Echeverría's campaign. All the camarillas used middlemen controlling local offices and peasant or worker organizations to turn out the vote — a practice still alive and well in Mexico today and known as *acarreado* (carrying). The active (and illegal) participation of officeholders in Canto Echeverría's campaign led supporters of Cebada Tenreiro in Progreso to condemn the attempts of the "bourgeois gang" of the "fifí" and "reactionary" mayor Alberto "The Big Shrimp" Peniche Barrera to impose Canto Echeverría and insult Cebadista local officials as they paraded through the streets. Similarly, Gualbertistas of the hacienda Yaxhá complained that the mayor of Muna threatened to punish those who did not support Canto Echeverría. Government workers, like Mérida's municipal band, city gardeners, and employees of the lottery, the hospital, and the asylum, campaigned and voted early and often for the official candidate. Many ballots for Canto Echeverría were attributed to the dead and to flying squadrons of drunk municipal employees, vagrants, and policemen, who were trucked to numerous bogus union meetings to multiply their effect. The pressing need to turn out thousands for Canto Echeverría in the face of widespread apathy forced government employees to interrupt a meeting of the barbers' *gremio* (religious confraternity) and force its members to vote for Canto Echeverría. The campaign of independent Emilio Guerra Leal reported that despite "the complaints of the fervent adulators of Christ," the PNR delegate dutifully registered the unwilling barbers as supporting Canto Echeverría. The state government reportedly paid voters to attend conventions and cast ballots for Canto Echeverría — the going rate for votes was four pesos, with an additional peso paid to attend rallies.[21]

The process of the 1937 gubernatorial election proves that much of the passion that regional politics once aroused on the grassroots level was gone. The push of machine politics still propelled voters to the polls, but the pull of parochial interests that once animated campaigns had for the most part vanished. The forms of Yucatán's revolutionary political culture remained, yet its ritual was increasingly divorced from popular consciousness or even interest. And, worse for the Open Door Plan, Cardenista ideology played little or no role in mobilizing voters.

Even though opposition candidates failed to stir up much popular support, the official camarilla still used the coercive power of state government to guarantee Canto Echeverría's victory. The printing press of Guerra Leal's newspaper, *La metralla,* fell victim to crowbars wielded by plainclothes policemen, but the Gualbertistas, the main threat to Canto Echeverría, bore the brunt of state harassment. Rank-and-file supporters of Gualberto Carrillo lost jobs in government and on haciendas. State policemen dressed as peasants frequently attacked partisans of Carrillo Puerto trying to meet or to put up propaganda. Official candidates for state congress led the town council of Xocchel in breaking up a Gualbertista rally, and government goon squads roughed up Gualbertista Pedro Ek in Opichén.[22]

The official campaign did not, however, have a monopoly on violence. In municipalities with Gualbertista town councils, the tables were turned. Supporters of Canto Echeverría in Tizimín feared for their lives when the Gualbertista mayor told partisans "to sharpen their machetes and get ready to do away with some sons of Tizimín." Some areas remained beyond the reach of the official camarilla, but most town councils and ejidal commissioners closed opposition headquarters in their jurisdictions, fearing the loss of their jobs or a worse fate, like that of Kanasín's murdered Gualbertista mayor. The crackdown against Gualbertistas prompted charges that mayors were acting like "lords of the manor" and that politics was returning to the days of the Porfirian dictatorship before the Revolution.[23] Such exaggerated rhetoric clearly indicates frustration on the part of Carrillo Puerto's clique. But, in the end, the Gualbertistas were stymied less by government suppression than by their own inability to generate the kind of outpouring of grassroots support that they had enjoyed in 1933 and 1936.

The top-down imposition of Canto Echeverría did provoke a degree of popular rancor, but nowhere near the levels registered in the two most recent statewide elections. Many local chapters of the PSS resisted its state directorate's orders to support Canto Echeverría, but it was much more a mutiny by petty politicos than a popular insurrection. Gualbertistas gained support from some old Socialists in Motul, while supporters of opposition candidate Cebada Tenreiro claimed that, in the southern village of Mani and the western towns of Hunucmá and Maxcanú, members of the Socialist party, ejidatarios, and "the people in general" rose up against imposition of the "unpopular and proclerical" Canto Echeverría.[24] But the majority of archival and periodical accounts of the election suggest that apathy, not outrage, was the predominant response of the electorate to the imposition of Canto Echeverría.

Ironically, the official camarilla triumphed, not only through the traditional techniques of fraud — cacique tactics, corrupting monitors, tossing out opposition votes — but also by adapting old methods of cooking elections to the new Open Door system. Palomo Valencia's clique had already unified many worker and peasant organizations into a "Cardenista" electoral front called the Popular Alliance of Yucatán. But it was a unification based, not on state response to popular demands, but on the co-optation of union and ejido leadership, achieving political stability at the cost of popular alienation. The official camarilla running Canto Echeverría's campaign had already cut deals with *líderes* (labor bosses, rural caciques) of popular organizations, who traded patronage and state offices for their members' support. Under the Open Door system, these tame unions and peasant organizations provided an easily managed supply of votes for Canto Echeverría.[25]

In another disappointment for Cardenismo, leftist popular organizations played an especially important role in the official camarilla's campaign. Hernán Labordé, a former railroad worker who headed the entire Communist Party of Mexico, came from Mexico City to personally assist his close friend Palomo Valencia in the election of Canto Echeverría, bringing national Communist notables like Carlos Sánchez to assist him. Not only did the conversion of Communist teachers into state-subsidized campaigners for Canto Echeverría draw charges of imposition, but it also caused many parents to accuse instructors of abandoning their jobs.[26]

The FSI formed a key component of the Left's popular base at the disposition of Canto Echeverría's campaign. Since 1934, the Communist-led labor federation unionized peons on haciendas, mainly in the western half of the henequen zone. With the culmination of agrarian reform, many of these FSI peon unions had been left underemployed because of the economic teething problems of the new ejidos. The FSI capitalized on resentment among the peons, encouraging them to vote for Canto Echeverría as a protest against the pro-Gualbertista federal Agrarian Bank. Surviving information from the rather murky electoral process suggests that Left-Cardenista organizations supplied much of Canto Echeverría's margin of victory. Kinchil, a small western town that had strong Communist peasant organizations, cast 1,375 votes for Canto Echeverría, even though the male population in the municipality in 1940 numbered only 1,070 and there is no suggestion that women voted there. The FSI Union of Stable Employees in Mérida was reregistered as the League of Stable Employees, doubling its impact, while the FSI's Union of Carriage Operators was triple-registered as the League of Drivers and Owners of Carriages and the Syndical League of Drivers of Carriages.[27]

Even with such support as well as the formidable weight of the state government apparatus and money diverted from state coffers, the election of Canto Echeverría by the official camarilla was not a sure thing. Three potential obstacles remained. First, members of the henequen ejidos mainly depended on federal, not state, patronage, and their votes were swayed by federal agrarian engineers backing Gualberto Carrillo. Second, urban labor proved especially difficult to swallow by the official political machine — a situation to be examined shortly. Third, the federal government would ultimately certify the results of the election, and, in the past, it had nullified gubernatorial elections in other states and the 1936 senatorial campaign in Yucatán in order to weaken regional camarillas.

At the polls, Canto Echeverría scored an easy victory. Between 23 September and 16 October, approximately 665 worker and peasant organizations representing (on paper) over seventy thousand members convened in small assemblies, which in turn elected delegates to nine district conventions, where they cast votes on behalf of their unions, ejidos, or other groups. Monitors from the national PNR and representatives of each candidate attended the conventions to verify that at least two-thirds of the members were present and duly registered and that no drinking went on during the assemblies. On 21 October 1937, the delegates from the district conventions met and elected Canto Echeverría the winner with 52,758 votes; Carrillo Puerto took second place with 14,325 votes, followed by Agustín Franco Villanueva (a renegade Socialist who parted company with the official camarilla) with 4,711 votes, Emilio Guerra Leal with 1,007 votes, and Rafael Cebada Tenreiro (who finished fifth and last) with 831 votes.[28]

In the light of widespread fraud and abstention, the absence of any candidate who could be considered as representing popular forces, and the persistent influence of the official camarilla over the electoral process, the Open Door system clearly failed. Drinking, multiple voting, and violence — the practices that had sustained the influence of caciques and camarillas over past elections — continued, and perhaps even increased, under the new system. Not only did national Cardenismo fail to build a popular base, but some of its representatives overseeing the election also proved vulnerable to bribery and co-optation by the very regional interests that they were charged with subduing.

The failure of the Open Door electoral reforms raises an important question: Why did Cárdenas accept the flawed outcome of the fraudulent election? He could have chosen to decertify the elections and simply impose Gualberto Carrillo Puerto, as Candelario Reyes advised. Or he could have selected another candidate to run on the PNR ticket, as he did in other states. His decision to allow Palomo Valencia to impose his handpicked successor points to a quid pro quo between the national Cardenista regime and the governor's camarilla: the official camarilla kept the governorship and in return supported agrarian reform. By late 1937, the political cost of dismantling regional machines like Palomo Valencia's was simply too high because it risked upheavals that could possibly endanger agrarian reform.

Indeed, the national Cardenistas's inability to directly mobilize peasants and peons, even after most had been transformed into ejidatarios, signaled the fundamental weakness of Cardenismo in the countryside. Agrarian reform clearly failed to strengthen agrarian Cardenismo. Paradoxically, rather than building a popular base, agrarian reform forced the Cardenista state to limit popular participation in politics for fear of a backlash. Instead of supporting the national regime, Left-Cardenismo sustained the official camarilla. However, peasants were only half the classic clasista "worker-peasant" alliance of the Cardenista project. The weakness of Cardenismo in Yucatán can be fully understood only by considering the failure of Cárdenas to mobilize the other half of the political equation: urban labor.

Alliance Failed: Labor Politics in Cardenista Yucatán

The question of why urban workers of Yucatán failed to take advantage of the Open Door system to elect a candidate to represent them deserves serious consideration. While a full history of urban labor in modern Yucatán is beyond the scope of this work, the relation between Cardenismo and urban labor in Yucatán is a crucial one that merits a closer examination. The question of why Yucatecan urban labor did not mobilize in favor of national Cardenismo is an especially puzzling considering that workers across most of Mexico had rallied to Cardenismo and in many states acted as Cardenista shock troops.[29] Historically, urban labor in Yucatán was potentially both a very strong and an ideologically radical force. Mérida was the nation's fifth largest city at the time, with thousands of jobs in service industries, transportation, and manufacturing (mainly in the henequen cordage factories and, to a lesser extent, the foodstuff and beverage industries). Workers in these sectors alone numbered over twenty thousand in the 1930s—large enough to decide Mérida's three seats in the nine-seat state congress as well as Mérida's city council. And, with the total turnout in most statewide elections between thirty and seventy thousand, this bloc could easily determine the outcome of gubernatorial and senatorial elections. Both Mérida's workers and those of the port of Progreso had a militant labor tradition that dated from the turn of the nineteenth century, with a strong anarchosyndicalist undercurrent that had survived both Porfirian oppression and Socialist harassment. Compared to the countryside, urban Yucatán had higher literacy rates, a more open social structure, and a tradition of political independence — all formidable obstacles to the usual techniques of machine politics.

In spite of all these advantages, Cárdenas's outreach to urban workers in Yucatán fell flat. The absence of a Cardenista-labor alliance was a decisive factor in the outcome of the Open Door election. Underlying this failure are five factors. First, patron-client ties subordinated many labor leaders to elements of the old hacendado class as well as to the official camarilla, a sort of labor caciquismo that blocked a horizontal, class-based workers bloc. Second, national Cardenismo never recognized, much less incorporated, the *local* anarchosyndicalist tradition of the workers of Mérida and Progreso. Third, the national Cardenista state proved incapable of acting as a neutral and effective arbiter in labor disputes and thus was unable to set up labor organizations linking Mérida and Progreso unions to Mexico City. Fourth, the national Cardenista labor federation, the CTM (Confederación de Trabajadores de México), repeatedly failed to bring together the various factions of Yucatecan labor. Fifth and finally, Cárdenas's emphasis on agrarian reform caused him to turn a deaf ear to worker demands during the crusade.

Moreover, the Cardenistas had to deal with a historically fragmented working class in Yucatán. The political attitudes and orientation of organized urban labor in the Cardenista era had taken shape in the previous two decades. In the early 1920s, a fundamental polarization occurred between supporters and opponents of the postrevolutionary state in Yucatán. Some unions and associated cooperatives had become economically and politically linked to the state government and its official party, the PSS. The nobility of Socialist labor were undoubtedly the drivers of the Union of Truckers and the Alliance of Truckers. They enjoyed a government-sponsored monopoly of bus and transportation routes as well as receiving a school, a headquarters, and other concessions from the state. One of the two unions of cordage factory workers, known as the League of Workers of Henequen Articles (LTAH, or Liga de Trabajadores de Artifactors de Henequen), some unions of artisans, bakery employees, and, of course, government employees had historically backed the PSS and the state government, although their leaders enjoyed more benefits than did the rank and file. All these unions generally turned out in elections to support the PSS, and the state government rewarded its leaders with seats on the town councils of Mérida and Progreso as well as in the state congress.[30] Despite the black legend of Yucatecan Socialism fomented by anti-Socialist opposition politicians and unwittingly spread by Vicente Lombardo Toledano and North American researcher Ruth Clark (and continued by some later historians), organized labor in Yucatán was not completely subordinated to the state or universally suffering from depressed wages in the 1920s and early 1930s.[31] However, the close relationship between the governors and some Socialist labor bosses—busing honchos Gonzalo López Manzanero and Fernando Vargas Ocampo and LTAH chief José Pérez Rosado—did resemble the *charrismo* of the 1950s, in which labor bosses loyal to the state reaped rewards while bottling up worker demands. Moreover, it seems that the Great Depression hurt Mérida's workers especially hard, as the henequen-related trades suffered greatly.

Independent (non-Socialist) labor activists, by contrast, suffered harsh repression during this same period. The experience of a worker turned organizer in the cordage sector suggests the kinds of obstacles that some labor activists faced in Yucatán before Cárdenas. The García Correa administration accused Enrique Núñez González of being Communist, a Cristero (a rebel against anticlerical legislation), and an enemy of the Revolution; he served several jail terms and paid a fine of five hundred pesos for the crime of publicizing the Federal Labor Code in Yucatán. Only President Abelardo Rodríguez's intercession finally released him from jail.[32]

With the intervention of the national government on the side of independent labor after 1933, the kind of repression that García Correa had exerted against embattled trade unionists like Núñez González was no longer possible. In the cordage factories, in the railroads, on Progreso's docks, and in many sectors of Mérida's working class, independent unions emerged. By 1934, this new generation of stubbornly autonomous labor unions overtook the Socialist labor movement. In terms of their size, militancy, and ability to paralyze the state's economy by striking, the workers of Mérida's cordage factories (SCY) and the laborers of the state railroads of Yucatán (SFP) were by far the most important independent workers' organizations. Both had adopted an aggressive policy opposing the Callista-era politicians of the PSS and, true to their anarchosyndicalist heritage, called for their industries to be handed over to the workers. The SCY and the SFP seconded the many truck and taxi drivers who formed an independent drivers union (the Frente Unico de Trabajadores de Volante, or FUTV) in mid-1936. The

Independent Unions, as these anti-Socialist unions were known, at times collaborated with the CGT and non-Communist teachers to organize peons and peasants, most notably in the 1936 FUTV strike.[33]

The PSS and the state government reacted to these independent unions with both attacks and attempts at co-optation. Given the power that the SFP and the SCY displayed in the October 1935 strikes, Governor López Cárdenas had hoped to incorporate them into a "United Front" of workers. He turned over the state-run railroads to the SFP and offered the SCY a new headquarters and a factory to run as a cooperative. Such concessions, however, failed to lure the SFP and the SCY into López Cárdenas's camp, and both helped oust him as governor.[34]

As seen in the fall of López Cárdenas, in spite of the ideological distance between the anarchosyndicalist labor unions and the conservative regional bourgeoisie, the latter supported urban unions in order to forward their own agenda. As a result, some labor leaders became entangled in dependent relationships with hacendados. Although their unions' anarchist heritage rejected electoral politics, between 1934 and 1936 some directors of the independent unions of truckers, cordage factory hands, and railroad workers accepted invitations to run for the town council of Mérida and the state congress on slates beholden to the upper class. And, after mid-1936, at a time when Cardenismo most needed urban labor as an ally in Yucatán, some independent labor leaders joined the official camarilla and ran on its slates.

Los Hermanos *González Inurreta, Labor Caciques*

The growing involvement of independent unions in politics can be seen in the careers of the SFP's preeminent leaders: the brothers Carlos, César, and (José) Mamerto González Inurreta. Their labor dynasty began in the 1910s, when Mamerto joined a Masonic lodge that included other politically conscious railroad workers as well as ambitious middle-class politicos.[35] Capitalizing on his Masonic contacts, Mamerto joined the PSS and became the leader of its railroad union, which he represented at the second PSS congress in 1921. Aided by brothers Carlos and César, who like him had immigrated from the state of Tabasco, Mamerto consolidated his hold over the railroad union. The SFP was born when most members of the old Socialist railroad workers' league "Torres and Acosta" abandoned it in 1933 over repeated cuts in wages and layoffs. The brothers together led the victorious strike of October 1935 and the subsequent worker takeover of the railroad.[36] Not only did the SFP-run railroad cooperative reinvest profits in improving infrastructure, but César González also used SFP funds for a trucking cooperative to protect workers from competition from road transportation.[37]

But, for many, the *hermanos* González epitomized, not the growing independence of urban labor, but the stereotypical labor boss. Many other labor leaders shouldered aside by them came to see Carlos, César, and Mamerto as extraordinarily greedy, prone to violence, and likely to ally themselves with class enemies for personal gain. To union dissidents, the SFP pact with conservative leader Enrique Aznar Mendoza was a betrayal of the SFP's historical tradition. Nine months after the July 1936 strike, César had to resign from his office as secretary general when he could not account for over forty thousand pesos of union funds.[38] Enemies accused Mamerto of being only slightly less venal; his own in-laws charged him with stealing their small henequen farm of Santa María in Kinchil.[39] The third González brother, Carlos, took advantage of his ties to their cousin, the governor of Tabasco, to set up a lucrative trade importing cattle, grain, and chickens from Tabasco to the entire Yucatán peninsula, allegedly using his control over rail lines and the SFP trucking cooperative to line his own pockets.[40]

Violence — another hallmark of the cacique — was a favored part of the González brothers' repertoire. During the July 1936 strike, they led a goon squad that beat several politicians and tried to assassinate Communist leader Antonio Betancourt Pérez.[41] Eloy Cáceres Reyes, who fought the González brothers for control of the SFP, accused Carlos of "yanking the ears of Mario Ojeda, Gregorio Misset, and Vitilano Avila, slapping José Cano, [and] kicking Fernando Bojórquez"; and Mamerto of "pistol-whipping Benjamín Cervera in the neck, punching out Rafael Sacramento, roughing up Paulino Suárez, and scratching Agusto Gutiérrez's face up with his gun."[42] Such dubious fame earned the González brothers many enemies inside and outside the SFP.

Governor Palomo Valencia tried to block the rise of the González brothers, jailing Carlos and exiling his brothers in late 1937 to bring the SFP under the sway of his official camarilla.[43] However, their aggressive and independent stance had attracted the attention of CTM head Lombardo Toledano; Lombardo stood by them against the governor and the anti-González faction within the SFP.[44] Francisco Mújica, head of the federal transportation ministry and a power within the Cárdenas cabinet, also appreciated their political value in Yucatán and had already backed them in the railroad strike of October 1935 against Alayola. He later urged them to oust interim governor Palomo Valencia and even hinted that he would back one of them for governor in 1937. National Cardenistas like Lombardo and Mújica might not necessarily have approved of the cacique-style rule of the González brothers over the SFP, but they saw them as important allies in the attempt to weaken the regional bloc headed by the governor and strengthen urban unions.[45]

Even with such powerful protectors in Mexico City, much of the SFP's membership was unwilling to tolerate the González brothers' abuses, and, by 1938, they had been largely rejected by the union's rank and file. But the tumultuous circumstances of Yucatecan politics in the latter 1930s would allow the brothers another opportunity to regain control of the SFP.[46]

Anarchism against Cardenismo

The resiliency and clout of the González Inurreta brothers shows the potential power of urban labor in Yucatán but also reveals how the personalistic nature of their rule so typical of caciquismo prevented the formation of a truly autonomous, class-based labor movement. Other independent unions also experienced turmoil and internal dissension because of their leaders' involvement in politics.

Patron-client ties between Socialist union leaders and the old PSS, on the one hand, and some anarchosyndicalist union leaders and hacendados, on the other, explain why urban labor's leadership had preexisting loyalties that prevented it from leading a regional labor movement on behalf of national Cardenismo in Yucatán. But, beyond the question of political alignments, Cardenismo also had ideological problems in mobilizing urban labor in Yucatán. In spite of its radical promise, Cardenismo failed to tap the strong revolutionary undercurrent of Yucatecan urban labor.

Historically, anarchosyndicalism had given many Mérida and Progreso labor unions a radical worldview. Anarchism rejected not just capitalism but the state itself; any notion of liberation of the working class implied smashing not just the market, but the national government of Mexico as well. The architects of the modern, postrevolutionary Mexican state from Alvaro Obregón to Cárdenas, on the other hand, shared a suspicion of untrammeled laissez-faire capitalism and believed that Mexico needed a strong organized labor movement as an economic and political counterweight to international investors and the national bourgeoisie. As a result, the postrevolutionary state claimed to champion the working class against the rich and employed other "classist" terminology (the Federal Labor Code of

1931 borrowed the terms *cámara de trabajo* and *sindicato* from anarchosyndicalism, transforming the latter from a free association of workers into a
constituent unit of official labor organizations). Cárdenas believed that the
promise of the Mexican Revolution had to be fulfilled by an activist state
with a social conscience.

For the Cardenistas to do more than simply co-opt the radical rhetoric of
urban labor and actually incorporate urban workers into their project, they
would have to forge meaningful mediating agencies to overcome anarchosyndicalist suspicions. The Cardenistas tried to do just that by creating
effective federal arbitration boards and a national labor confederation. The
success or failure of these efforts represents the third factor shaping relations between Cárdenas and urban labor in Yucatán.

The Cardenista promise of unbiased arbitration of labor conflicts by the
federal state never became a reality. Urban labor unions like the SCY continued to face unreliable and often corrupt federal labor boards, just as they
had suffered from similar problems with state arbitrators dominated by the
hostile PSS since the late 1910s.[47] Lacking that, the main means of bringing
Yucatecan labor into the Cardenista camp was Cárdenas's pact with national
labor leader Vicente Lombardo Toledano, which resulted in the creation of
a national labor federation, the CTM.

The CTM's Failures in Yucatán

While the CTM set up effective regional labor organizations to support
Cárdenas in many states, in Yucatán it failed miserably. From the beginning,
Yucatecan urban labor saw any government-sponsored labor federation
based in Mexico City as a threat to its own independent, anarchosyndicalist
tradition. When the PNR first tried to set up an official workers' organization in 1934, Mérida's truckers, restaurant workers, bricklayers, and other
laborers and artisans adamantly refused to join, fearing a loss of control
over their own affairs.[48]

After Cárdenas broke with Calles and embraced Vicente Lombardo Toledano, a major radical labor organizer in Mexico, it seemed that the ground-
work had been laid for Yucatecan labor to join Cardenismo. The president
and his national party, the PNR, adopted a clasista and obrerista (class-
based, pro-worker) doctrine, and the national state pledged to support
Lombardo Toledano's campaign to organize an authentic pro-labor national federation of workers. Because of its radical labor tradition and
worker resentment of the labor policies of Callista governor Bartolomé

García Correa, Yucatán seemed to be fertile ground for Lombardo Toledano. He had first visited the state in March 1934 and condemned the PSS both for its betrayal of Socialism and for its opposition to independent (non-Socialist) unions.[49]

At its first national congress in February 1936, the CTM approved a motion from the Yucatecan delegation calling for the dissolution of the PSS for its attacks on the workers and its continuation of the "nefarious epoch of García Correa." Toledano saw the FUTV-SFP mobilizations of April and May 1936 as an opportunity to finally rally enough urban (and possibly rural) support to destroy the old PSS and bring Yucatecan workers firmly under the CTM aegis.[50]

But, in spite of the political ferment among urban workers in Yucatán, the CTM repeatedly failed to unify Yucatecan workers under its authority. Early on, the CTM's delegate to the state gained the support of the SFP (led by Cesár González Inurreta), Porfirio Pallares and the CGT, the anti-Communist faction of teachers led by Arturo Albertos, and even a few unions formerly affiliated with the PSS. However, the inclusion of Porfirio Pallares and Arturo Albertos (both of whom were reportedly on the take from hacendados) in the CTM alienated many labor groups. The CTM's endorsement of Gualberto Carrillo Puerto for the senate further offended the leftist and Socialist workers. Not until 13 June 1936 could the planned CTM congress of worker unification take place. Given the acrimony between pro– and anti–state government unions, and considering the divisions among the independent labor leaders, it is not surprising that the congress failed to resolve disputes among the organizations. The PSS walked out, effectively preventing a single CTM affiliate from forming. This enraged the national CTM's young delegate, Fidel Velázquez, who stormed out of the meeting.[51]

Undaunted by these false starts, the CTM redoubled its efforts to expand into Yucatán in 1937, motivated by the prospect of a seat in the national congress to be elected in the spring of 1937 under the new Open Door electoral system. Because Yucatán's first district, encompassing all of Mérida, had been earmarked for the CTM, national organizers needed to rapidly establish the CTM in the state before the PNR primary scheduled for 4 April 1937. To encourage the SCY and the SFP to participate, the national PNR published a "Manifesto to the Proletarian Classes of Mexico," promising workers historically wary of electoral activity that the plan was, not an attempt to exploit workers, but a means for the PNR to share in the activities of—but not subordinate—ejidos and unions.[52]

Both the PNR and the CTM hoped that the Open Door Plan would allow them to finally bring together Mérida's workers and elect a Cardenista congressman from Mérida. However, in yet another demonstration of the weakness of the CTM as well as the PNR in Yucatán, no CTM convention was held. Instead, the Popular Alliance of Yucatán (Alianza Popular Yucateca, or APY), the political front of the official camarilla, ran the primary. Just as he would do in the 1937 gubernatorial election, national PNR head Silvano Barba González implicitly recognized that the APY, not the CTM or the national PNR, would control popular organizations in Mérida when he allowed "proletarian" organizations besides the CTM to take part. The fate of the first congressional district provided yet another indication that the CTM still lacked a strong presence in Yucatán.[53]

To deny the CTM a political foothold in the state when it tried to run a nominee in Mérida, Palomo Valencia funneled state money to his favored candidates.[54] Furthermore, Governor Palomo Valencia jailed the CTM's candidate, Florencio Avila Sánchez, twice and harassed his propagandists. Such treatment of candidates who ran for office without the backing of the governor was not unusual, and a candidate with enough popular support and/or pull in Mexico City could overcome it. But Avila had neither. More damaging to the CTM's man in Yucatán was the opposition of regional leftists, labor, and even peasant organizations. Hernán Morales, a key ally of Cárdenas's in Yucatán and head of the Young Socialists, considered the naming of candidates from Mexico City a violation of Cardenista doctrine, which stressed respect for the vote. He vociferously protested to Cárdenas the fact that Lombardo Toledano leaned on CTM members to impose a "total unknown."[55] Cardenista corporatism fell victim to both Cardenista democracy and resurgent machine politics.

Hostility to the CTM by groups linked to and subsidized by the official camarilla could not have come as a surprise — after all, many of these same groups, especially those affiliated with the PCM, had already fought the expansion of the CTM into Yucatán. Less understandable was the refusal of the strongest regional affiliate of the CTM in Yucatán and a group patronized by Lombardo Toledano, the SFP, to back the CTM candidate. The SFP declared that, despite Lombardo Toledano's endorsement of Avila Sánchez, its principles prevented it from interfering in electoral politics. The general secretary of the transportation workers of the FUTV, another independent union supported by Lombardo Toledano, ran an advertisement supporting Avila Sánchez, but the same day the rest of the union's executive committee publicly criticized its highest officer for endorsing the CTM's candidate without their approval. The FUTV's members then voted to join the railroad union in refusing to back the national labor federation's candidate. The motives for the FUTV's and the SFP's neutrality are unclear. Had key leaders been paid "walking-around money" by the official camarilla to keep their members away from the polls? Or had the old anarchosyndicalist suspicion of electoral politics kept these two key unions out of the election? Had Lombardo Toledano erred by not naming a more well-known candidate, or a leader of the SFP or the FUTV, as the CTM's man in Yucatán? No evidence exists to prove or disprove any of these possibilities. With weak organizational backing and virtually no popular support, the CTM candidate received an embarrassing seventy-four votes out of some forty-five hundred cast in the PNR primary for the first federal congressional district.[56]

The most objective appraisal of the federal congressional elections, the confidential report filed by the national Ministry of the Interior's observer Manual Ríos Thivol, analyzed the inability of Cardenismo to cultivate a strong base of politically active workers in the state. Classifying Yucatecan politics as "anarchic," Ríos Thivol reported that, even though the Callista forces — by which he meant supporters of Callista-era governor Bartolomé García Correa (1930–33) — had been banished, popular forces failed to triumph because of the power of the "bureaucratic-political elements, morally amorphous and lacking in ideals." In other words, the official camarilla used control of regional-level bureaucratic entities, patronage, and clientelistic networks to prevent Cardenista, class-based politicking. Its manipulation of individual líderes and front groups divided and misled workers and peasants. Ríos Thivol attributed the failure of a worker-peasant popular front to the nebulous "official party" headed by a series of governors who, along with more than a few hacendados, had controlled the state's administration for the past twenty years. Even more tellingly, he blamed the weak turnout of workers on the federal government, which failed to give Mérida's workers incentives to support Cárdenas. Because national authorities failed to enforce the Federal Labor Code and execute the Six-Year Plan (Cárdenas's platform calling for more worker cooperatives), disputes proliferated among rival labor groups and allowed capitalists to exploit workers.[57]

Ríos Thivol's glum assessment of Yucatecan labor's lack of Cardenista sentiment should have served as a warning to the president's collaborators. The congressional elections in the spring of 1937 had revealed the flaws in both the Open Door electoral system and the national government's labor policy. Serious problems remained in relations between Cárdenas and the workers. The SFP voted down a federal offer to take over the state-run railroads — a snub to Cárdenas and the SFP's national patron, Mújica.[58] The FUTV had rejected a call to join the welcoming committee for Cárdenas during the crusade as a ploy by corrupt politicians.[59] Old habits of suspicion of the state died hard among Mérida's railroad workers and truckers, and the president still had yet to find a following among Yucatecan labor.

Still, there was reason for the national Cardenistas to hope for a strong labor mobilization, even after the CTM's debacles. After all, by mid-1937, the president was belatedly turning his attention southeastward, and the crusade promised a fresh start for relations with organized labor. Urban unions like the SFP, the SCY, and the FUTV were strong enough to influence Mérida and even state-level elections decisively, and they could be induced to lend their political support to Cárdenas in return for concrete concessions. Indeed, momentum seemed to be building for a labor offensive in the state: the railroads had been in the hands of the workers for almost two years, waterworkers struck just before the crusade, and the day before Cárdenas landed on the Yucatán peninsula federal mediation helped the historically strong electricians of Mérida win a strike for the right to co-manage power production in the state.[60] This growing labor militancy suggested that a Cardenista groundswell among Mérida's workers might well rise up to meet the president.

Labor and the Crusade of the Maya

Buoyed by the triumph of the electricians and stimulated by the impending presidential visit, Yucatecan workers bombarded Cárdenas with appeals for help. The volume and enthusiasm of unions' correspondence with the president hinted at the possibility of a Cárdenas-labor alliance and revealed the concerns and goals of the workers of Mérida and Progreso. Virtually every major organized labor group appealed to the president, offering loyalty and asking that attention be paid to its plight.

The factory workers of the SCY, a key potential constituency for Cárdenas, once again asked for federal intervention in long-running, contentious disputes with cordage factory owners and a rival, pro-PSS union. Besides help with a new headquarters and land for a new workers' neighborhood to provide decent housing, they voiced two more radical demands. First, they asked for worker control of the state government–run Cordelería Yucateca factory through a federally supported cooperative. Second, they asked Cárdenas to arm the SCY, creating a worker's militia to second the existing Agrarian Militia and "be prepared to support your government, whenever it is necessary." The most martial organization that the SCY ever got, however, was a drum-and-bugle corps. While Cárdenas saluted the cordage workers' "conciencia obrera" or "working-class consciousness," no help from Mexico City was forthcoming on either count.[61]

Workers' desire to control production was powerful in other Yucatecan unions with a strong anarchosyndicalist heritage as well. Numerous labor organizations in the state's only major port of Progreso asked the national government for help organizing maritime cooperatives, as shipping and warehousing were long monopolized by politically connected businessmen. Dockworkers also requested federal resolution of disputes among unions from the same sector. For instance, the Union of Land (Dock) Workers (Union de Trabajadores Terrestres), "Piedad Luna," asked for protection against its bitter rival, the Union of Workers in Henequen (Union de Trabajadores Henequeneros), the "Martyrs of Chicago," as well as for federal help in regaining a share of the henequen transportation business. The stevedores of Piedad Luna also reminded the president that his assistance would at least enable them to build a library and a recreation center.[62] Their nemesis, the Martyrs of Chicago, also sought presidential aid to build and run their own warehouse. They invoked Cárdenas's Six-Year Plan by pointing out that it would allow workers to retain a greater share of the costs of transporting henequen; although Cárdenas conceded an audience to them, once again no federal help was forthcoming.[63]

Another cooperative of transportation workers in Progreso, "La Antorcha" (The Torch), wrote the president that its members supported his "proletarista y cooperatista" (pro-worker and pro-cooperative) policy and asked for federal help to organize a collective to transport cargo and thus increase worker control over the docks. La Antorcha also requested subsidies to buy a warehouse and tariff reductions to encourage more maritime trade.[64] The largest labor organization in Progreso, the Federation of Workers of Progreso (Federación Obrera de Progreso, or FOP), made the most ambitious request: federal help to buy and run its own small merchant marine to ship henequen and to take over shipping insurance currently monopolized by the Chamber of Commerce. Over a month later, Cárdenas's office cabled the FOP regrets that the president could not attend to their telegram and suggested writing a letter.[65]

Another large urban union, the FUTV, sent a delegate to Cárdenas just before his visit to explain the economic problems plaguing bus and taxi drivers as well as to protest against physical attacks at the hands of the state government. There were no responses.[66] Many other, smaller unions asked for federal help and reiterated their support for the president. The federal government snubbed them all. The case of the bricklayers is instructive. They telegraphed Mexico City asking for an audience with Cárdenas during the crusade to explain workers' complaints that had arisen because of "the inclement condition of capitalism" in Yucatán; they did not receive even a cursory reply until almost two months later, long after Cárdenas had departed the state.[67]

Although Cárdenas kicked off the crusade by announcing that Mexico would soon become a "workers' democracy," he consistently passed over the concerns and grievances of urban labor during his visit to Yucatán. Agrarian reform, not the workers of Mérida and Progreso, merited presidential attention. Although he briefly met with the scy personally, Cárdenas sent his minister of labor, Antonio Villalobos, to meet with most urban workers so as to free up more time to deal with the land question. On 6 August 1937, Villalobos huddled with assembled representatives of workers' groups, relaying to them the importance of land distribution, and asking on Cárdenas's behalf that they avoid any strikes as they might threaten land reform. Cárdenas did promise that the National Workers' Bank of Industrial Development (Banco Nacional Obrero de Fomento Industrial) would in the future invest millions in worker-run industry, but his refusal to respond to specific requests for federal help in creating cooperatives sent a much stronger and unmistakably negative message to urban labor.[68] Cárdenas's attention to industry and transportation was limited to their roles in the henequen industry; he restricted all concrete pledges of support to those sectors of the economy directly related to sisal. Cardenista industrial policy stressed modernization and improvement, not worker-run cooperatives. As Jonathan Brown has argued in his study of Mexican oil workers, the president increasingly emphasized "labor discipline" in his dealings with unions; during the crusade, the president sent orders back to central Mexico to halt wildcat strikes by petroleum laborers.[69]

Cárdenas's failure to meet the demands of urban Yucatecan labor for meaningful federal help might seem to reinforce revisionist claims that his obrerista rhetoric was hollow and manipulative. However, to dismiss Cárdenas as a Machiavellian politico is to ignore both the genuine attempts by Cárdenas to change Mexico and the very real limits on Cardenismo. Simply put, the Crusade of the Mayab aimed to complete land reform, and Cárdenas was willing to make trade-offs in other areas in order to achieve his agrarian goals. At the same time, economic factors severely constrained his ability to commit federal resources. Rising inflation and pressure from conservative interest groups forced Cárdenas to carefully choose which sectors of the economy to nationalize.[70] And in Yucatán, the need to conserve both economic and political capital for costly agrarian reform in the henequen zone meant that Progreso and Mérida workers had little chance of receiving the kind of national investments necessary to make a go of a worker-run enterprise. The national government had, after all, already stepped in to help railroad workers acquire the state's railroads in the October 1935 strike, and this intervention had not yielded many political gains for Cárdenas in Yucatán. Breaking up the economic might of the often-belligerent Yucatecan hacendados and addressing the problems of poverty and political instability in the countryside appeared much more pressing than the demands of the less numerous and relatively better-off workers of Mérida and Progreso. Cárdenas and his collaborators designated agrarian reform as the priority of the crusade and let the opportunity to forge closer ties with Yucatecan labor pass.

Cárdenas's inability to build a strong base among urban labor in Mérida and Progreso during the crusade would, however, have serious long- and short-term results. Fallout from the failed alliance between Cárdenas and urban labor included growing apathy among urban unions toward Cárdenas and the national state and the increasing alienation of union leadership, which remained enmeshed in regional camarillas. The short-term costs for Cárdenas were painfully apparent in the 1937 Open Door gubernatorial election.

Urban Labor in the Open Door Election: The Price of Failure

National Cardenistas hoped that the Open Door Plan would increase popular participation and limit the ability of conservative regional camarillas to control state-level elections. In the case of Yucatán, this was an especially important goal, given the strength of regional cliques and the previous failures of the CTM and the Agrarian Bank to mobilize a strong worker-peasant coalition.

The gubernatorial election of 1937 represented a crucial test for the Cardenista state. Aware of the centralizing strategy of Cardenismo, the official camarilla had successfully blocked it in the countryside via the co-optation of Left-Cardenismo and the neutralization of agrarian Cardenismo.[71] However, the official camarilla controlled few urban unions in 1937.[72]

Without a mass base among urban unions, the official camarilla fell back on a tried-and-true formula in Mexican politics: *pan o palo,* "bread or the stick." Even the threat of gubernatorial candidate Humberto's brother Mario Canto Echeverría, head of the state labor arbitration board, to legally decertify unions that did not back his sibling, failed to badger urban labor, and he fined the Union of Cordage Workers of Yucatán for not endorsing Canto Echeverría. The bread was doled out mainly to leaders, and, by such measures, the official camarilla won over more than a few labor chieftains who agreed to run on official slates for state congress and municipal councils.[73]

Although the governor's group lured many leaders into endorsing Canto Echeverría, not only did the rank and file refuse to follow, but they often denounced their own leaders. Members of the SFP, for instance, were not swayed by some of their leaders' endorsements of Canto Echeverría and preferred to abstain in mass. Some dissident members known as the Companions of the Railroad Workers went so far as to publicly attack Canto Echeverría as a "clerical reactionary." Most of the leadership of the Workers Federation of Progreso refused to endorse Canto Echeverría, and its constituent organizations censured some of their officers for endorsing him without consulting them. Members of Mérida's FAREYS (a union of actors, entertainers, and restaurant workers) condemned their leadership's "ambitious and egotistical behavior" for taking the same unauthorized action.[74]

Two of the largest and most influential urban unions in Mérida, the drivers of the FUTV and the cordage factory hands of the SCY, were deeply divided by the campaign. The legal counsel of the FUTV tried to convince the union to support opposition candidate Arturo Cisneros Canto's abortive gubernatorial campaign, a move firmly rejected by the base. The SCY suffered much more serious internal turmoil when Julio Osorio, a leader in the SCY since its founding in 1933, resigned from its executive committee in 1937 after rival leaders supporting the official candidate Humberto Canto Echeverría attacked Osorio. Cordage worker committees were fielded by at least two other rival gubernatorial candidates, a divisive development for a union with a strong independent tradition.[75] The spreading corruption of labor leaders during the gubernatorial campaigns created serious internal upheavals in most urban unions, an unintended result of the Open Door campaign.

Some workers resented not just the selling out of their leadership to the official camarilla, but the very concept that unions should participate in politics. Juan Peña, a Progreso union leader, expressed anger that Canto Echeverría claimed that his union voted for him by forging members' names on telegrams. Ironically, Peña invoked the Federal Labor Code of 1931 in declaring, "This league does not participate in politics or religion." At the same time, Peña's language reflected a strong anarchist tradition among Yucatecan port workers. A few months earlier, another Progreso union, the Martyrs of Chicago, as well as the Workers' Federation of Progreso felt strongly enough about the bogus endorsement of a gubernatorial candidate by their corrupted leaders to take out paid announcements protesting the involvement of any union in politics as a violation of ideological principles as well as the Federal Labor Code.[76]

Given the attitude of many workers toward political participation, it was no surprise that, during the Open Door electoral process, assemblies convened by the national PNR delegates of stevedores, railroad laborers, cordage workers, truckers, and electricians were poorly attended. Rather than participate in meaningless conventions after their leader had already bartered away their votes, most workers preferred to stay home.[77]

The gubernatorial election in the fall of 1937 underscored the fact that Cárdenas never incorporated the strong urban unions of Mérida and Progreso into his political base. Some of this reticence could be traced to the anarchosyndicalist heritage of Yucatecan labor, which instilled an instinctive suspicion of elections, or perhaps even the federal government's Federal Labor Code of 1931, which expressly forbade unions from involving themselves in elections.[78] However, it seems difficult to believe that workers truly believed that the federal labor codes bound them to stay out of politics. Adolfo Trujillo Domínguez, a leader in the anarchosyndicalist typesetters' union, wrote that history and struggle, not the bourgeois state, gave workers their rights and power.[79]

It is much more likely that, in the eyes of the workers, the Cardenista state had given them precious few reasons to support it and that the Federal Labor Code served as a tactful way for unions to refuse to participate in politics without directly antagonizing Cárdenas. Workers had been disappointed by previous federal failures to effectively intervene in labor disputes. Most urban laborers correctly perceived that the "proletarian president" (Trujillo's words) might have sympathized with their situation but could do little for them.

The widespread abstention of workers and the internal dissension in many urban unions evident in the gubernatorial campaign underscored the distance between the Cardenista vision of an emerging workers' democracy and the reality of Yucatán. Far from being the advance guard of popular Cardenismo, urban labor was fractured and alienated. The Open Door election highlighted the cost of the decisions that Cárdenas and his national collaborators had made. Agrarian reform had finally been completed in the henequen zone, but economic and political necessity forced Cárdenas to back away from the meaningful overhaul of electoral practices that the Open Door promised as well as to ignore the pleas by urban labor for federal aid to realize the dream of worker-run cooperatives and fair arbitration. Perhaps the realities and contingencies of the day offered Cárdenas no other possibilities. Only the future would reveal whether agrarian reform could continue without political reform and whether Cardenismo could survive in Yucatán as a viable political movement without a strong urban component.

6

The Retreat of Cárdenas:
The Great Ejido Plan and the New
Political Equilibrium in Yucatán

ONLY A FEW DAYS after the completion of Cárdenas's Crusade of the Mayab, hacendados took out a public announcement warning that the Agrarian Bank's newly expanded influence would give Candelario Reyes virtual control of the state.[1] Such fears mirrored the hopes of the national Cardenistas, who believed that only the "federalization" of Yucatán would free the supposedly quiescent Maya peasantry from centuries of oppression. Both the anxiety of Yucatecan landowners and the optimism of national Cardenistas were misplaced.

The Crusade of the Mayab was in fact the swan song of Cardenismo, as Governor Palomo Valencia and the official camarilla would soon roll back federal power in Yucatán. Regional politicos had already scored key victories in the creation of independent ejidos outside federal control and in the manipulation of the Open Door gubernatorial election to impose Humberto Canto Echeverría. As governor, Canto Echeverría (February 1938–February 1942) moved to finish off federal influence in Yucatán and re-regionalize politics by gaining control of the henequen ejidos in Yucatán through the Great Ejido Plan, a development charted in the first part of this chapter.

As we shall see in the middle portions of this chapter, the governor and his official camarilla did not go unchallenged. They had to battle a heterogeneous coalition of opportunistic politicos on the "outs," more than few resurgent hacendados, and the last coalition of pro-Cárdenas labor, peasant, and leftist organizations. This movement, headed by the Committee for the Defense of the Ejido (Comité Pro-Defensa Ejidal, or CDE), almost succeeded in toppling Canto Echeverría and the official camarilla in the name of Cardenismo, not once, but twice. Invoking Cárdenas's mandate of economic democracy—allowing ejidatarios the right to manage the henequen ejidos on their own—and exploiting the hostility of many national Cardenistas to Canto Echeverría, the CDE's popular mobilizations represented the last (if imperfect) opportunity to correct the serious problems with agrarian reform and forge a direct link from the Cardenista national regime in Mexico City to the Yucatecan countryside.

The concluding portion of this chapter reveals how the political necessities of the 1940 presidential succession and the errors of the CDE's leadership allowed Governor Canto Echeverría and the official camarilla to finally regain control over regional politics and the henequen ejidos. The new political equilibrium in Yucatán came about, not because the governor and his group championed the Cardenista agenda or incorporated popular forces, but because they exploited the president's weaknesses and revived the kind of machine politics and cacique tactics that only a few years earlier Cardenistas denounced as Callismo.

The Birth of the Great Ejido

Since at least late 1936, state officials had been floating an alternative to the federal agrarian reform program that would concentrate all the ejidos in the henequen zone into a single administrative unit, later known as the Great Ejido.[2] Centralization, they claimed, would resolve the financial and technical problems of the henequen ejidos. Their rational alternative to the Agrarian Bank was to manage all two hundred or so ejidos with one single bureaucracy instead of dozens of individual credit societies and to turn control over to experts familiar with the peculiar needs of henequen cultivation—that is to say, Yucatecans, not the Agrarian Bank. This plan had languished until early 1938, as Cárdenas continued stubbornly to support Reyes and federal agrarian authorities.

However, the political and economic costs of agrarian reform forced the president to rethink his commitment to the original federal land reform blueprint. The decision to allow independent ejidos and include thousands of peons in ejidos, and the toleration of Palomo Valencia's imposition of Canto Echeverría as governor convinced Candelario Reyes that he no longer enjoyed Cárdenas's full confidence. In a signal victory for Palomo Valencia and the official camarilla, a demoralized Reyes resigned in late 1937. By early 1938, national events presented the new governor, Canto Echeverría, with the opportunity to put forward the so-called Great Ejido Plan. Canto Echeverría chose a most opportune moment to approach Cárdenas, knowing that, even though the president had staked much on finally solving Yucatán's agrarian problem, Cárdenas might well be ready to give in to the governor.

Indeed, much had changed since the Crusade of the Mayab in the early fall of 1937. Even though the next president would not take office until the end of 1940, there was already much anxiety among leading national Cardenistas over the upcoming struggle to replace the president. Fears of a disputed election and of an armed rising by rightists (realized when Saturnino Cedillo rebelled) forced Cárdenas to be much more conciliatory in his relations with regional interests.

Economically, Cárdenas simply could not meet all the tremendous commitments that the national government had assumed. To fund the costs of agrarian reform in the northern cotton region of La Laguna, the Cardenista financial team headed by Minister of the Treasury Eduardo Suárez had forced a large loan on the Bank of Mexico, hoping that a good harvest on the new cotton ejidos would allow the national government to pay off the mounting national debt quickly. A poor cotton crop in 1937 complicated these plans. Moreover, Cárdenas's farsighted but expensive program of investments in infrastructure absorbed much of the national treasury. Most ominously for the president, the oil expropriation of March 1938 and the subsequent need to compensate foreign owners pushed Mexico's finances to the breaking point.[3]

It was in the midst of this fiscal crisis, in March 1938, that Cárdenas quietly approved Canto Echeverría's Great Ejido Plan in order to reallocate federal resources away from Yucatán to meet more pressing needs. In a meeting in Veracruz with Cárdenas and federal advisers, Canto Echeverría won the president over when he promised that the Great Ejido Plan would eliminate the need for federal subsidies. Most national Cardenistas had argued vociferously against the plan; they felt that it violated the spirit of Cardenismo and effectively ended reform in Yucatán. But they were undercut by the fact that the national government had already begun retreating from Cárdenas's commitments in the henequen zone; the federal treasury had been forced to suspend payments to the henequen ejidos because of its own economic crisis. This provoked a depression in Yucatán of which Canto Echeverría took full advantage to promote the Great Ejido.[4]

Beyond the economic logic, Canto Echeverría justified the Great Ejido in a number of original ways. He went so far as to compare the Great Ejido to the petroleum expropriation, calling it another "economic emancipation." The governor, however, never explained the similarity between the federal Agrarian Bank and foreign oil companies. Canto Echeverría even managed to link the Great Ejido to indigenism: he claimed that his inspiration for it came from Sylvanius Morley, the North American archaeologist who told him that the Maya worked the land collectively, not individually. Following this logic, the Great Ejido represented a return to "traditional" Maya agricultural practices by creating one collective farm out of hundreds of ejidos.[5]

The Great Ejido promised even more. As an engineer, Canto Echeverría argued that centralizing the hundreds of ejidos would make their administration much more efficient and "restore discipline and organization." This would in turn raise the quality of production, allowing Yucatán to regain the world market share lost to foreign rivals in Africa and Asia. Canto Echeverría reminded Cárdenas that quality-control problems on federal ejidos were so bad that a foreign buyer inspecting sisal in Progreso found part of a mule carcass inside a bale. Besides boosting exports, Canto Echeverría also claimed that his plan would correct problems created by the rapid execution of the hundreds of land grants decreed during the Crusade of the Mayab by equitably redistributing resources among all the ejidos.[6]

With little exaggeration, Canto Echeverría argued that the Agrarian Bank's federal engineers had lost authority to ejidal caciques and *líderillos* (petty leaders) who had taken over day-to-day operations of the ejidos, naming favorites to the managerial jobs like checkers and organizing riots to force the Agrarian Bank to remove objectionable supervisors. Under the Great Ejido Plan, by contrast, ejidatarios would follow the orders of supervisors and mind the new slogan — "Order, Organization, and Work."[7]

Perhaps to balance the autocratic structure of the Great Ejido Plan, Canto Echeverría promised Cárdenas that peasants could train in new schools to become managers, overseers, and quality-control specialists and that, starting in 1940, they would begin taking over the staffing of the Great Ejido. Similarly, the governor also pledged that ejidatarios would have "direct involvement in the henequen industry" by giving them seats in the governing body of the Great Ejido; this would fulfill the presidential decree of August 1937 that mandated full rights for peasant producers. To give Canto Echeverría's project the appearance of grassroots backing, a hastily organized "popular" convention rubber-stamped the Great Ejido Plan. To further bolster popular support, the state simultaneously announced price controls on beef and maize, imported and distributed eleven thousand tons of maize at subsidized prices, and raised advances paid to ejidatarios on state-supported independent land grants.[8]

Although the Great Ejido would soon encounter serious problems, it did not immediately demonstrably worsen the precarious position of ejidatarios in the henequen zone, who already suffered from low advances, intrusive bureaucrats, and a feeling of disenfranchisement. Unfortunately, the Great Ejido never came close to fulfilling Canto Echeverría's promise of economic improvement and social liberation for the ejidatarios. Despite raising henequen taxes in April and again in July 1938, the Great Ejido continued to need national subsidies, and Canto Echeverría had to cut state funding for education and medical care. Another casualty of the Great Ejido's economic crisis was the planned state technical school, which would have trained peasants to fill administrative posts.[9]

Financial problems multiplied as anticipated savings under the Great Ejido Plan failed to materialize. Even when all the ejidos were administratively unified, the optimal two-to-one ratio of land in cultivation to land out of cultivation was not achieved, which complicated planning. Although Canto Echeverría initially planned to reduce the number of mechanized raspers in operation to save money, transportation and administrative problems meant that many ejidos could not process their harvest. Mounting losses from waste thus forced Canto Echeverría to reverse course and try to expropriate more processing machinery from the hacendados in April and again in October 1938, but legal stays frustrated his plans.[10]

The Great Ejido's great expectations were also dampened by "discipline problems" with workers. Canto Echeverría was professionally trained as an engineer and had a notoriously stubborn personality; he believed that human productivity could be raised through careful planning and the force of his own will. Despite his lip service to Cárdenas's goals of peasant empowerment, he was determined to overcome problems of líderisimo and poor productivity by browbeating field managers and simply ignoring peasant complaints.[11] Despite the rhetoric of Cardenista democratization that Canto Echeverría used to sell the Great Ejido to Cárdenas, the plan's administrators soon came to rely on the same kind of heavy-handed tactics that federal engineers used. This is not surprising, considering that the managers of the new Great Ejido were mainly recruited from among former employees of the Agrarian Bank, along with middle-level politicians and bureaucrats from the old Socialist Party and even former hacienda foremen.

Reregionalizing Politics

If the Great Ejido failed to realize its ambitious economic and social goals for ejidatarios, it achieved a vitally important political one for the governor and the official camarilla. It got the federal government out of the henequen zone, and it allowed Yucatecan politicos, above all Governor Canto Echeverría, to reclaim control over the state, reregionalizing politics.

The Great Ejido became a valuable asset for the governor and his group.

Staffed by the governor (its director) and his followers, many of its ejidatarios were organized by official camarilla subsidiary groups, the PSS, the
FSI, and the CGT. They, in turn, filled the political vacuum left by the
departure of the Agrarian Bank.[12] The governor sent out federal teachers,
by now another cog in the regional political machine, to convince the
ejidatarios of the benefits of the Great Ejido and to counteract hacendado
propaganda that agrarian reform was a failure by blaming all the ejidos'
problems on hacendado sabotage.[13] At the same time, Canto Echeverría
shrewdly divided the hacendado class by offering some families posts in the
administration of the Great Ejido while threatening hostile clans with further expropriations of land or machinery.[14]

The Great Ejido also served to fend off the expansion of the national
peasant (CNC) and labor (CTM) federations as well as the national ruling
party (Partido de la Revolución Mexicano, or PRM, formerly known as the
PNR) in Yucatán.[15] The Great Ejido's control over jobs and economic
resources gave Canto Echeverría leverage over local politics. Many municipalities controlled since 1935 by supporters of the federal Agrarian Bank
were quickly captured by allies of the official camarilla.[16]

The success of Canto Echeverría and his official camarilla against the
central state is nowhere more apparent than in the fate of the political,
worker, and peasant arms of the national state in Yucatán: the PRM, the
CTM, and the CNC. To bolster the national party, Cárdenas announced
in early 1938 that the PNR would adopt a new name and a new structure.
Now designated the PRM, it adopted a "functional" structure clearly mod-
eled after corporatism. Four branches embraced almost all society: the
workers (basically the CTM, along with the CROM [Confederación Regional Obreros Mexicanos], the CGT, and some independent unions), the
peasants (the CNC), the military, and the popular sectors. The last was
something of a default category, including government employees, young
people, and women's groups. The PRM, then, aimed not only at giving the
national government/party a strong popular base, but also at increasing
Mexico City's influence over regional affairs.[17]

The CTM's attempts to organize urban labor were not directly blocked by
the Great Ejido, but Canto Echeverría threw up other obstacles to the
national labor federation. Most importantly, he gained the allegiance of
some Yucatecan unions, using state patronage and political posts to establish a precarious modus vivendi with leaders of urban labor. Canto Echeverría co-opted the leadership and courted rank-and-file members with
economic concessions, a strategy once again facilitated by the state govern-

ment's control over the Great Ejido. For example, he won over the independent FUTV drivers' union with the lucrative contract to transport henequen for the Great Ejido; by 1940, the FUTV fully supported the official camarilla's candidates in elections. As a result of these efforts, the national CTM never built a strong regional affiliate in Yucatán during these years. Yucatecan labor federations that joined the CTM in name continued to maintain their distinct identities (the PSS refused to drop its name on grounds of tradition). More importantly, the larger CTM affiliates, like the FSI, the CGT, the FROC, and the PSS, harbored close ties to and remained financially dependent on the state government, while the CTM's Yucatecan affiliation (the FTY, or Federación de Trabajadores de Yucatán) remained a weak organization, to say the least. It lacked a headquarters, a functioning directorate, a treasury, a newspaper, or any seats in either the state congress or the Yucatecan delegation to the national congress.[18]

National peasant confederations achieved even less success in Yucatán. Attempts to set up regional peasant confederations fizzled in late 1935, in late 1937 during the Crusade of the Mayab, and yet again in March 1938 when the PNR became the PRM.[19] In August 1938, Governor Canto Echeverría and such national notables as David Vilchis of the CTM, Carlos Terrazas, secretary of agricultural affairs of the national PRM, and Vicente Salgado Páez, the federal Agrarian Department's representative in the state, convened peasant delegates from ejidos across the state to finally form a Yucatecan affiliate of the CNC (Confederación Nacional Campesina), the peasant wing of the PRM. This organization would be known as the League of Agrarian Communities (Liga de Communidades Agrarias, or LCA). But, as in the case of the CTM, the state government and local caciques greatly circumscribed the CNC's influence. The LCA's lack of economic resources and political clout hindered its ability to build strong local affiliates in the countryside. In December 1939, over fourteen months after its founding, the LCA had functioning affiliates in only one-quarter of Yucatán.[20]

Given the weakness of the national peasant and worker federations in Yucatán, the PRM's only means of building a true base in the state seemed to be the popular sector, which, following the corporatist doctrine of the party, took in just about everything that was not included in either the military or the worker and peasant sectors. But, in Yucatán, the PRM's popular sector was dominated by affiliates of the PCM, like the FUPDM and the JSUM, which by this time were firmly tethered to the state government. The other major groups in the PRM's popular sector were closely linked to existing organizations also controlled by the governor's camarilla: government employees, from state and municipal executive agencies as well as the state congress and supreme court, down to gardeners and laborers on public works projects; house intellectuals of the old PSS (writers, artists, and journalists of the José María Iturralde Socialist League) and its Constituents Bloc; and the powerful Union of Baratilleros (street vendors, long a pillar of the old PSS in Mérida). For good measure, Governor Canto Echeverría also stacked the PRM's popular sector with shadowy organizations dependent on subsidies and public-sector jobs and run by old Bartolista-era politicos, like the Front to Defend Workers and Peasants (Frente Defensor de Obreros y Campesinos, or FDOC) and the State Social Committee of Workers and Peasants (Comité Estatal Social Obreros y Campesinos, or CESOC).[21]

The ineffectiveness of the PRM was apparent from its first test in managing elections in the fall of 1938. The national PRM ordered its state branch to supervise the selection of candidates for town councils for the 1939–40 term, making sure to exclude reactionary elements and to balance the input of peasant, worker, and popular organizations. But, in practice, town councils continued to be selected in traditional ways. The governor's camarilla chose candidates in consultation with local factional leaders in informal meetings led by congressional deputies and representatives of official popular organizations like the FSI and the PSS. The governor's clique and local caciques intervened in local elections while effectively nullifying the role of the national party as arbiter. Indeed, the PRM's co-optation by regional networks caused Emilio Pacheco, head of Izamal's ejido and an old agrarian Cardenista leader, to lament that the PRM "is unknown [in] Yucatán."[22]

Neutralizing or co-opting federal institutions allowed Canto Echeverría to fend off challenges from above. However, there were other problems from below. Many towns and villages continued to be ruled by the same caciques for years on end. Rather than oust entrenched caciques, Canto Echeverría recognized the authority of Antonio Aranda Méndez over Cansahcab and Sóstenes Carrillo over Muna in return for their fealty but continued to rely on popular organizations like the FSI and the PSS to deal with grassroots problems on most henequen ejidos. Outside the henequen zone, the governor relied less on labor federations and unions. Instead, he built a network of new caciques made up of state deputies elected in 1937: Félix Vallejos took over Valladolid and surrounding villages in the eastern corner of the state, while Ricardo Marín ran the southern town of Tekax and its hinterland as his own fief.[23]

In 1938 and early 1939, Canto Echeverría scored notable success in weakening the federal government's influence in Yucatán, in no small part due to the state government's control over the Great Ejido. Yet this new mega-bureaucratic entity that ran the production, processing, and export of henequen became the target of a concerted takeover bid from within by a coalition of peasant leaders, renegade bureaucrats, caciques, and a few land-owners.[24] The rise of this cross-class alliance was made possible by Cárdenas's determination to give peasant ejidatarios a stake in the running of the Great Ejido, a democratic opening that would mark the ill-fated last phase of Cardenismo in Yucatán.

Economic Democracy and the First Fall of Canto Echeverría

Since the start of agrarian reform, Cárdenas had advocated giving peasants across Mexico not only the means of material improvement, but also eman-cipation from dependency on either landlords or bureaucrats, a policy here termed *economic democracy*.[25] For henequen ejidatarios, economic democ-racy meant the right to elect managers, the ability to train to take over more specialized jobs, and the chance to decide through plebiscites and elected representatives how to financially manage their collective future. Although the problems and setbacks experienced by agrarian reform in the henequen zone greatly complicated its implementation, evidence of Cárdenas's desire to reform the agrarian system along these lines can be found in two key decisions made in late 1937 and early 1938. First, in August 1937, Cárdenas gave ejidos the right to declare independence from the federal Agrarian Bank and run their own affairs without federal supervision. Second, Cár-denas rescinded the bank's oversight of the henequen zone because Canto Echeverría promised that ejidatarios themselves would eventually coad-minister the Great Ejido. Together, these presidential decisions promised ejidatarios the ability to control their own economic fates and emancipation from overseers, bureaucrats, and agrarian engineers.

To be sure, economic democracy was not realized immediately. Rather, it evolved slowly, starting in an unimpressive way with the first ejidatario convention during the Crusade of the Mayab.[26] This assembly did, how-ever, set the important precedent of requiring ejidatarios' participation in the agrarian reform process. When Canto Echeverría began to lobby Cár-denas for the Great Ejido Plan, a second convention of ejidatarios was held in early January 1938. Although this convention, like the first, was to some degree stage-managed to produce the results that the governor wanted (a ringing endorsement of his plan), it reinforced the process of democrat-ically summoning delegates from each ejido to ratify important decisions.[27]

It was not until April 1939 that truly democratic assemblies of ejidatarios were finally held. Although some peasant representatives asked for the expropriation of remaining haciendas, delegates' demands focused on the low advances and mismanagement of the Great Ejido. For instance, Francisco Cardos Dorantes of Motul asked for the employees of the Great Ejido to take a 25 percent pay cut to allow ejidatarios to buy basic goods.[28]

From the governor's point of view, these forums demonstrated his own desire to give ejidatarios a greater share in running their affairs — Cardenista economic democracy in its purest form. Of course, Canto Echeverría might well have hoped simply to let ejidatarios share in the blame as henequen prices dropped by giving them some responsibility in running the Great Ejido. A few months later, in late August 1939, the governor again held a series of meetings with ejidatarios, who passed resolutions urging the governor to lobby Cárdenas to give them more autonomy. Peasant delegates also voted to use their surplus revenues to raise advances instead of repairing houses.[29] For the first time, peasant delegates actually made decisions on how the Great Ejido as a whole would be managed.

At the same time, these assemblies provided an opportunity for opponents of Governor Canto Echeverría to organize and mobilize popular support against him. Cardenista economic democracy was finally achieving more participation by ejidatarios, but it also created another arena where camarillas would battle for regional supremacy. The CDE united ejidatarios against Canto Echeverría by building on the momentum generated at these meetings. The CDE, however, also served the political interests of a nascent camarilla set on controlling regional politics.

The leader of the CDE was Arsenio Lara, a veteran PSS cacique of Tixkokob known for his humble origins from the middle, mestizo stratum of his provincial hometown, his popular touch, as well as his success as an alcohol vendor and a rancher. But many believed that the true head of the CDE was Lara's mentor and in-law Antonio Gual García, an influential lawyer with links to a series of governors since the late 1910s. These two, along with a number of local Tixkokob politicians, ranchers, and merchants, made up the nucleus of the CDE, known as the Tixkokob group. Ejidatarios around Tixkokob strongly opposed the Great Ejido Plan because their land grants were better than most, and members of these "rich" ejidos resented seeing their profits taken to subsidize "poor" ejidos in the south and west. Small henequen producers upset over their political marginalization in the Great Ejido structure as well as some wealthy henequen barons seeking to regain lost cloud and settle scores with the governor also supported the CDE.[30]

Letters written to Cárdenas by peasants affiliated with the CDE suggest the depth of popular grievances against the Great Ejido. Disgruntled ejidatarios of Hunucmá who enlisted in the CDE demanded a raise to two pesos daily or for all the haciendas in the area to be turned over to the peasants.[31] On 23 August 1939, over two thousand pro-CDE ejidatarios met in Tixkokob and wrote to Cárdenas, their letter serving as kind of *cahier* of ejidatarios. They demanded nothing less than an end to the Great Ejido and the return of the federal Agrarian Department, along with higher advances, medical service, and a more responsible bureaucracy. The language of their letter reveals popular outrage over Canto Echeverría's betrayal of Cardenista economic democracy: "The ejidatarios, being the legitimate owners, have to obey the orders of the employees, who in most cases treat us worse than what happened in the past."[32]

To contest the rapid spread of the CDE across the henequen zone, Canto Echeverría assembled a grassroots base of his own. To this end, he created the Committee for Agrarian Fairness (Comité Pro-Equidad Ejidal, or CPEE) on 3 September 1939. Its very name encouraged peasants to resist the CDE on the grounds that it was concerned only for the "rich" ejidos of Tixkokob at the expense of the rest of the state. Geographically, its limited base reflected Canto Echeverría's weak position against the CDE. Ejidatarios from around Mérida and the poorer henequen areas just to the south and west of the state capital dominated its leadership. But it had only a weak presence in the central, northern, and eastern parts of the henequen zone.[33] The CPEE's overall debility was apparent when it had to bring in peasants from outside the henequen zone to stage demonstrations against the CDE.[34]

The CPEE recruited local power brokers such as town councilmen and members of ejidal commissaries and, through them, tried to reach out to common ejidatarios. In appealing to peasants, it attacked the CDE as a hacendado front and a class enemy. The checkered past of CDE president Arsenio Lara also provided much ammunition for the CPEE; it accused Lara of masquerading as a Yucatecan Mahatma Gandhi who advocated the defense of the humble while selling alcohol and speculating in maize to exploit peasants.[35]

Even as it attacked the CDE, the CPEE mimicked its reformist message. The CPEE claimed that it would fulfill Cardenismo's economic-democratic mandate in the running of the ejidos. But the progovernor group said that it was committed to turning over the ejidos to the ejidatarios, not to the "nabob" Lara and his shadowy mentor, Antonio Gual García. And, like the

CDE, it advocated a "cleansing" of current Great Ejido employees who bullied ejidatarios. Undoubtedly, the fact that many employees of the Great Ejido campaigned for the CDE hardened Canto Echeverría's resolve to purge the ejidal bureaucracy. Moreover, the CPEE revived Canto Echeverría's unfulfilled promise to educate ejidatarios so that they could eventually manage the ejidos themselves. More realistically, it denounced the CDE's promise to raise wages as a deceptive plot that would only put ejidatarios further into debt given the shaky price of henequen on global markets — although the CPEE at times also pledged to raise advances. Finally, the CPEE harped on the prominent roles played by people "outside the ejido" (railroad workers, electricians, etc.) in the CDE's leadership.[36]

The rise of the CDE revealed both the strengths and the weaknesses of mature Cardenismo. Although the president had effectively given up on meaningful political reform after the Open Door election, he continued stubbornly to advocate economic democracy, believing that peasants could and should be allowed to manage their ejidos. He made this a condition in accepting the Great Ejido and pressured regional actors to comply. The shifting of power away from national authorities in Yucatán, however, made it very difficult to achieve this noble goal, although Cardenista policy did force the camarillas to take popular demands into account. Politicos of the Tixkokob group sought to seize the Great Ejido by exploiting Cardenista economic democracy. To be sure, their means of doing so, the CDE, was not simply manipulating ejidatarios — its discourse and program articulated popular demands, and it opened its leadership to peasant representatives. The embattled governor, for his part, also had to make some concessions to ejidatarios to try to broaden his base, and, just like the CDE, his CPEE claimed to champion economic democracy.

Considering the importance of the Great Ejido to the state's economy and the tremendous amount of political patronage that it controlled, it was inevitable that the battle between the governor and the CDE would dominate the region until the end of Cárdenas's term. Initially at least, it seemed that Cardenista economic democracy would force both sides to repair the errors of the agrarian reform project in a way that would make a meaningful difference in the lives of over thirty thousand ejidatarios and their families.

The CDE against the Official Camarilla

In its conflict with Canto Echeverría's camarilla, the CDE aligned with foes of the governor in the henequen zone, Mérida, and Mexico City. The leader of Left-Cardenismo in Yucatán, state congressman and FSI president Diego Rosado broke with Canto Echeverría to bring most Communist organizations into the CDE camp in the autumn of 1939 after many leftist groups rejected the governor's authoritarian management of the Great Ejido.[37] The CDE reached out to independent urban labor unions grouped in the Union Alliance for Collective Defense (Alianza Sindical de Defensa Colectiva, or ASDC). The ASDC included the SFP and the old Socialist truckers' cooperative, which wanted to regain the lucrative rights to transport henequen that the governor had given to the FUTV. The SCY, another ASDC affiliate, wanted the Cordelería Mayapan for a workers' cooperative. Other labor groups, such as the workers of Mérida's water and electrical plants, also demanded control of their industries. Another labor ally of the CDE's, employees of the Great Ejido, demanded the right to unionize and the reinstatement of those fired by Canto Echeverría. Arsenio Lara even found allies among the teachers, backing the faction opposing the Communist group that controlled the education bureaucracy in Yucatán.[38]

In challenging Canto Echeverría for de facto dominance of Yucatán, the CDE accumulated a formidable list of allies in Mexico City. Many Yucatecan politicians in the national capital held grudges against Canto Echeverría: both Yucatecan senators, Bartolomé García Correa and Gualberto Carrillo Puerto, federal congressman Miguel Angél Menéndez, as well as Fernando López Cárdenas, ex-governor and supreme court justice. The latter embarrassed Canto Echeverría by publishing charges of corruption in the Great Ejido in Mexico City's *La Prensa* newspaper. Moreover, there were national Cardenistas smarting over the ejection of the federal agrarian bureaucracy from the state — most notably the head of the CNC, Gabino Vázquez, and the Agrarian Bank. They saw the CDE as a means of regaining federal control of the henequen zone.[39]

With this strong support in Mexico City, the ASDC and the CDE joined in a general strike that threatened to shut down the henequen industry and jeopardized the Canto Echeverría administration. To resolve the strike, Cárdenas sent a trusted envoy, Colonel Ramón Beteta, to mediate. In an agreement worked out by Beteta and signed in September 1939, the beleaguered governor agreed to most of the demands of the CDE and the ASDC. Canto Echeverría conceded that the CDE represented the "immense majority of ejidatarios" and disbanded the CPEE. Most importantly, he stepped down as general director of the Great Ejido, and his allies in its bureaucracy resigned as well. Under the accords, the direction of the Great Ejido was to be put in the hands of a popularly elected directorate. Beteta also promised that Cárdenas would come to Yucatán in person to hear complaints and resolve disputes — an open challenge to Canto Echeverría's authority interpreted by many to mean that the governor no longer had the president's favor.[40]

On 21 September 1939, as guaranteed under the agreement, a convention of ejidatarios of the henequen zone took place in Tixkokob, the stronghold of the CDE. The CDE leadership invited representatives of unions of the ASDC along with delegates from all 272 henequen ejidos. Divisions between the minority supporting the governor and the pro-CDE majority led to rowdy debates. After heated floor discussions, the ejidatarios elected Ramiro Ancona, meat merchant of Tixkokob and ally of CDE jefe Arsenio Lara Puerto, as director of the Great Ejido. The CDE-dominated convention pressed for the immediate election of peasant directorates for the Great Ejido, but the governor managed to stall the vote for two more months.

Although the CDE dominated the convention, cracks were already apparent within its broad coalition. Especially divisive was the prominent role of the foremen and managers of the Great Ejido in the CDE. While peasant supporters of the Tixkokob group endorsed CDE motions to fire 119 "favorites" of the governor from the henequen bureaucracy, many peasants did not support the CDE directorate's resolutions backing higher wages for Great Ejido employees. After all, they were already doing much better economically than the ejidatarios in spite of their often poor performance. Many ejidatarios also demanded that they get the well-paid bureaucratic posts filled mainly by urban employees — a promise that both the governor and the CDE had made but that neither was quick to honor. The CDE leadership eventually overcame disputes between ejido employees and peasants and united the assembly in a commitment to strike in eight days to force Governor Canto Echeverría to turn over the Great Ejido to them immediately. Only one day later, the strike had shut down the export of henequen.[41]

Despite scattered shows of support for the governor from urban unions and some peasants and attempts by federal military zone commander General Jesús Benignos to use federal troops to keep the CDE out of Mérida, between 27 and 29 September special trains arranged by the SFP brought thousands of protesting ejidatarios to Mérida.[42] As in October 1935 and July 1936, demonstrations by thousands of peasants and workers gave the CDE a strong argument to remove Canto Echeverría: the governor had lost control of the state, and he had no popular support. Moreover, Canto Echeverría had repeatedly backpedaled on his promise to Cárdenas to implement economic democracy. Under both traditional political practice and Cardenista doctrine, he was a liability for the national government.[43]

Realizing that continued protests would finish him, the governor responded with both conciliation and coercion. On the one hand, he offered to remove many Great Ejido bureaucrats, and he once again promised to turn over all supervisory and administrative posts to peasants, a belated conversion to Cárdenas's economic democracy. At the same time, Canto Echeverría and General Benignos moved to disarm the Agrarian Reserves of Tixkokob, which had protected the Tixkokob group, dispatched federal troops to prop up the unpopular, progovernor mayors of Acancéh and Hunucmá, and halted trains bringing pro-CDE "agitators against public order" into Mérida. But the federal troops and the governor's Cheka (plainclothes policemen and employees disguised as peasants) could not seal off the capital because of the SFP's support for the CDE. Rather than endanger his governorship, the governor swallowed his pride and stepped down from his executive directorship of the Great Ejido. His only hope for salvation was now in the hands of the president.[44]

With the threat of political and economic crises hanging over the state, Cárdenas arrived in Mérida on 21 November 1939 to arbitrate the dispute for control of the Great Ejido personally. The CDE greeted Cárdenas with several public demonstrations against Canto Echeverría. Cárdenas mediated a resolution to the strike in which the governor once again lost power to the CDE. Cárdenas named Senator Gualberto Carrillo Puerto, no friend of Canto Echeverría's, as federal representative to the Great Ejido. Most importantly, the presidential resolution dictated that the day-to-day management would be in the hands of the peasants themselves through democratically elected territorial councils, a central committee, and its oversight committee. This agreement shifted much more power over the running of the Great Ejido to the ejidatarios and seemed finally to realize Cárdenas's cherished goal of economic democracy for the Great Ejido. But it also significantly altered the regional balance of power in Yucatán. Because the CDE now had organized most of the ejidatarios in the henequen zone, it had indirect control over the Great Ejido through its elected organs, and power was thus split in the state between the CDE and the governor.

If the November convention of ejidatarios convened by the president seemed to fulfill the Cardenista goals of economic democracy, it also publicly aired many of the bottled-up grievances of the peasants. Cárdenas left the convention shaken by the outpouring of complaints by ejidatarios against their poor economic conditions and by the lack of deference shown the president.[45] We can never know for sure, but the aggressiveness with which peasants condemned the shortcomings of agrarian reform might well have caused the president to have second thoughts about economic democracy. In any event, the November 1939 convention led, not to a peasant takeover of the henequen ejidos, but to a new conflict between the CDE and the official camarilla and a new reticence by Cárdenas to intervene on the side of the ejidatarios.

Fearing a landslide victory for the CDE candidates in the upcoming elections of the Great Ejido councils, the official camarilla pressured municipal governments to crack down on CDE organizers. The governor set loose the Cheka and ordered caciques to silence the CDE branches. As in past elections, the official candidates for Great Ejido posts relied on the inducement of alcohol to attract voters.[46]

Canto Echeverría and the CDE both realized the importance of courting caciques — testimony to how little Cardenista corporatism and democratization had meaningfully changed regional politics. Their control over voting in many (but by no means all) locales would mean that the outcome of the December 1939 election to choose the peasant councilors for the Great Ejido would be in the hands not just of the voters, but also of petty bosses. The rural chieftains, for their part, were wary as either the CDE or Canto Echeverría could prevail and joining the loser might mean being deprived of their local fiefs. The actions of Antonio Aranda, boss of the town of Cansahcab on the eastern fringes of the henequen zone, typified the often-erratic and volatile behavior of local bosses in this uncertain environment.

In October 1939, when the CDE tried to organize in Cansahcab, Aranda used strong-arm tactics to squelch its efforts, seeing the CDE as a possible challenger.[47] But as the CDE grew in strength, and as national power seemed to endorse it, Aranda apparently joined the CDE, sensing that he might well be deposed should it prevail. On 1 November, he was among the dozen "peasant" representatives who met with Canto Echeverría on behalf of the CDE.[48] However, in trying to counter the CDE, Canto Echeverría sought out Aranda's help just as he approached other bosses. Now back in the official camarilla, Aranda ran on the slate of progovernor candidates against the CDE for the territorial council of Cansahcab.[49] In January 1940, a riot on the ejido by disgruntled peasants served as a pretext for the Arandista mayor to fire suspected CDE supporters. In August of that year, the CDE's subcommittee in Cansahcab wrote to the governor complaining that "the malevolent casique [*sic*] and dictator Antonio Aranda" had been propped up in power by Yucatecan governors since 1924. Because of his "political influences," they complained, "he served [previous governors] in order to iniquitously exploit the humble working classes of this unfortunate pueblo." The authors of the letter asked the governor to finally remove Aranda, saying that for years he had "provoked the estrangement of the laborious sons of Cansahcab, in order to live off their sweat." Finally, the CDE of Cansahcab invoked the "ideals and postulates of our sacrosanct Revolution, which gave rights and liberties to the pueblos, winning for them their social liberation" in their fruitless efforts to topple Aranda.[50] The CDE's inability to co-opt or roust provincial bosses like Aranda would complicate its attempts to build a strong popular base in the henequen zone even after it seized control of the Great Ejido.

Although the Tixkokob group included some caciques, the broad popular base of the CDE and the widespread belief among ejidatarios that Canto Echeverría bore responsibility for the economic ills of the Great Ejido forced the governor's group to rely more and more on bosses like Aranda. Failing to build a rival organization in the countryside, the governor had no alternative but brute force to try to stave off CDE victories in elections for the Great Ejido administrative councils. In Kanasín, for instance, official politico Gonzalo López Manzanero overthrew Kanasín's elected town council and imposed Teodoro Ricalde as mayor. During previous unelected service in town hall, Ricalde had earned a reputation as a petty tyrant and a thief, having reportedly stolen the town clock. Back in the saddle again, Ricalde and CPEE leader Ignacio Canché jailed CDE organizers. In Izamal and Tekal, veteran PSS organizer Professor Eustaquio Avila led a gang of toughs to intimidate CDE organizers before the election. CDE organizers in Tahmek, Maxcanú, Halachó, and Chuburná complained that, before the vote, progovernor gangs jailed, beat, and otherwise intimidated them.[51]

The governor's support for bosses and the arming of several hundred ejidatarios under the Agrarian Militia program heightened factional disputes in many communities. On the eve of the election for Great Ejido councilors, Tekantó had split into two hostile bands with irreconcilable antagonisms and a potential for violence that required federal troops to keep order. This situation was all too common across the henequen zone in late 1939. The governor's network of bosses and enforcers was implicated in the deaths of five peasant leaders active in the CDE between late November 1939 and April 1940.[52]

The struggle between the CDE and the official camarilla was not just an intraelite feud. The fact that local authorities propped up by the governor held onto power against the will of much of the community created tense situations in many henequen towns. When leaders of the CDE were killed by outsiders, apparently on the orders of the governor, ejidatarios felt that their communities had been invaded. In Hoctun, support for the CDE ran high, although the embattled town council stayed loyal to the governor and the local strongman, Renán Ricalde. On 23 November, agents of the governor assassinated Manuel Reyes Hu, recently elected on the CDE slate to the Great Ejido's directorate, which provoked a wave of popular resentment. The murder and the impunity that his assassins enjoyed sparked protests and eventually a general strike by most of Hoctun, from ejidatarios to merchants. Protesters came to see the death of Hu as emblematic of larger problems, from the interference of reputed cacique Renán Ricalde in the local affairs of Hoctun for years to the mismanagement of its henequen ejidos by the Great Ejido. On 9 August 1940, an estimated three hundred of Hoctun's citizens took advantage of the temporary removal of Governor Canto Echeverría from office (see below) to storm town hall and jail the mayor and town treasurer.[53]

Despite intimidation from the Cheka, federal troops, and caciques and the efforts of the teachers to "orient" the peasants about the governor's "revolutionary labor," CDE candidates triumphed overwhelmingly in the elections for Great Ejido directive committees held in the first ten days of December 1939. Participation was high, and the CDE received a convincing 21,184 of 30,911 ballots (only members of henequen ejidos could vote, meaning that only roughly half the state's men could), a victory margin probably artificially lowered by fraud in Izamal, Muna, and Ticul. The balloting gave the CDE control of the Great Ejido's central committee and seven of nine territorial councils. It also won leadership of the organizations representing both large and small henequen producers in the Great Ejido.[54] The net result was that the Great Ejido's management, staffing decisions, and budget would all be in the hands of the Tixkokob group and allied popular leaders.

To oversee the transfer of power and calm the tense situation in Yucatán, Cárdenas returned to Mérida on 16 December 1939. He warned assembled ejidatarios and CDE leaders against "sterile agitation" and told them in no uncertain terms to cease and desist in their efforts to oust the governor. To that end, Cárdenas left Canto Echeverría the crucial authority to remove the director of the Great Ejido. This gave the governor a de facto veto over the CDE's management of it.[55] Such a concession reflected Cárdenas's growing concerns about keeping the governors loyal in the upcoming presidential election. The political calculus of the presidential succession, and quite possibly his fears that unchecked economic democracy might lead to another outpouring of peasant anger against agrarian reform like the one that he had only recently witnessed in November, forced Cárdenas to end his tilt toward the CDE and prop up Canto Echeverría. Clearly, Cardenista economic democracy did not mean political democracy — the governor still served at the will of the president, not the people.

As in the past, battles for control of regional politics were fought, not just in Mexico City and Mérida, but at the grassroots level. Cardenismo's power was clearly receding, even as the struggle for local and regional power intensified. When Canto Echeverría's official camarilla faced off against the CDE, both sides claimed to have a popular mandate, and the CDE actually had a fairly broad base of worker and peasant support. Cárdenas could not command the unquestioned support of the camarillas and lacked a direct means of mobilizing a popular base in the countryside, but he could and did force regional camarillas to take popular demands into account by brandishing his power to remove and install governors. Even this limited influence over regional politics failed when Cárdenas had to rely on his governors' loyalty in the approaching presidential election.

Sensing Cárdenas's dependence on him, Canto Echeverría could use the police and caciques to stem the rise of popular mobilizations triggered by the CDE, as well as to ignore Cárdenas's call for economic democratization without fear of retribution. Bolstered by presidential decisions that weakened the CDE even as the Great Ejido was handed over to it, Canto Echeverría prepared to strike back.[56]

The ability of the CDE to fill Mérida's streets with thousands of protesters had already forced the governor to relinquish control of his cherished Great Ejido in September 1939. Another such strike could push him out of power, just as Alayola and López Cárdenas had been toppled. Canto Echeverría's first move to neutralize the CDE threat was to uncouple urban labor from the ejidatarios by co-opting its leadership.

Canto Echeverría went to Carlos González Inurreta, the former cacique of the SFP, to make a deal. Canto Echeverría agreed to back the González brothers' efforts to regain control of the union, which they lost over charges of corruption and violence. In return, Carlos González agreed to take the SFP out of the ASDC, the pro-CDE labor alliance, thus depriving the CDE of its ability to move large numbers of protesters to Mérida by rail. To hold up his end of the bargain, the governor convinced the federal commander in the state (a friend) to withdraw troops guarding the SFP headquarters where the anti-González "Renovating" leadership held sway and, on 28 October 1939, sent in the Cheka to join the supporters of the González brothers in chasing out their opponents.[57] Simultaneously, Canto Echeverría co-opted other urban unions and split them off from the ASDC. Because of the governor's support for González Inurreta, the CTM's ninth national congress declared Canto Echeverría the defender of Cardenista agrarian reform against so-called reactionary forces.[58]

The Official Camarilla Counterattacks

To dampen grassroots enthusiasm for the CDE, allies of the governor attacked its management of the Great Ejido, launching the same sorts of charges of corruption and nepotism that the CDE had used to good effect against the governor in the past. The CDE's exploitation of the Great Ejido as a source of patronage allowed Canto Echeverría to accuse its employees of trying to make themselves a "permanent bureaucracy." Supporters of the governor charged that Arsenio Lara threw an excessive number of parties at the Great Ejido's expense, including his recent birthday party, which featured two orchestras, a train rented for two thousand pesos, and a sumptuous meal. The governor also took advantage of the continuing poor economic situation in the henequen zone by encouraging peasants to ask for raises in order to embarrass the CDE. The official camarilla took up the banner of popular Cardenismo, calling for economic democracy to be realized by reforming the Great Ejido — now that it was in the hands of the CDE.

While weakening the CDE, Canto Echeverría looked to Mexico City to regain control of the Great Ejido. With the PRM facing a strong opposition candidate in the presidential election, Canto Echeverría raised the specter of opposition candidate General Juan Andreu Almazán to get the CDE out of the Great Ejido. The official camarilla and the governor charged that Arsenio Lara and the CDE were in fact supporting Almazán. Before and after the presidential elections of June 1940, they would blame the surprisingly strong showing by Almazán on the CDE. In fact, Canto Echeverría wrote to Cárdenas shortly after the vote that 95 percent of henequen ejidatarios voted for Almazán against Cárdenas's candidate, General Manuel Avila Camacho. If true, the charge would have given the opposition candidate at least half the votes in the state. In spite of the drumbeat of charges by the governor's clique that Arsenio Lara and his supporters (including General Juan B. Izaguirre Payan, briefly federal military commander in the state) were Almazanistas, there exists little evidence to substantiate these attacks.

Although there might well have been some preliminary negotiations between the CDE and Almazanistas in Mexico City, Arsenio Lara publicly endorsed Cárdenas's man, Avila Camacho, in Tixkokob in April 1940.[59] Nevertheless, the governor took full advantage of the doubts surrounding Lara's loyalties. The fact that Canto Echeverría had two years of experience in dealing with the national capital and his own staff of lobbyists in Mexico City while Lara had no national political experience proved to be a decisive advantage for the governor.

To press his advantage in Mexico City, Canto Echeverría convinced national Cardenistas to make him head of the Avila Camacho campaign in Yucatán.[60] The PRM would need a lot of help from regional power brokers like Canto Echeverría to install its nominee. The candidacy of the little-known general (nicknamed "the unknown soldier" by his own supporters) had attracted such anemic support that the Yucatecan state government offered ejidatarios one peso each to attend rallies in his favor.[61] Special trains had to bring peasants from the southern corn-growing zone to Mérida demonstrations in favor of Avila Camacho because of so much resentment toward the national government in the henequen zone. In one case, these imported peasants were directed to sack the CDE offices in Mérida. This gave Avila Camacho the mistaken impression that the henequen ejidatarios rejected the CDE and genuinely supported his candidacy.[62]

More than once, Canto Echeverría used Cárdenas's fear of Almazanismo in Yucatán as a pretext to attack the CDE. During the presidential campaign, supporters of the governor killed Cecilio Cab, CDE organizer and member of the regional ejidal council in Mérida, and thugs intimidated ejidatarios into renouncing their support for the CDE, all in the name of subduing Almazán. In late April 1940, PSS delegates began visiting ejidos around the state to pressure peasant leaders to publicly denounce the CDE. The governor's intermediaries recruited ex-hacienda foremen to campaign against partisans of the Tixkokob group. Congressman and official enforcer Félix Vallejos demanded the resignations of municipal officials not backing the governor and threatened town councils that supported Diego Rosado and the CDE.[63]

The main thrust of the official camarilla's counteroffensive was aimed squarely at the CDE home base of Tixkokob. Taking advantage of Arsenio Lara's absence on a trip to Mexico City, the state congress legally dissolved the municipal government of Tixkokob and, on the night of 7 May 1940, ordered the state police to occupy its town hall and church and the Great Ejido's medical center. Leaders of the CDE fled to the offices of the federal military for protection. When Arsenio Lara returned from Mexico City, the governor's goons allegedly kidnapped him, drove him out of town, and released him with orders not to come back for two weeks. Enemies of Arsenio Lara questioned his account of the kidnapping, suggesting that, just as Lara allegedly faked his own death in the past to avoid liquor taxes, he staged an "autokidnaping" as an elaborate hoax to gain Cárdenas's sympathy and embarrass Canto Echeverría.[64]

With Lara temporarily neutralized, Canto Echeverría worked to seize control of the Great Ejido and divide the CDE. He exercised the privilege that Cárdenas had given him to replace the elected pro-CDE director of the Great Ejido, Ramiro Ancona. He rehired former supervisors with orders to rout the CDE. In this dangerous atmosphere, several of the pro-CDE peasants elected as directors of the Great Ejido resigned in fear of their lives.[65]

While Canto Echeverría took advantage of the national political situation to strike at the CDE, his bold plan had been executed without specific permission from Cárdenas; moreover, these actions violated the agreements brokered by Beteta and Cárdenas in late 1939. Consequently, the Tixkokob group took advantage of Canto Echeverría's error to strike back at the official camarilla.

The Second Fall and Rise of Canto Echeverría

Governor Canto Echeverría overplayed his hand by clumsily bludgeoning the CDE, invading Tixkokob, and (apparently) abducting Arsenio Lara without Cárdenas's approval, leaving himself open to a counterattack. The Tixkokob group knew, however, that removing the governor would require the acquiescence of the federal commander in the state, and General Benignos had proved himself steadfastly loyal to the governor. Benignos himself was vulnerable to being removed because he had committed an unpardonable political sin against Cárdenas: He had used his influence to convince the Great Ejido's administration to grant its lucrative insurance contract to Roberto Sarlat, who was Almazán's campaign manager in the state. The CDE's national allies convinced Avila Camacho to pressure Cárdenas into removing Benignos in reprisal. The new military commander of Yucatán, General Juan B. Izaguirre Payan, proved to be much less sympathetic to the governor, and the Tixkokob group could now move against Canto Echeverría.[66]

The CDE then shifted its focus to the national capital, where Senator Laureano Cardos Ruz (who had replaced Gualberto Carrillo Puerto when he became Cárdenas's representative to the Great Ejido) moved to wrest the governorship from Canto Echeverría. On 13 May, only two days after the change of federal military commanders, Cardos Ruz announced that Manuel Avila Camacho had appointed him his representative to Yucatán, replacing Canto Echeverría.[67] Over the next two weeks, the leaders of the CDE and the pro-CDE CNC (the official national peasant confederation) published manifestos in the Yucatecan press calling for the resignation of Canto Echeverría because of his attacks on peasant leaders and elected local officials as well as his failure to implement economic democracy in the Great Ejido.[68]

The strategy of appealing for presidential intervention in the name of Cardenismo was also used by FSI president and state congressman Diego Rosado, who criticized the governor's reliance on the notorious Cheka. Canto Echeverría's growing unpopularity, he warned, might plunge the state into an "ungovernable" situation.[69] Rosado reminded the president of the political danger for Cárdenas should Canto Echeverría remain — political chaos on the eve of the presidential succession that threatened the henequen ejidos — and of the fact that the governor was opposed by Cardenista groups with strong popular support: the CDE, with ejidatarios organized across the henequen zone; Left-Cardenismo, with strong peasant, youth, and women's group support; as well as urban unions. But, given the president's imperative to keep the support of governors for the upcoming presidential election, Cárdenas was inclined to give Canto Echeverría a chance to ride out the storm despite the barrage of complaints. The Tixkokob group still needed to prompt the national government to take action, and in May and June, Arsenio Lara and the CDE, backed by Military Zone commander Izaguirre, began assuming functions of the state government to force Cárdenas's hand. The CDE appointed municipal councils to places like Maxcanú that had been overthrown by the governor and organized efforts to counter a locust plague on its own. With the help of federal troops, the CDE regained its control of the administration of the Great Ejido, and, on 19 June, the Great Ejido announced that it would withhold 50 percent of the taxes that it paid to the state.[70]

Deprived of his main source of revenue, facing attacks on all fronts, deserted by some of his own camarilla, lacking support from presidential candidate Avila Camacho (who would take office in five months), and unable to contact President Cárdenas, Canto Echeverría submitted an indefinite leave of absence to the state congress. It was accepted, and, in deference to the shifting political winds in Mexico City, the congress named

Senator Laureano Cardos Ruz, who appeared to be future president Avila Camacho's choice, as interim governor.[71]

The day before Canto Echeverría took leave of office, the presidential election took place. The balloting was marred by widespread fraud, which masked both a strong opposition showing by Almazán's Partido Revolucionario de Unificación (PRUN), and massive abstention by members of progovernment labor, peasant, and popular organizations. As was usually the case, these circumstances prevent an accurate reconstruction of the vote. However, the size of the fraud that gave Avila Camacho the triumph in Yucatán indicated how serious a threat Almazán presented to the PRM candidate. The final vote count gave Almazán only a fraction of an impossibly high number of 100,000 votes cast. Large numbers of PRUN votes were thrown out, and PRUN partisans were turned away in Valladolid, Motul, Temax, Maxcanú, and several polling places around Mérida. Typical electoral tactics of the official camarilla nullified widespread Almazanista support: caciques intervened, state employees and elected officials ran the polling places, and federal monitors turned a deaf ear to protests.[72]

The surprising strength of Almazanismo in Yucatán confirms the conclusions of recent studies of Cardenismo in other regions of Mexico that reveal widespread popular dissatisfaction with Cardenismo often fueled Almazán's candidacy. In Hidalgo, many agraristas, frustrated with Cárdenas's support for a conservative, antiagrarian reform camarilla, turned to Almazán.[73] In Puebla, peasants seeking individual parcels and relief from oppressive agrarian reform officials also embraced Almazán in record numbers.[74] True, in Yucatán, Almazanista support was strong among the middle class and hacendados—landowners in Tecoh threatened ejidatarios that, when Almazán won, he would return the ejidos to them.[75] But not only did Almazán garner the support of frustrated office seekers and the regional bourgeoisie; peasants also supported him, although apparently more as a reaction against the economic problems that they blamed on Cárdenas and his government than from any affinity for Almazán's program. One confidential envoy of the governor visited the henequen town of Sinanché and found a large majority of workers and peasants backing Almazán, along with the mayor, the schoolteacher, and the heads of the ejido and the Socialist league.[76] The failure of Cardenista agrarian reform resulted in a massive rejection of Avila Camacho across the henequen zone.

Of course, Cárdenas could have stolen Almazán's thunder by naming a more popular successor. General Francisco Mújica, Avila Camacho's main rival for the PRM's nomination, had a strong following among both Yucatecan Left-Cardenistas and the SFP. Avila Camacho, on the other hand, had no reliable clients in the state and found himself drawn into divisive camarilla struggles and scapegoated for the problems of agrarian reform.

If Avila Camacho was hurt by this wave of popular resentment against Canto Echeverría, new interim governor Laureano Cardos Ruz benefited from it. He was given a warm greeting on 14 July 1940 at a huge rally organized by virtually every major labor, peasant, female, and youth organization in Yucatán. These same groups pledged to unify the working classes "in a spirit of conciliation" under the new governor. However, in the aftermath of his swearing in, revenge, not harmony, was the order of the day. Those who were on the "outs" during the Canto Echeverría administration got back "in" at the expense of the official camarilla, returning to the leadership of the SFP, the FROC labor federation, the teachers' union, and — most importantly — the Great Ejido.[77]

From its start, however, the brief Cardos Ruz administration was marked by ugly fights among his own supporters over spoils, a situation that his enemies quickly exploited. When the interim governor refused the demands of CDE potentates Ramiro Ancona and Arsenio Lara to appoint Antonio Gual García as secretary of government, they cut off the flow of henequen tax revenue to the state government to punish him.[78]

The clique of veteran politicians and bureaucrats who had run the official camarilla for years was suspicious of the new governor. While publicly supporting Cardos Ruz, these men privately used bureaucratic stalling tactics to weaken his administration. Gonzalo López Manzanero, head of one of the official trucking cooperatives, president of the PSS, and a key state congressman, set the course for the stealth opposition. He symbolically removed Canto Echeverría's portrait from PSS headquarters but postponed the scheduled election of a new party directorate, thus blocking the new governor from appointing loyalists to head the party. Supporters of Canto Echeverría in the state congress blocked action against anti-CDE mayors, which prevented the new governor from turning over town halls to his supporters.[79]

 Because the rear guard of the official camarilla managed to prevent Cardos Ruz from consolidating his hold over regional power, questions of control over local political power and ejidos continued to be resolved violently. In Akil and Tekax, the police had to restore order when supporters of the CDE, bolstered by pro–Cardos Ruz cacique Pedro Romero Solís, clashed with supporters of the mayor, who stayed loyal to Canto Echeverría. Similarly, in Tzucacab, another town south of the henequen zone, pro-CDE *chicleros* (seasonal workers who collected sap for chewing gum) challenged the pro–Canto Echeverría municipal council and the ejidal commissary.[80]

The interim governor's support in the henequen zone was undercut by the same factors that dogged Canto Echeverría and his official camarilla. Simply put, cuts in advances for ejidatarios were attributed to the governor, although the global price of henequen or the national government was often responsible. This dynamic had favored opponents of Canto Echeverría in the past, but with his departure, the new governor now took the blame.[81]

The most dangerous contingency that Cardos Ruz faced, however, remained the ambiguous position of President Cárdenas toward the change of governors in Yucatán. The president allowed his heir, Avila Camacho, to remove Canto Echeverría but had yet to recognize the change. These mixed messages gave Canto Echeverría a possible means of returning to power. After intense lobbying in Mexico City, the former governor began reasserting his claim to the governorship. He briefly returned to Yucatán on 2 August, and his supporters staged a public demonstration to convince Cárdenas of the popular support for him. The once and future governor finally got an audience with Cárdenas in Queretaro on 5 August and persuaded him to back his return to the governorship. Canto Echeverría attributed Cárdenas's support to the president's respect for state's rights, a newfound conviction for a president who had removed most of the governors he had inherited from previous presidents.[82] It seems much more likely that Cardos Ruz and General Izaguirre had failed to consult with Cárdenas before asking for Avila Camacho's support — a violation of political etiquette as well as an insult to Cárdenas's authority.[83]

Cárdenas's decision to return Canto Echeverría to power had important ramifications for the attitude of peasants and workers toward Cardenismo. Both the Left and the CDE spoke for most Yucatecans when they asked Cárdenas not to reinstall the unpopular Canto Echeverría to office — appeals that Cárdenas ignored in favor of maintaining his own authority during the last months of his presidency.[84] To counter support for Cardos Ruz, Canto Echeverría tried to whip up popular backing of his own; a female teacher supporting Canto Echeverría got illiterate peasants to sign a petition demanding his return by telling them that they were signing a request to bring a teacher to their village.[85]

On his return to the governorship in late August, Canto Echeverría took advantage of a new, sympathetic federal military commander to purge pro-CDE leaders from unions, ejidos, and municipal governments across the state. Apparently, his promise to govern "without either hatreds or reprisals" did not extend to political foes.[86]

But, after taking revenge, Canto Echeverría needed to create a degree of stability in Yucatán, and that required ending the continuing turmoil in the Great Ejido by wresting it, once and for all, from the hands of the CDE. The governor craftily used the same tactics that the CDE had once used against him. In early October 1940, official groups staged demonstrations and wildcat work stoppages protesting corruption and nepotism in the Great Ejido's CDE bureaucracy and its recent cut in advances. With the support of Cárdenas. Canto Echeverría took advantage of the absence of the CDE's Great Ejido director Ramiro Ancona in Mexico City to name a new interim director. Finally, on 19 November, Canto Echeverría published decree 303 against "leaderism" in the Great Ejido, stripping its directive council — held by pro-CDE elected representatives since December 1939 — of control over the henequen ejidos.[87]

Cardenismo without Cárdenas

While Canto Echeverría was retaking the governor's chair and regaining control of the Great Ejido, the war between the official camarilla and the CDE-Left-labor coalition continued over the election of town councils and the state congress scheduled for mid-October 1940. Uniting under the leadership of Arsenio Lara, on 26 September 1940 the CDE, Left-Cardenismo, the antigovernor factions of the SFP, the PSS, and the FROC, and various labor groups (from barbers to government employees) formed the Independent Democratic Front (Frente Democrático Independiente, or FDI). Since the FDI embraced almost every ideological current and socioeconomic group in Yucatán, its program could be defined by only two principles: opposition to Canto Echeverría and the claim to represent "true" Cardenismo in Yucatán. Because of the presence of many Communists at a time when the national atmosphere was fast becoming virulently anti-Communist, the FDI was careful to proclaim its support for democracy and freedom of political and even religious thought.[88]

Although Canto Echeverría had regained Cárdenas's backing, many of the president's inner circle still nursed old grievances against the headstrong governor and were willing to try to bolster the FDI in the fall elections. Gabino Vázquez, head of the federal Agrarian Department and long a supporter of the CDE, ordered federal agrarian engineers in the state to campaign for the FDI and vigorously lobbied Cárdenas to support the FDI's candidate for mayor of Mérida, Mario Negrón Pérez. By this time, Canto Echeverría was so strong that he politely defied the president's wishes that Negrón be elected mayor, writing to Cárdenas that he regrettably could not "force" Negrón Pérez's candidacy on Mérida without "dividing" the workers, 90 percent of whom he claimed backed the candidates already selected by the governor's official camarilla.[89] The governor's open defiance of the president indicates that the fabled Cardenista centralization of power had far to go, at least in Yucatán.

Canto Echeverría's group launched an all-out offensive against the opposition during the October 1940 election. Operating under the Open Door system, voting took place through conventions of unions, ejidos, and various "popular" organizations, which chose delegates to regional conventions where the actual nomination of the PRM candidates (and presumed winners) took place.[90] As in the 1937 gubernatorial election, the official camarilla controlled state and local PRM committees, bullied and bribed electoral monitors from Mexico City, and refused to count votes of opposition organizations (especially ejidal commissaries affiliated with the CDE) while creating phony groups staffed by state employees to inflate support for official candidates. Canto Echeverría increased turnout among employees of the Great Ejido by granting them a fat *aguinaldo,* or Christmas bonus, despite the cooperative's financial crisis.[91] Federal troops under General Aureo Calles and a confederation of local caciques backing Canto Echeverría used coercion to negate much of the FDI's potential support.[92] Fortunately for Canto Echeverría, Gualberto Carrillo Puerto ran his own slate of candidates separately from the FDI's, splitting the opposition.[93]

After a questionable vote, the governor's candidates triumphed over the FDI slate in a suspiciously overwhelming fashion, claiming the support of 84,959 members of some 629 unions and ejidos.[94] Having been swept in the local and district conventions, the FDI appealed to Mexico City. The national PRM overturned the election, registered the FDI slate as the PRM candidates, and appointed federal deputy Rafael Granja Lizarraga to head a provisional, pro-FDI PRM executive state council in Yucatán. Federal officials charged Granja with ensuring that the governor's supporters remained "disciplined" to the national PRM's decision and dutifully supported the FDI/PRM candidates in the general election in November.[95]

The response of Canto Echeverría once again proved that the national government's power in Yucatán was weak and waning. The governor openly warned national PRM president General Heriberto Jara that his decision violated "majority will" and was "causing useless and lamentable confusion and seriously harming the prestige of the PRM."[96]

The governor's words were not empty threats; he backed them up by flexing his political muscle on the streets of Mérida. Organizations linked to the official camarilla—mainly the PSS—struck on 24 October against the national PRM decision. The strike not only demonstrated Canto Echeverría's control over Yucatán but also allowed him to claim a Cardenista popular mandate to defy the national party. More directly, it warned Jara and the national government that spurning the governor would indeed lead to PSS activists and the Cheka roaming the streets in trucks and cars adorned with black-and-red banners, attacking store owners who did not honor the strike, and forcibly preventing peasant women from coming to Mérida to market vegetables.[97] Only a few years previous, the Cardenista national state had used popular mobilizations to topple conservative regional interests. Now, Canto Echeverría used Cardenista tactics to flaunt the will of the national Cardenista state.

In an even more blatant act of political mutiny, Canto Echeverría announced that the (official) worker and peasant organizations of Yucatán would temporarily withdraw from the PRM and form a Revolutionary Confederation of Yucatán (Confederación Revolucionaria de Yucatán, or CRY) to challenge the FDI candidates who now enjoyed their status as the PRM's candidates in the November general elections.[98] In another example of chutzpah, the governor invoked a proposal supposedly made by the national CTM, the CNC, the FROC, and petroleum workers to form a Popular Front directly under Cárdenas's leadership on the incredible grounds that the national PRM had been infiltrated by Almazanistas.[99] But behind the bravado was keen political instinct: the national PRM directorate headed by General Jara resigned on 24 November, and the rumored dissolution of the national party served to distract attention from the regionalist insurgency in Yucatán against the national party.[100]

While the official camarilla exploited confusion in Mexico City to defy the national government, it reached back into the past of Yucatán to legitimize its actions and try to build up support against the strong popular base that the CDE, urban labor, and the Yucatecan Left had mobilized behind the FDI. The CRY's propaganda revived the red triangle symbol of the PSS and referred to it by its old name of Partido Socialista del Sureste rather than its unwieldy formal title of the Confederación Ligas Gremiales de Obreros y Campesinos (Confederation of Gremial Leagues of Workers and Peasants). The radical, regionalist rhetoric of the CRY called on Yucatecos to join it on the barricades defending "the Socialists of Yucatán and the people" against unnamed—but presumably non-Yucatecan—enemies. The messages of regionalism and states' rights were coded in Canto Echeverría's claim that the

CRY was defending state sovereignty against external tyranny with the slogan "The People of Yucatán: These are your candidates. Do not accept the imposition." The CRY claimed to be the spiritual heir of the PSS, as it styled Canto Echeverría as the successor of Felipe Carrillo Puerto, continuing the struggle against unspecified "rightist" enemies. This nostalgic invocation appealed to the hallowed tradition of the PSS and the legend of Felipe Carrillo Puerto to counter the weak appeal of the national PRM. But, even while trafficking in the old symbols and slogans of Socialism, Canto Echeverría assembled a collection of politicos hostile to the PSS, including Mamerto and César González of the SFP (the CRY called the latter a Cincinnatus) and Porfirio Pallares of the CGT.[101] Significantly, while the CRY's discourse stressed Yucatán's regional identity and the faded glory of the PSS, it avoided any open identification with Cardenismo.

As the second round of voting neared, the FDI complained to sympathetic members of the federal congress that the governor and the official camarilla planned to use repression and electoral fraud to defeat them in the general election, in which the FDI's slate would run as the official PRM candidates against the "independent" slate of pro–Canto Echeverría candidates. It seemed that the FDI might prevail when a delegation of federal deputies sent to Yucatán to supervise the election urged PRM members to support the slate of FDI candidates and condemned supporters of the governor as "reactionary and impositionist."[102] Despite the presence of the federal congressional commission and a visit by the new general secretary of the national PRM, Gustavo Cárdenas Huerta, all trying to prevent the governor from again flouting the rulings of the PRM, Canto Echeverría ordered local officials to refuse to register the FDI slate in all but ten municipalities. And, in another open and successful challenge to national authorities, the governor ordered local officials to ignore the national PRM's cancellation of the registration of his CRY candidates in six of the largest towns in Yucatán.[103]

As in previous confrontations with national authorities, Canto Echeverría backed obstinacy with violence. His Cheka invaded and occupied opposition campaign headquarters.[104] And, as in the first round of voting, government employees, caciques, and aguardiente all helped magnify the CRY's vote total and keep pro-FDI votes out of the urns. The state PRM had already been institutionally neutered by Canto Echeverría; it now lost control over the district conventions, which often disintegrated into riots between rival factions. Once again, the governor's candidates triumphed in all but a handful of Yucatán's ninety-five municipalities (including the hotly disputed Mérida election) and claimed victory in all nine seats in the state congress. The national PRM argued that the FDI candidates had triumphed despite widespread fraud and violence. As in the primary balloting in October, the exact numbers are hard to ascertain, although the support of the CDE alone would probably have carried the election for the FDI.[105]

In a repetition of the primary election, the FDI, the CNC, and the PRM appealed the vote in the federal congress. The federal congressmen sent to monitor the election themselves testified to the fraud and violence in the election.[106] The CNC's delegation of federal deputies, led by Cuáhtemoc Ríos Martínez continued to accuse Canto Echeverría of imposition and violence. But it was not the hollow institutions of Cardenista corporatism but the federal military commander in the state who represented Cárdenas in political matters, and General Aureo Calles vouched for the fairness of the vote and ratified his friend Canto Echeverría's victory. One of Mexico City's leading newspapers, *La Prensa,* headlined its 25 November edition with an accurate assessment of the main political arm of Cardenismo: "The PRM was totally defeated in Yucatán. With this blow, the decay of the Political Institute is palpable."[107]

On 4 December, the governor won his final battle against the FDI and its CDE-Left-labor base. On that day, new president Avila Camacho took away the right to resolve regional political disputes from the national PRM and gave it to the Interior Ministry, held by a man sympathetic to the governor.[108] To seal his triumph, Canto Echeverría's allies in Mexico City—federal congressmen José María Bolio Méndez and Antonio Mediz Bolio—arranged to have a new, pro–Canto Echeverría federal congressional delegation sent to resolve the disputed election. The delegation dutifully ruled that the governor's CRY had won all but two seats in the state congress, a questionable decision reportedly made in exchange for a sizable sum withdrawn from the Great Ejido's coffers.[109] Realizing the futility of fighting Canto Echeverría, the FDI withdrew its protests, receiving only two of nine seats in the state congress and a handful of town councils.[110]

Cardenismo Conceded

The Cardenista era in Yucatán ended with a whimper, not a bang. In the three years after the climactic Crusade of the Mayab, Cardenismo suffered a string of defeats. Cárdenas's acceptance of the Great Ejido Plan in March 1938 represented the most obvious retreat.

Although the Great Ejido Plan allowed Cárdenas and the national government to extricate themselves from weighty financial responsibilities, Cárdenas remained committed to giving the ejidatarios a modicum of economic security and more control over the ejidos through economic democracy. This commitment gave the governor's opponents a political space in regional affairs. In late 1939, the first of a series of agrarian protest movements emerged in the form of the CDE, headed by the Tixkokob camarilla. The CDE and its allies among urban labor, joined by Left-Cardenismo, mobilized a broad popular base to (temporarily) drive Canto Echeverría from office and seize control of the Great Ejido.

However, Cardenista economic democracy conflicted with yet another important goal of the president: securing the election of Avila Camacho and maintaining political control of Mexico during the remainder of his term. When forced to choose between supporting popular demands for Canto Echeverría's exile and keeping his own hold over national power, Cárdenas chose the latter. In the last act of the drama of the Great Ejido, Canto Echeverría overcame both widespread popular resistance and the opposition of many national Cardenistas to throw the 1940 elections to his own slate of candidates.

In Yucatán, the CDE and the FDI found themselves representing the ideals and base of Cardenismo against Cárdenas's own indifference; his refusal to oust Canto Echeverría doomed popular mobilizations led by the FDI to defeat. While the opposition leadership's own missteps helped seal their fate, and while conservative elements could be found in the CDE, Cárdenas clearly placed political stability and his own presidential prerogatives over economic democracy and the creation of a popular base for the postrevolutionary state.

The case of Yucatán, moreover, was not exceptional. In Campeche, where a Left-Cardenista movement even stronger than that in Yucatán had emerged under Mújica's aegis, Cárdenas refused to support that movement in the gubernatorial election of 1939, allowing a conservative regional machine to stay in power.[111] In some states, Cárdenas's support for conservative elements began even earlier. In Sonora, Cárdenas backed the conservative regional strongman Yocupicio against more radical alternatives for reasons of national political expediency.[112] In Puebla, Cárdenas had come to terms with the right-leaning Avila Camacho brothers in 1935 and tolerated their regional camarilla that only tepidly supported agrarian reform and squelched radical popular mobilizations.[113] In Zacatecas, Cárdenas refused to intervene against the governor, General J. Félix Bañuelos, a champion of landowners against agrarian reform, when he imposed unpopular

but loyal candidates and sustained local caciques over the vociferous protests of progressive elements, including the CTM, the CNC, and a strong,
independent miners' union in state congressional elections in July 1939 and
municipal elections in December 1939. From the middle of 1939 to the end
of his term, Cárdenas sacrificed not just Cardenista popular mobilizations,
but much of his own corporate political apparatus (the PRM, the CNC, the
CTM) to impose Avila Camacho.[114]

The tumultuous events of 1939–40 undermined and to some extent undid the legacy of Cárdenas in Yucatán. Agrarian reform ended with the
transfer of the henequen ejidos to a state government with limited economic and social resources and little concern for the peasants. Thousands
were still landless, and the new ejidatarios faced a stalled income and a bleak
future. Politically, the official camarilla fended off centralizing institutions
like the PRM, the CNC, and the CTM by supporting regional organizations
against them. Seen from the point of view of the provinces, regional elites
tended to co-opt national institutions, rather than the reverse. The cost of
imposing Avila Camacho instead of selecting a candidate with strong support from Cardenista organizations like Francisco Mújica is apparent when
regional politics is examined. Still, it would be hasty to judge Cardenismo
in Yucatán on the basis of only the events of 1939–40, and it is to the long-
term effect of Cardenismo in Yucatán that I will now turn.

7

Cárdenas Compromised: Cardenismo's
Legacy in Yucatán

THIS STUDY BEGAN by asking four questions about Cardenismo in Yucatán: Who were the Cardenistas in Yucatán, and who opposed them? To what extent did Cárdenas succeed in mobilizing popular support and building an enduring worker-peasant base for the postrevolutionary regime? How much success did Cárdenas have in centralizing power in Mexico City? And what did Cardenismo change?

The first question is the easiest to answer. There was no single, homogeneous Cardenista bloc in Yucatán.[1] Rather, there were four major groups that could at various times claim to represent Cardenismo in the state: agrarian Cardenismo (1935–38), Left-Cardenismo (1935–40), Gualbertismo (1933–37), and the CDE–Left–independent labor alliance (1939–40). At various times, each mobilized significant popular support in the countryside in the name of Cárdenas, and each to some extent challenged the hold of camarillas and caciques over power. Agrarian and Left-Cardenismo challenged the old hacendado class, which continued indirectly to influence state and local government and Yucatecan society in general.

The question of who opposed Cardenismo is a much more complicated one. Certainly, the threat of agrarian reform unified almost all the old Yucatecan oligarchy against Cárdenas, and its ability to corrupt federal intermediaries and regional politicos weakened Cardenismo in Yucatán. For the most part, Yucatecan governors waged a covert war against Cardenismo, with the notable exception of López Cárdenas. The role of Gualbertismo and independent labor is more ambiguous. National Cardenistas often backed both, in order to undermine governors' camarillas and thus increase federal influence in Yucatán, yet the links of Gualbertismo and independent labor to hacendados probably prevented a broader pro-Cárdenas popular movement from forming.

The second question—the extent to which Cardenismo, or the various Cardenismos, succeeded in mobilizing popular support and uniting a worker-peasant alliance — is more difficult to answer. Certainly, strong popular mobilizations existed, but the fact that they were divided by the contradictions within Yucatecan Cardenismo — especially the Left's rivalry with the Agrarian Bank and Gualbertismo — lessened their effect. The elusive worker-peasant alliance came together three times: in the October 1935 and the July 1936 general strikes that toppled Governors Alayola and López Cárdenas, and in the 1939–40 CDE–Left–independent labor movement. In the first two cases, the intervention of camarilla politics and the hacendados impeded these movements from evolving into a popular base for Cárdenas. In the last case, the national political and economic situation prevented Cárdenas from supporting the grassroots movement that opposed Governor Canto Echeverría.

The focus of much of the literature on (male) urban worker–rural peasant alliances, however, may itself be misplaced. Left-Cardenismo, which had the strongest grassroots base in Yucatán, brought together young people, women, and rural workers (peons). This popular leftist coalition not only supported agrarian reform (although not always the agrarian bureaucracy) and the right of workers to organize, but also challenged the patriarchal, conservative rural culture of Yucatán. The inability of national Cardenismo to incorporate this leftist base in Yucatán was a significant failure for Cárdenas.

As to the success or failure of Cárdenas in centralizing power in Mexico City, the case of Yucatán presents a clear and not unique case of the Cardenista national state's inability to subordinate regional interests.[2] The start of the Cardenista era began with a strong offensive by the national state in Yucatán. The overthrow of two governors and the growing strength of independent urban labor, peasant, and peon organizations suggested that Cardenismo would soon triumph in Yucatán. However, the problems of agrarian reform and the breakdown of alliances linking national Cardenistas to Left-Cardenismo and independent labor gave the regional politicos and the Yucatecan hacendados a respite. Under Palomo Valencia's interim administration and the succeeding Canto Echeverría regime, the federal government's influence shrank dramatically, most notably in the gubernatorial election of 1937 and the acceptance of the Great Ejido Plan. By 1940, the national government had no more influence over Yucatán than it did in 1934.

Finally, the question as to what Cardenismo did or did not change in Yucatán is the most difficult to answer. Clearly, Yucatán in 1940 was still far from the revolutionary new society that Cárdenas envisioned in 1934 and tried to create from above in the Crusade of the Mayab in 1937. The economic predicament of agrarian reform and the persistence of boss politics and traditional practices that sustained it (drinking, violence) siphoned off popular support for Cardenismo.

However, revisionist interpretations of Cardenismo that argue that Cárdenas's grandiose project changed very little or served principally to strengthen the postrevolutionary state miss important changes. The popular mobilizations of the Cardenista era, the strikes and demonstrations, the adult literacy classes and political rallies, altered Yucatán's polity and society in often subtle but meaningful ways. Caciques and camarillas still existed, but they had to make more popular concessions and could rely less on intimidation and a norm of deference among subaltern groups. True, peasants in the post-Cárdenas henequen zone were dependent on an agrarian bureaucracy instead of landowners, a kind of *neopeonage,* as Othón Baños terms it.[3] But they were part of a more open society with more means of political redress and more economic and social options. Moreover, from the general strike of 1935 to the CDE-FDI mobilizations in 1940, politicians and the old upper class had been forced to accept these two Cardenista principles: that they must admit some degree of popular participation (if not democracy) and that officials had to maintain a degree of popular support (although not always at the ballot box).

Cardenismo did largely fail to reform Yucatán, but the questions remain of why and how the president's project fell short.

Cardenismo Compromised

The Cardenista project for Yucatán tried to implement a very ambitious project of sweeping transformation. Most importantly, it aimed to replace the henequen plantations with self-sustaining peasant collectives while allowing the survival of privately owned small properties. National Cardenistas also hoped to displace regional camarillas and petty rural bosses in favor of a corporate political structure integrating workers, peasants and peons, and women and young people into the ruling party state. Finally, Cardenista planners wanted to replace traditional, patriarchal rural culture — above all men's recreational drinking and religious festivals — with a new constellation of social institutions (such as the school), symbols (i.e., the Mexican flag), and practices (including sports). On all these counts, Cardenista reform largely failed in Yucatán.

As we have seen, agrarian reform encountered a series of serious delays and by mid-1936 was a near disaster. The predicament of Guatemalan President Jacobo Arbenz in the early 1950s as described by Jim Handy resembles Cárdenas's situation in Yucatán: both ran up against a "complex interlacing of jealousies and feuds" in the countryside that superseded the ethnic- and class-based mobilization that their reforms hoped to achieve.[4] Microhistorical analyses of communities like Muxupip suggest the variety of difficulties that Cardenismo faced in forging horizontal linkages to overcome factionalism, caciques and landowners, and peasant-peon antipathy.

The problems of agrarian reform dragged down the rest of the Cardenista project in Yucatán. In the Crusade of the Mayab in 1937, political and social reform were largely abandoned to try to save land reform in a kind of strategic triage, as Cárdenas desperately tried to focus scarce resources on the henequen ejidos. It should not be forgotten that, by this point, death had removed the two most effective Cardenista leaders in Yucatán, General Rafael Cházaro Pérez (January 1936) and Rogerio Chalé (September 1936). Although neither death resulted from conspiracies by enemies of Cárdenas, these men were probably the only two loyal Cardenistas capable of governing the state, and their absence seriously limited Cárdenas's options. By early 1938, facing other economic commitments (above all oil nationalization) and the need to create an elite political consensus for his successor, Cárdenas abandoned agrarian reform in Yucatán entirely, returning all authority over the henequen ejidos to the state government in the Great Ejido Plan.

The complex history of Cardenismo in Yucatán suggests that there is no one cause as to why the Cardenista project failed, nor was there any preordained, structural reason that it had to fail. Although the high transition cost of collectivizing henequen proved daunting, in the end Cárdenas prioritized other national goals ahead of it. Cardenismo was a historical process that evolved over time, and its trajectory was shaped both by choice as well as structural conditions. In 1935 and 1936, when Cardenismo's focus was squarely on agrarian reform, it is clear that lack of federal resources, the contradictions within the Cardenista coalition in Yucatán, and the success of the regional oligarchy in exploiting both these factors frustrated the Cardenista project. The rise of Left-Cardenismo and independent labor, however, offered a new potential popular base for Cardenismo. But first independent labor and then the Left became enmeshed in camarilla politics and alienated from national Cardenismo. By the time Cárdenas returned to Yucatán in 1937, little Cardenismo from below still existed.

As late as 1937, the possibility of successful reform still existed, a pos-

sibility that Cárdenas grasped and moved to take advantage of. Rapid fulfill-
ment of stalled agrarian reform backed with large federal outlays and the
election (or outright imposition) of a popular, Cardenista governor would
probably have saved Cardenismo in Yucatán. Sustained, patient efforts by
Cárdenas and the national state during the last three years of his term could
have overcome many of the economic and political obstacles to agrarian reform and dislodged resistant regional politicos and recalcitrant hacendados
from power in Yucatán. Yucatán could have become a political and economic success for Cárdenas, similar to that in the northern Laguna region.

In the end, the failure of the Cardenista project in Yucatán was due more
to a tragic chain of events than stubborn structural barriers. First, the tim-
ing of the Crusade of the Mayab *after* most popular mobilizations had been
co-opted or suppressed greatly complicated Cardenista reform. The lack of
a unified popular base or reliable and strong intermediaries like Chalé and
Cházaro Pérez forced Cárdenas to rely on questionable allies such as Gualberto Carrillo Puerto and Governors Palomo Valencia and Canto Echeverría, which undercut what remained of popular Cardenismo in the state.
Most damagingly, when mounting costs and diminished resources forced
Cárdenas to husband scarce resources, he chose agrarian reform over political reform and peasants ahead of urban labor. By shelving plans for a truly
inclusive political system, and by failing effectively to support urban unions
against the regional political machine, agrarian reform continued for the
moment but was ultimately doomed.

Ironically, reform in Yucatán was also harmed by reform in the rest of
Mexico. By the time the Crusade of the Mayab was finally launched in late
1937, Cárdenas's national administration had run up a dangerously high
deficit in funding the cotton ejidos of La Laguna and expensive infrastructure improvements.[5] The oil expropriation of March 1938 added a new
financial burden to the Cárdenas administration, one that probably sank
once and for all the federal solution to Yucatán's "agrarian problem." Consider the fact that, of the 205 million pesos that the Agrarian Bank lent to
ejidos across Mexico from 1936 to 1938 and in 1940, 99 million went to the
Laguna and only 17 million to Yucatán (the second most important commitment for most of this period), with very little reaching the peninsula
after 1938.[6]

Had Cárdenas lavished as much funding on Yucatán as he had on the La
Laguna, and had he continued supporting the ejidos throughout his presidency, the outcome in the henequen zone would have been quite different.
With enough rasping machinery, and with federal support for seven years
until newly planted fields came into cultivation, the ejidos created by the

crusade in the fall of 1937 would have come into production in time to catch the boom in henequen prices triggered by World War II. These same fields would still have been flourishing when the Korean War stimulated another bonanza. Instead, state authorities systematically looted the Great Ejido during these boom years, and few benefits of the recovery of the henequen sector reached the ejidatarios.[7] Cardenismo in Yucatán was in the end compromised by a series of decisions and political conflicts that prematurely closed the revolutionary laboratory in Yucatán.

The experience of Yucatán in the Cardenista era forces us to rethink accepted views of Cardenismo held by both neopopulists and revisionists. In the first place, the failure of Cardenismo in Yucatán was not the result of heroic popular resistance to a Leviathan-like central state, as some would have it. Nor should we trace it to a violent conspiracy or white terror, funded and planned by recalcitrant hacendados.[8] Cárdenas was compromised not so much by popular or elite resistance—although both played a role in the failure of reform—as by faulty decisions and by other demands (La Laguna, oil, infrastructure) that overrode Cárdenas's commitment to Yucatán.

Second, the conventional view that Cardenista land reform politically stabilized and centralized power in Mexico by ending social tensions in the countryside and forging a social compact between the postrevolutionary state and the peasants can no longer be accepted, at least in the case of Yucatán. Most scholars of Yucatecan history conclude that agrarian reform demobilized peasant and peon protests that toppled governors and paralyzed the state in the mid-1930s.[9] Yet, as we have seen, mobilizations continued after the culmination of agrarian reform in the fall of 1937. The struggle between supporters of Governor Canto Echeverría and the CDE from late 1939 until the end of Cárdenas's term—almost two years *after* the completion of land reform—involved as many popular mobilizations and as much violence as those in the first three years of Cardenismo. As historians begin to venture into archival sources for the 1940s in other regions, it will be interesting to see to what extent they find the Mexican countryside calmed by land reform.

On a related point, agrarian reform is assumed to have been a way of strengthening the federal government. Once again, the experience of Yucatán suggests that the conventional wisdom must be rethought. Generally, Cardenismo is believed to have created enduring corporatist institutions that integrated peasants/ejidatarios and workers into the modern state. Yet we have seen how a parade of Yucatecan governors and the official cliques that they headed frustrated attempts to create strong peasant and worker groups affiliated with the national state. The situation in Yucatán in the late 1930s is strikingly similar to that of Sonora as described by Adrian Bantjes, where Governor Yocupicio defied the national government repeatedly.[10]

Third, Cárdenas's agrarian reforms in Yucatán are widely believed to have modernized the economy by destroying the supposedly feudal, antimodern mentality of the old landowning class and thus freeing up capital and social niches for new actors with more modern characteristics. This idea, which has currency, not just in Yucatán, but in Mexico as well, claims that Cárdenas destroyed the old Porfirian landowning oligarchy and thus created conditions necessary for industrialization and a more modern society. In the case of Yucatán, it has been most forcibly argued by Jose Luis Sierra Villarreal and José Antonio Paoli Bolio, who see Cárdenas's reforms as directed squarely against "the most backward sector of the bourgeoisie." In their account, these reforms forced the old hacendados to seek new, more productive investments.[11]

This is exactly what Cárdenas hoped would happen, and in fact some of the upper-class families did preserve their fortunes by taking them out of agriculture and putting them into industry and commerce.[12] But two factors render the Cardenista modernization theory null in Yucatán. First, the Cardenista reforms produced some unexpected results that set economic modernization back in Yucatán. Second, not all socioeconomic changes can be attributed to Cardenismo. The supposedly feudal, backward-looking hacendado class in Yucatán had for years *before* 1934 been diversifying into industry and banking. Since the 1920s — long before Cardenista agrarian reform — the landowners had been displaced from their positions of leadership atop the regional bourgeoisie by bankers, although more than a few bankers were landowners (and vice versa).[13] Certainly, the Great Depression had already done an effective job of weeding out the least economically run hacendados long before the Crusade of the Mayab, which was not aimed at poorly run haciendas. Much of what industry there was in Yucatán depended on the protected market of the peninsula, shielded from competition by the high costs of shipping through Progreso; and, once the railroad connecting Yucatán with the rest of Mexico that was begun under Cárdenas was completed in 1951, Yucatecan industry was swamped by "foreign" competition from the rest of the country. When henequen finally died in Yucatán, it was plastics, not Cárdenas's reforms, that killed it, and federal subsidies had already prolonged its life artificially.[14] For the most part, tourism and other agricultural products, not industry, replaced henequen. And, as the acerbic rightist journalist Roque Armando Sosa Ferreyro noted, the Revolution spawned a generation of *new* landowners — ex-governors, high functionaries, and lesser politicos.[15]

All in all, reports of the death of the old Yucatecan "Casta Divina" of great landowners were greatly exaggerated. Historically, the Crusade of the Mayab had much less effect on the henequen industry than both critics and supporters of Cárdenas believe. The federal reform undertaken in 1935 and finished in late 1937 by the crusade took away some 500,000 hectares of land, mainly from the great landowning families, and much of it from the henequen zone. Some hacendados escaped with more than 150 hectares; a few hacendados escaped the reform entirely. But, most importantly, Cárdenas left the most valuable part of the estate — the defibrating machinery — untouched. Those hacendados who did hold on to their land and machinery instead of diversifying would be richly rewarded in the 1940s and early 1950s when the price of henequen rebounded. Under the state-directed Great Ejido that administered the henequen ejidos from 1938 to 1956, many hacendados enjoyed an economic renaissance. Others threw their lot in with the CDE movement, where they maintained some influence over regional politics. World War II boosted sisal prices, and, in 1942, the Great Ejido returned over two hundred defibrating machines to their old owners and agreed to give them 52 percent of the value of the ejidos' product that would be processed there.[16] Many hacendados did even better. Even though the Manzanilla's San Francisco had been reduced to 212 hectares of land by the crusade, until 1967 it got 60 percent of the price paid for ejidatarios' henequen that it rasped.[17]

The survival and partial recovery of many hacendado clans is evident in Yucatán today. The heirs of the Manzanilla, Molina, and Peón hacendados can be found in prominent positions in business, the liberal professions, even politics. This is not to say that regional society did not change over time. The great-grandchildren of the Porfirian elite have to share power and prestige in contemporary Yucatán with the grandchildren of the Socialists, the Cardenistas, and even a few Communists as well as the offspring of successful Lebanese immigrants. And the collapse of many old oligarchic families cannot be attributed primarily to Cárdenas.[18]

Finally, Yucatán presents an important exception to the widespread belief that, in regions where the Cardenista state tried to transform society, it created a legacy of Cardenista sentiment that is leftist, populist, and nationalist. Land reform, oil nationalization, and support for strikes all helped create an enduring leftist tradition that Lázaro Cárdenas's son Cuáhtemoc (the former mayor of Mexico City and presidential candidate in the year

2000) has revived in the Left-center Party of the Democratic Revolution (Partido de la Revolución Demócrata, or PRD). In the other four regions where Cardenista agrarian reform took place on a large scale, a strong leftist and Cardenista tradition is reflected in the popularity of the current PRD. Likewise, in other poor southern states with a large indigenous presence, the neo-Cardenismo of the PRD has found a stronghold—Yucatán again excepted.[19] Other Gulf Coast states such as Yucatán with a radical, revolutionary tradition stretching back to the nineteenth century, like Veracruz, Tabasco, and Tamaulipas, have been hotbeds of the PRD—but again Yucatán is exceptional.[20] The failure of the Cardenista reform to create an enduring leftist-nationalist-populist tradition meant that the Left that once thrived in Yucatán withered. The PSS, founded by radical governor Alvarado (1915–18) and nurtured by Felipe Carrillo Puerto (1922–24), weakened, eventually being absorbed into the PRM-PRI and the CTM in the second half of the twentieth century. The PCM, present in Yucatán since the early 1920s, flourished in the 1930s, sprouting youth, women's, and peasant branches, also largely vanished by the 1940s.[21]

Even if the failure of Cardenista reform has prevented the growth of neo-Cardenismo in Yucatán, it would be wrong to say that Cardenismo left no political legacy in Yucatán. Fundamentally, the great contribution of Cardenismo in Yucatán was to create forms of popular protest and means for peasants and workers to pressure the state to make concessions. The CDE continued to protest the state government's management of the Great Ejido throughout the 1940s. Later, after the collapse of henequen prices following the end of the Korean War, new mobilizations of ejidatarios protested their poor economic status and unresponsive and corrupt bureaucrats. Like their forerunners in the 1930s, these protests made claims (the right of ejidatarios to a decent standard of living and the freedom to run their own ejidos) on the state based largely on Cardenismo: Cardenista economic democracy. The same language of ejidal "autonomy," the same condemnations of corrupt and uncaring state agents, reappeared in the 1960s, 1970s, and 1980s. The Association of Autonomous Henequeneros took the name General Lázaro Cárdenas in 1979 to demand justice for their "independent" ejidos.[22] Most famously, a protest movement by students, workers, and ejidatarios in the early 1970s took the title Frente Sindical Independiente in memory of the Left-Cardenista labor federation.[23] Even the practices of peasant protests—the marches through Mérida after arriving in caravans from the henequen zone and the occupation of the Casa del Pueblo (now the headquarters of the CNC and the PRI)—can be traced back to the Cardenista era.[24]

Cárdenas set out to reform Mexico with decisive state action from above and by mobilizing grassroots support from below. Yet the outcome of the reform in Yucatán fell far short of Cárdenas's dream. The henequen ejidos that were finally created never achieved the economic emancipation and social liberation of the rural poor that Cárdenas had envisioned. The national state created nominally centralized political institutions and reduced the size of the great henequen estates, but regional camarillas continued to control Yucatecan politics, and the old landowning class for the most part survived and in many cases prospered. In the end, after jettisoning political and sociocultural reform, Cárdenas was forced to curtail agrarian reform only a few years before a global boom in henequen demand would have rescued the ejidos. Even though the Cardenista reforms failed to achieve most of their stated goals, and even though this failure denied future leftist and neo-Cardenismo movements a historical heritage on which to build in Yucatán, the legacy of popular empowerment and the memory of the democratic opening that Cárdenas briefly created has not yet been erased.

Notes

In referring to archival material, the Archivo General de la Nación is abbreviated as AGN, followed by either LC (Presidente Lázaro Cárdenas) or AR (Presidente Abelardo Rodríguez), or DGG (Dirección General de Gobernación) and then the number of the expediente (exp.) or legajo (leg.) if necessary. Material from the Archivo General del Estado de Yucatán is cited as AGEY, followed by either MA, signifying Archivo Municipal or PE, indicating Poder Ejecutivo, followed by the seccíon (SG for Seccion Gobernación or SJ for Seccion Judicial).

Introduction: Cárdenas, the Mexican Revolution, and Yucatán

1. Sanjuana Martínez, "Vargas Llosa: La democratización mexicana, ilusoria," *Proceso* 1219 (12 March 2000) (www.proceso.com.mx/1219/1219n06.html); Frank Ralph Brandenburg, "Mexico: An Experiment in One-Party Democracy" (Ph.D. diss., University of Pennsylvania, 1956).

2. The literature on Cardenismo is too voluminous to be surveyed here, but, for an exhaustive, critical summary, see Alan Knight, "Mexico, c. 1930–1946," in *The Cambridge History of Latin America,* vol. 11, *Bibliographical Essays,* ed. Leslie Bethell (Cambridge: Cambridge University Press, 1994).

   The classic populist histories of Cárdenas are Frank Tannenbaum, *Mexico: The Struggle for Peace and Bread* (New York: Knopf, 1950); and William Townsend, *Lazaro Cardenas: Mexican Democrat* (Ann Arbor, Mich.: George Wahr, 1952).

   Notable revisionist works include Jorgé Basurto, *Cárdenas y el poder sindical* (Mexico City: Era, 1983); Paul Friedrich, *The Princes of Naranja* (Austin: University of Texas Press, 1986); and John Gledhill, *Casi Nada: A Study of Agrarian Reform in the Homeland of Cardenismo* (Austin, Tex.: Institute of Mesoamerican Studies, 1991). Friedrich and Gledhill both study Cárdenas's home state, Michoacan. Norah Hamilton's *The Limits of State Autonomy* (Princeton, N.J.: Princeton University Press, 1982) remains one of the most important revisionist national syntheses of Cardenismo.

3. Gilbert M. Joseph and Daniel Nugent, "Popular Culture and State Formation in Revolutionary Mexico," in *Everyday Forms of State Formation,* ed. Gilbert M. Joseph and Daniel Nugent (Durham, N.C.: Duke University Press, 1994), 3. Along with the recently reissued compilation *Rural Revolt in Mexico: U.S. Intervention and the Domain of Subaltern Politics,* ed. Daniel Nugent, 2d ed. (Durham, N.C.: Duke University Press, 1998), *Everyday Forms* showcased many of the leading neopopulists.

The pure neopopulist case has been best made by Mary Kay Vaughan, *Cultural Politics in Revolution: Teachers, Peasants, and Schools in Mexico, 1930–1940* (Tucson: University of Arizona Press, 1997). Alan Knight has supported many of the conclusions of the neopopulist school in a number of articles, including "Cardenismo: Juggernaut or Jalopy?" in *Texas Papers on Mexico* (Austin: Institute of Latin American Studies, University of Texas at Austin, 1990), but, in "Popular Culture and the Revolutionary State in Mexico, 1910–1940," *Hispanic American Historical Review* 74, no. 3 (1994): 393–444, he argues that a new, revolutionary popular culture never truly sank deep roots across Mexico, although there were many locales where it did take. Stephen Lewis's "Revolution and the Rural Schoolhouse: Forging State and Nation in Chiapas, Mexico, 1913–1948" (Ph.D. diss., University of California, San Diego, 1997) explores the successes and failures of Cardenista educators in forging a new political culture in Chiapas. Marjorie Becker's interpretation of Cardenismo has evolved from the critical, revisionist perspective expressed in "Black and White and Color: *Cardenismo* and the Search for a *Campesino* Ideology," *Comparative Studies in Society and History* 29 (1929): 453–65, to a more nuanced one, exceptional in its attention to the relation between gender and Cardenismo, in *Setting the Virgin on Fire: Lázaro Cárdenas, Michoacán Peasants, and the Redemption of the Mexican Revolution* (Berkeley and Los Angeles: University of California Press, 1995). For a reexamination of Cardenista Michoacan, see Chris Boyer, "The Cultural Politics of Agrarismo: Agrarian Revolt, Village Revolutionaries, and State-Formation in Michoacán, Mexico" (Ph.D. diss., University of Chicago, 1997).

Two recent works have added new dimensions to analyses of Cardenismo by demonstrating its limits without employing revisionists' economic structuralism. In his *Mexico between Hitler and Roosevelt: Mexican Foreign Relations in the Age of Lázaro Cárdenas, 1930–1940* (Albuquerque: University of New Mexico Press, 1998), Friedrich Schuler demonstrates how Cárdenas's presidency was shaped by international diplomatic and financial pressure. Adrian Bantjes, on the other hand, convincingly argues that regional, conservative interests forced Cárdenas to moderate his reforms (see *As If Jesus Walked on Earth: Cardenismo, Sonora, and the Mexican Revolution* [Wilmington, Del.: Scholarly Resources, 1998]).

Cardenismo continues to be the subject of new research. Jocelyn Olcott's "Las Hijas de La Malinche: Women's Organizing and State Consolidation in Postrevolutionary Mexico, 1934–1940" (Ph.D. diss., Yale University, in progress) promises to deepen our understanding of the relation between gender and Cardenismo.

4. Jennie Purnell, *Popular Movements and State Formation in Revolutionary Mexico: The Agraristas and Cristeros of Michoacan* (Durham, N.C.: Duke University Press, 1999).

5. Eric Van Young, "Are Regions Good to Think?" in *Mexico's Regions: Comparative History and Development,* ed. Eric Van Young (San Diego: Center for U.S.-Mexican Studies, University of California, San Diego, 1992), 5–6.

6. Yucatán has not been untouched by the recent boom in regional history. In fact, several studies touching on various aspects of the Cardenista period in Yucatán have been published. These studies have not, however, used archival sources to any great extent — if at all. See Fernando Benítez, *Kí: La historía de una planta y un pueblo,* 2d ed. (Mexico City: Fondo de Cultura Economica, 1956); Luis González Navarro, *Raza y tierra: La guerra de castas y el henequén,* 2d ed. (Mexico City: Colegio de México, 1969); and José Luis Sierra and José Antonio Paoli Bolio, *Cárdenas y el reparto de los henequenales* (Mérida: Gobierno

del Estado de Yucatán, 1986). While his research on agrarian reform did not draw on archival resources, Othón Baños Ramírez offers a suggestive interpretation of the social and political changes behind the upheavals of the era (see "El trasfondo politico de la reforma agraria: El caso de Yucatan, 1933–1937," *Revista de la Universidad Autónoma de Yucatán* 172 [January–March 1990]: 80–95, and "Agrarismo estatal y poder en Mexico (1915–1940): El caso de Yucatán," *Revista de la Universidad Autónoma de Yucatán* 165 [April–June 1988]: 20–39). For an insider's account of Cardenista-era politics, see Antonio Betancourt Pérez, *Memorías de un combatiente social* (Mérida: Instituto de Cultura de Yucatán, 1991). Maria Lapointe and Lucie Dufrese have drawn on some archival sources but focus on economic and ethnic issues rather than political, social, and cultural history (see Marie Lapointe, "El estado mexicano y las elites del henequén en Yucatán," *Gazeta universitaria* 12 [1991]: 13–30; and Marie Lapointe and Lucie Dufresne, "El Cardenismo en Yucatan," in *Sociedad, estructura agraria, y estado en Yucatán,* ed. Othón Baños Ramírez [Mérida: Universidad Autonoma de Yucatán, 1990], 341–62).

7. Despite the relative abundance of Cardenista studies, only recently have regional and local archives been tapped. Over the past thirty years, studies of postrevolutionary Mexico have focused on center-region dynamics. National studies of Cardenismo include Alicia Hernández Chávez, *Historia de la Revolución,* vol. 16, *La mecanica Cardenista* (Mexico: Colegio de Mexico, 1979); and Octavo Ianni, *El estado capitalista en la época de Cárdenas* (Mexico City: Serie Popular Era, 1977). Two recent regional studies of Cardenismo focusing on elite politics are Alex M. Saragoza, *The Monterrey Elite and the Mexican State, 1880–1940* (Austin: University of Texas Press, 1988); and Mark Wasserman, *Persistent Oligarchs: Elites and Politics in Chihuahua, Mexico, 1910–1940* (Durham, N.C.: Duke University Press, 1993). More recently, scholars have delved deeply into rural microhistory but, for reasons of academic economy, have left unexcavated other locales and urban areas within particular regions. See Becker, "Black and White and Color"; Ann Craig, *The First Agraristas: An Oral History of a Mexican Agrarian Reform Movement* (Berkeley and Los Angeles: University of California Press, 1983); Friedrich, *Princes of Naranja;* Gledhill, *Casi Nada;* David Ronfeldt, *Atencingo: The Politics of Agrarian Struggle in a Mexican Ejido* (Stanford, Calif.: Stanford University Press, 1973); and Frans J. Schreyer, *The Rancheros of Pisaflores: The History of a Peasant Bourgeoisie in Twentieth-Century Mexico* (Toronto: University of Toronto Press, 1980).

8. See, e.g., Manuel Escoffie Z., *¡Ya!: Libro de los buenos yucatecos* (Mérida, 1954), 166–67.

9. Roberto Zamarripa, "Ana Rosa Payán: 'Salinas no quiere que Yucatán sea gobernado por el PAN,'" *Proceso* 862 (10 May 1993): 17. This and all other translations from the Spanish are, unless otherwise noted, my own.

10. The dean of this school was Antonio Betancourt Pérez, once a young Communist and supporter of Cárdenas in the 1930s, who influenced an entire generation of contemporary Mexican scholars, most notably Sierra.

11. See, e.g., Pedro Echeverría, *La política en Yucatán en el siglo XX: 1900–1964* (Mérida: Maldonado, 1985).

12. Hernán R. Menéndez, "H_2O, el virus historiográfico que ha contaminado la investigación regional: Herencia oligárquica e historia oficial," *Unicornio,* 24 March 1996, 3–7.

13. For a suggestive rethinking of ideas of the state in postrevolutionary Mexico, see Joseph and Nugent, "Popular Culture"; Claudio Lomnitz-Adler, *Exits from the Labyrinth: Culture and Ideology in the Mexican National Space* (Berkeley and Los Angeles: University of

California Press, 1992); and Jeffrey Rubin, "Decentering the Regime: Culture and Regional Politics," *Latin American Research Review* 3, no. 3 (fall 1996): 85–126.

14. Alan Knight, *The Mexican Revolution* (Lincoln: University of Nebraska Press, 1986), 1:315, 559 n. 386; Jeffrey Rubin, *Decentering the Regime: Ethnicity, Radicalism, and Democracy in Juchitán, Mexico* (Durham, N.C.: Duke University Press, 1997), 11–13.

15. My findings in Yucatán agree with Mary Kay Vaughan's research in Sonora and Puebla and Adrian Bantjes's work in Sonora, both of which stress Cárdenas's need to compromise with conservative, regional interests, as well as Rubin's notion of Cárdenas forging a "multitude of regional arrangements" (Rubin, *Decentering the Regime,* 13).

16. For a different view, one that emphasizes structural limits on Cardenismo, see Hamilton, *Limits of State Autonomy.*

17. Joseph and Nugent, "Popular Culture," 8–9; Knight, *The Mexican Revolution,* 1:x–xi.

18. On Yucatecan caciques before Cárdenas, see Gilbert M. Joseph, *Revolution from Without: Yucatán, Mexico, and the United States,* 2d ed. (Durham, N.C.: Duke University Press, 1983), 204–13. On caciquismo elsewhere in Mexico, see Schreyer, *Rancheros,* 10–11; and Friedrich, *Princes of Naranja.*

19. Lomnitz-Adler, *Exits from the Labyrinth,* 297.

20. Guillermo de la Peña, "Poder local, poder regional: Perspectivas socioantropológicas," in *Poder local, poder regional,* ed. Jorge Padua and Alain Vanneph (Mexico City: Colegio de México/CEMCA, 1993).

21. Gilbert Joseph and Allen Wells, "Yucatán: Elite Politics and Rural Insurgency," in *Provinces of the Revolution: Essays on Regional Mexican History,* ed. Thomas Benjamin and Mark Wasserman (Albuquerque: University of New Mexico Press, 1990), 93–132. See also Manuel L. Carlos, "Peasant Leadership Hierarchies: Leadership Behavior, Power Blocs, and Conflict in Mexican Regions," in Van Young, ed., *Mexico's Regions,* 91; Roderic Ai Camp, *Mexico's Leaders: Their Education and Recruitment* (Tucson: University of Arizona Press, 1980), chap. 2; and Carlos Loret de Mola, *Los caciques,* 3d ed. (Mexico City: Grijalbo, 1979), 64.

22. I agree with Rogelio Hernández that the groupings termed *camarillas* here should be seen not as mini-Mafias subject to the iron discipline of a leader, but rather as coalitions of individuals sharing common interests (see *Amistades, compromisos, y lealtades: Líderes y grupos políticos en el estado de México, 1942–1993* [Mexico City: Colegio de México, 1998], 27–30).

23. Allan Wells and Gilbert M. Joseph, *Summer of Discontent, Seasons of Upheaval: Elite Politics and Rural Insurgency in Yucatán, 1876–1915* (Stanford: Stanford University Press, 1996), 223.

24. José Revueltas quoted in Federico Campbell, *La invención del poder* (Mexico City: Aguilar, 1994), 94.

25. John Kenneth Turner, *Barbarous Mexico* (Austin: University of Texas Press, 1969), chap. 1.

26. Antonio Mediz Bolio, *La tierra del faisan y del venado* (Mexico City: Costa Amica, 1974).

27. Ben Fallaw, "Cárdenas and the Caste War That Wasn't: Land, Ethnicity, and State Formation in Yucatán, 1847–1937," *The Americas,* 53, no. 4 (April 1997): 551–77.

28. Gabriel Antonio Menéndez, *Directorio general* (Mérida: Popular, 1941); Barbara Ellen Holmes, "Women and Yucatec Kinship" (Ph.D. diss., Tulane University, 1978), 22–23; Wolfgang Gabbert, "When 'Mestizos' Are Indians—Ethnicity and the State in Yucatan,

Mexico" (paper presented at the European Social Science History Conference, Noord-wijkerhout, the Netherlands, 9–11 May 1996), 10; Richard Allen Thompson, "Status, Ethnicity, and Mobility in a Yucatec Town" (Ph.D. diss., University of Texas, 1970), 120–23; Paul Sullivan, "Ethnicity," in *Ethnology: Supplement to Handbook of Middle American Indians* vol. 6 (Austin: University of Texas, 2000); Alvaro Gamboa Ricalde, *Yucatán desde 1910,* vol. 1, *1910–1914* (Veracruz: Standard, 1943), 30–31; Denise Fay Brown, "Yucatec Maya Settling, Settlement, and Spatiality" (Ph.D. diss., University of California, Riverside, 1993), 133–34.

29. Matthew Restall, *The Maya World: Yucatec Culture and Society, 1550–1850* (Stanford, Calif.: Stanford University Press, 1997), 61–83; Terry Rugeley, *Yucatán's Maya Peasantry and the Origins of the Caste War* (Austin: University of Texas Press, 1996), 8–21; Franco Savarino, *Pueblos y nacionalismo, del régimen oligárquico a la sociedad de masas en Yucatán, 1894–1925* (Mexico City: INEH, 1997), 89–144; Robert Redfield, *The Folk Culture of Yucatan* (Chicago: University of Chicago Press, 1941), 150–51.

30. Wells and Joseph, *Summer of Discontent,* 144–76; Pedro Bracamonte Sosa, *Amos y sirvientes: Las haciendas de Yucatán, 1789–1860* (Mérida: UNAM, 1993), 130–62; Allen Wells, *Yucatán's Gilded Age: Haciendas, Henequen, and International Harvester, 1860–1915* (Albuquerque: University of New Mexico Press, 1984), chap. 5; Savarino, *Pueblos y nacionalismo,* 98–114; Baños, "Trasfondo"; Siegfried Askinasy, *El problema agrario de Yucatan* (Mexico City: Botas, 1936), 74.

31. Askinasy, *Problema agrario,* 30; Gledhill, *Casi Nada,* 82–87.

32. Wells and Joseph, *Summer of Discontent.*

33. Joseph, *Revolution from Without;* Francisco Paoli and Enrique Montalvo, *El socialismo olvidado de Yucatán* (Mexico City: Siglo Veintiuno, 1977).

34. Robert Redfield and Alfonso Villa Rojas, *Chankom: A Maya Village* (Chicago: University of Chicago Press, 1962); Thompson, "Status, Ethnicity, and Mobility," 40.

35. Alvarado founded the Socialist Workers Party (Partido Socialista Obrero) in 1915, and its name was changed to the Yucatecan Socialist Party (Partido Socialista Yucateco) in 1917. In 1921, its name was changed again to Socialist Party of the Southeast (Partido Socialista del Sureste). To avoid confusion, and in recognition of the continuity of leadership and ideology of the party despite its nominal changes, I will refer to all three as *Yucatecan Socialism.*

36. Luis Aboites, *La Revolución mexicana en Espita, Yucatán (1910–1940): Microhistoria de la formación del estado de la Revolución* (Mérida: Maldonado, 1985), 84.

37. Joseph, *Revolution from Without.*

38. Luis Javier Garrido, *El partido de la Revolución institucionalizada: La formación del nuevo estado en México* (Mexico City: Secretaría de al Educación Publica, 1986), 184–219; Tzvi Medin, *El minimato presidential: Historia política del maximato (1928–1935)* (Mexico City: Era, 1981), 95; Heather Fowler-Salamini, *Agrarian Radicalism in Veracruz, 1920–1938* (Lincoln: University of Nebraska Press, 1971).

39. Hamilton, *Limits of State Autonomy,* 129–32. On corruption among the revolutionary elites, see Carlos Martínez Assad, Mario Ramírez Rancaño, and Ricardo Pozas Horcasitas, *Revolucionarios fueron todos* (Mexico City: Secretaría de Educación Pública, 1982).

40. Garrido, *El partido,* 199–200, 206–9.

41. Frente Ideológico Revolucionario, *El ejido en Yucatán* (n.p., 1935), 13–19.

42. Benítez, *Kí,* 233–34.

43. *Diario del Sureste,* 10 February 1934; *Historia documental del partido de la Revolución* (Mexico City: PRI, 1981), 3:51–52.
44. Knight, "Popular Culture," 393–96.
45. Albert Michael, "The Modification of the Anti-Clerical Nationalism of the Mexican Revolution by General Lázaro Cárdenas and Its Relationship to the Church-State Detente in Mexico," *The Americas* 26 (1969): 37–46.
46. Partido Nacional Revolucionario (PNR), *Primer informe anual que rinde el Comité Ejecutivo Nacional del Partido Nacional Revolucionario a todos los sectores sociales del país, junio 1936* (Mexico City: PNR, 1936), 29.
47. Benítez, *Kí,* 231, 233.
48. Memorandum, 12 May 1936, AGN LC 404.1/12 leg. 2.
49. Narciso Bassols, *Hoy,* 5 June 1937, quoted in Benítez, *Kí,* 129.
50. Luciano Kubli, *Sureste proletario: Apuntes de una jira fecunda* (Mexico City, 1935), 85, 111–12.
51. Moisés Gonzalez Navarro, *La confederacion nacional campesina: Un grupo de presión de la reforma agraria mexicana* (Mexico City: Costa-Amic, 1968), 115.

1 Agrarian Cardenismo, the Rise of the CGT, and the Fall of Governor Alayola, 1934–1935

1. Memorandum, 12 May 1936, AGN LC 404.1/12 leg. 2.
2. Benítez, *Kí,* 232; Gabino Vázquez to Alayola Barrera, AGN LC 404.1/12-1 leg. 1.
3. *Diario del sureste,* 9, 10, 27 March, 9 June, 19 December 1934; Posadas to President Rodríguez, 2 July 1930, AGN AR 011/11; Tzvi Medín, *El minimato presidencial: Historia política del Maximato (1928–1935)* 5th ed. (Mexico City: Era, 1991), 153.
4. Benítez, *Kí,* 211–12.
5. Askinasy, *Problema agrario,* 3–4.
6. Memorandum, 12 May 1936, AGN LC 404.1/12 leg. 2.
7. Enrique Manero, *Anarquía henequenera* (Mexico City, 1960), appendix.
8. *Diario de Yucatán,* 5 October 1935; "Oposición sindical revolucionario de la enseñanza," 24 September 1935, and "Trabajadores de Yucatan," 26 September 1935, AGN LC 432/219.
9. *Vibración,* May 1935, 3; "Puntos," AGN LC 404.1/12 leg. 1; Gustavo Molina Font, *El problema agrario en la zona Henequenera de Yucatán* (Mexico City, 1934), 34–37; Manero, *Anarquía,* 19.
10. *Diario del sureste,* 29 January 1934; Enrique Couh to governor, 17 December 1934, AGEY PE 981 SG 1.
11. AGEY PE 991 SJ; memorandum, 12 May 1936, AGN LC 404.1/12 leg. 2; *Diario del sureste,* 27 November, 23 December 1934; Pedro Cruz et al. to President Cárdenas, 13 December 1934, AGN LC 403/30; relación, AGEY PE 997 SG; Angel Posadas to secretary of the president, 15 February 1934, AR 011/11.
12. *Diario del sureste,* 2 February 1935.
13. *Diario del sureste,* 9, 28 April 1935, 1 May 1935.
14. *Diario de Yucatán,* 5 May, 2, 20 July 1935.
15. Sierra and Paoli, *Cárdenas,* 71.
16. Askinasy, *Problema agrario,* 68–69, 74–76.

17. *Diario del sureste,* 23, 28 May 1935.

18. *Diario del sureste,* 26 April 1935; *Diario de Yucatán,* 18, 29 May 1935.

19. *Diario del sureste,* 6 October 1935, 17 August 1937.

20. Benítez, *Kí,* 200–201.

21. Memorandum, 12 May 1936, AGN LC 404.1/12 leg. 2.

22. Julio Moguel to president, 16 February 1935, AGN LC 542.2/199.

23. *Diario de Yucatán,* 21 September 1936.

24. Ivan Menéndez, *Lucha social y sistema político en Yucatán* (Mexico City: Grijalva, 1981), 107–10.

25. *Diario del sureste,* 13 October 1935.

26. *Diario de Yucatán,* 7 February 1936; Candelario Reyes to López Cárdenas, 6 December 1935, AGEY PE 1022 SG 1; *Diario del sureste,* 14 October 1940.

27. *Diario de Yucatán,* 14 June 1936.

28. *Diario de Yucatán,* 13 December 1936.

29. *Diario de Yucatán,* 13 July 1936.

30. Reyes to Alayola, 3 October 1935, AGEY PE 1005 SG 1.

31. *Diario del sureste,* 6 September 1935.

32. Molina, *Problema agrario,* 37–40.

33. Gabino Vázquez to governor, AGN LC 404.1/12-1 leg. 1; Pascual Gamboa et al. to President Cárdenas, 25 February 1935, AGN LC 404.1/1-12 leg. 1.

34. *Diario de Yucatán,* 15 March 1936; Carlos Peralta to Lázaro Cárdenas, 17 April 1936, AGN LC 404.1/12 leg. 2.

35. "A los trabajadores de la ciudad y del campo," 3 October 1935, AGN LC 543.1/30; *Diario de Yucatán,* 3 September 1935; Saturnino Cedillo to president, 20 March 1936; AGN LC 404.1/12 leg. 2; Pablo Massone to Saturnino Cedillo, 26 December 1936, AGN LC 543.1/30; *El Yucateco,* 17 August 1935.

36. *Diario del sureste,* 26 January 1936.

37. AGN LC 404.1/12-1 leg. 1; *Diario de Yucatán,* 8 February, 14 March 1935.

38. A. Peralta to president, 30 October 1934, AGN LC 404.1/12-1 leg. 1.

39. John M. Hart, *Anarchism and the Mexican Working Class, 1860–1931* (Austin: University of Texas Press, 1978), 174–76; Hernández, *Historia de la Revolución,* 164; Jean Meyer, *Historia de la Revolución mexicana,* vol. 11, *Periodo 1928–1934: Estado y sociedad con Calles* (Mexico City: Colegio de Mexico, 1977), 88–89.

40. Stanley G. Payne, *Spain's First Democracy: The Second Republic, 1931–1936* (Madison: University of Wisconsin Press, 1993), 13–16; Daniela Spenser, "Workers against Socialism? Reassessing the Role of Urban Labor in Yucatecan Revolutionary Politics," in *Land, Labor, and Capital in Modern Yucatan: Essays in Regional History and Political Economy,* ed. Gilbert M. Joseph and Jeffrey T. Brannon (Tuscaloosa: University of Alabama Press, 1991); and Ramiro E. Peña's appendix in Betancourt, *Memorías,* chap. 7.

41. AGN LC 404.1/12-1 leg. 1; *Diario de Yucatán,* 26 June, 25 July 1935, 19 September 1936.

42. *Padron* (voting roll) from Chuburná de Hidalgo, AGN DGG 2.311S vol. 120 exp. 2; *Sindicato* Xcumpich to governor, 9 February 1935, AGEY PE 1004 SG 2.

43. Helidoro Peña to governor, 26 February 1936, and Federico Gutierrez to governor, 1 April 1936, AGEY PE 1018 SG 1; Eric Villanueva Mukul, *Así tomamos la tierra* (Mérida: Maldonado, 1984), 41–42, 47–48.

44. *Diario del sureste,* 4, 7 September 1935.

45. *Diario de Yucatán,* 20 May 1935.

46. Manuel J. Cano to president, 17 April 1936, AGN LC 404.1 / 12 leg. 2.
47. Sierra and Paoli, *Cárdenas,* 45–46.
48. *Diario del sureste,* 30 November 1935, 24 October 1936; *Diario de Yucatán,* 29 October 1936.
49. Benito Arceo, 21 May 1935, AGEY PE 1005.
50. Victor Goldkind, "Social Stratification in the Peasant Community: Redfield's Chankom Reinterpreted," *American Anthropology* 67 (1965): 872–73.
51. Malcolm Karl Shuman, "The Town Where Luck Fell: The Economics of Life in a Henequen Zone Pueblo" (Ph.D. diss., Tulane University, 1974), 131–32.
52. Venancio Narváez Ek, *San Antonio Too: Historia de una hacienda henequenera* (Mérida: Programa de Apoyo a la Cultura Municipal y Comunitaria y Consejo Nacional Para la Cultura y las Artes, 1992), 11–12, 49–50 (quotation), 50, 57–58.
53. Gledhill, *Casi Nada,* 87.
54. Candelario Reyes to Governor Alayola, 3 October 1935, AGEY PE 1005 SG 1; *Diario del sureste,* 13 October 1935.
55. "A los trabajadores de la ciudad y del campo," 3 October 1935, AGN LC 543.1 / 30.
56. Pedro Cruz et al. to president, 12 March 1936, AGN LC 404.1 / 12-1 leg. 2.
57. Chief of staff to Agrarian Department, 23 March 1936, AGN LC 404.1 / 12-1 leg. 2.
58. *Diario de Yucatán,* 3 September 1935; Saturnino Cedillo to president, 20 March 1936, AGN LC 404.1 / 12 leg. 2.
59. *Diario de Yucatán,* 2 September 1935.
60. Santiago Capetillo A. to president, 5 October 1935, AGN LC 404.1 / 12-1 leg. 1; Carmen Can et al. to president, 9 March 1936, and Nicolas Pech to president, 12 February 1936, AGN LC 404.1 / 12 leg. 2; "A los trabajadores de la ciudad y del campo," 3 October 1935, AGN LC 543.1 / 30; *Diario de Yucatán,* 2, 9 September 1935.
61. AGEY PE 1004; Pallares to Pedro Castro Aguilar, 26 September 1936, AGEY PE 1014 SG 1; *Diario de Yucatán,* 3 September, 18 October 1935.
62. Baños, "Trasfondo," 91.
63. *Diario de Yucatán,* 17 March 1936.
64. Sierra and Paoli, *Cárdenas,* 44; *Diario de Yucatán,* 9 August 1936.
65. *Diario de Yucatán,* 17 November 1936.
66. Benítez, *Kí,* 200–201.
67. Wells and Joseph, *Summer of Discontent,* 233–34, 246–47.
68. Francisco Paredes to governor, 24 February 1936, AGN LC 404.1 / 12-1 leg. 2.
69. Victoriano Chi et al. to president, 9 March 1936, AGN LC 404.1 / 12-1 leg. 2.
70. *Diario de Yucatán,* 11 April, 17 July 1936; Porfirio Pallares to president, 17 April 1936, AGN LC 404.1 / 12 leg. 2; Ildefonso Monforte to president, 2 February 1935, AGEY PE 1001 SG 1.
71. *La opinión,* 5 August 1921; Santos Domínguez Aké, *La vida de Felipe Carrillo Puerto y su memoria en Muxupip* (Mérida: Maldonado, Consejo Nacional para la Cultura y las Artes, Culturas Populares, 1992), 25–26; *El asesinato de Carrillo Puerto (discursos y articulos en elogio del ilustre martir, y protestas contra sus infames asesinos)* (Mexico City, 1924), 6.
72. Joseph, *Revolution from Without,* 239.
73. Domínguez, *Vida.*
74. Diego Domínguez Tacú, "Mis recuerdos como campesino henequenero," *Memoria historia de los henequeneros yucatecos,* ed. Concejo Nacional para la Cultura y las Artes (Mexico City: Dirección General de la Cultura Popular, 1992), 54–57.

75. Ibid., 58.

76. Mayor Pedro Chávez to governor, 24 August 1934, AGEY PE 991 SJ.

77. *Diario de Yucatán*, 18 January 1936; CGT manifesto, 3 October 1935, AGN LC 543.1/30.

78. *Quinto censo de población: 15 de Mayo de 1930, estado de Yucatan* (Mexico City: Secretaria de la Económica Nacional, Dirección General de Estadistica, 1930).

79. Domínguez Tacú, "Recuerdos," 57–58; Santos Dominguez Aké, *La historia de la sociedad ejidal de Muxupip* (Tlahuapan: Instituto Nacional Indigenista Sedesol, 1994), 42; *Diario del sureste*, 25 November 1935; Santos Chalé, letter, *Diario de Yucatán*, 25 August 1935.

80. *Diario del sureste*, 25 November 1935.

81. *Diario de Yucatán*, 2 September 1935.

82. Santos Chalé to president, 1 February 1936, AGN LC 404.1/12-1 leg. 2; Santos Chalé to president, 11 January 1936, AGN LC 404.1/12-1 leg. 1.

83. Domínguez Tacú, "Recuerdos," 57–58; Domínguez, *Historia*, 51–52.

84. AGN LC 402.2/88.

85. Candelario Reyes to governor, 17 July 1935, AGEY PE 1004 SG 1.

86. Lizarraga to governor, 30 July 1935, AGEY PE 992 SG 2.

87. Diego Domínguez Tacú to governor, 1 August 1935, AGEY PE 992 SG 2; *Diario oficial*, 13 August 1935.

88. Domínguez, *Historia*, 41; Lizarraga to governor, 3 August 1935, AGEY PE 992 SG 2.

89. Domínguez, *Historia*, 44–47.

90. Ibid., 43.

91. Santos Chalé, letter, *Diario de Yucatán*, 25 August 1935; Domínguez, *Historia*, 43.

92. Reyes to governor, 23 September 1934, AGEY PE 1004 SG 1.

93. "Memo executivo," n.d., AGEY PE 1018 SG 1.

94. *Diario del sureste*, 24 May 1936.

95. Santos Chalé, letter, *Diario de Yucatán*, 18 January 1936.

96. Domínguez, *Historia*, 44.

97. *Diario de Yucatán*, 24 May 1936.

98. Domínguez Tacú, "Recuerdos," 58; *Diario del sureste*, 22 June 1937; Domínguez, *Historia*, 52–53.

99. *Diario del sureste*, 3 September 1937.

100. Echeverría, *Política*, 58; *Diario de Yucatán*, 3 September 1935.

101. *Diario de Yucatán*, 2 September 1935.

102. *Diario del sureste*, 9 September 1935; *Diario de Yucatán*, 12 September 1935.

103. Julio Moguel to president, 1 September 1935, AGN LC 432.2/31.

104. Julio Moguel to president, 16 February 1935, AGN LC 542.2/199.

105. Casimiro Moo et al. to editor, *Diario del sureste*, 7 September 1935.

106. General Mújica to president, 29 June 1934, AGN AR 011/22.

107. Memorandum, AGN LC 543.1/30; Governor Alayola, "A la conciencia yucateca," AGN LC 543.1/30 leg. 2; *Vibración*, January 1935, 18–19.

108. *Diario del sureste*, 9 September 1935.

109. PNR, *Primer*, 50–52, 57–58.

110. Memorandum, 27 July 1935, AGN LC 543.1/30 leg. 1; *Diario del sureste*, 19 September 1935.

111. Santiago Loria to governor, 16 April 1935, AGEY PE 985 SG 1; *Diario del sureste*, 14 May, 15 September 1935.

112. *Diario de Yucatán*, 15 September 1935; AGN LC 414.2/2.

113. Laureano Cardos Ruz, *El drama de los Mayas: Una reforma social traicionada* (Mexico City: Editorial Libros de México, n.d.), 256; AGN LC 543.1/30; *Diario del sureste,* 6 October 1935.

114. AGN LC 432/219; *Diario del sureste,* 8, 9 October 1935; *Diario de Yucatán,* 8, 9 October 1935; *El Yucateco,* 12 October 1935.

115. *Diario de Yucatán,* 8 October 1935; AGN 543.1/30 leg. 2; Macario Cocom to president, 28 October 1935, and A. Escalante to L. Cárdenas, 14 November 1935, AGN LC 543.1/30.

116. General Otero Pablos to Senator Dámaso Cárdenas, 27 January 1936, AGN LC 543.1/30.

117. Various correspondence, 11–15 October 1935, from AGN LC 543.1/30 leg. 1 and leg. 2; *Diario de Yucatán,* 11, 12 October 1935.

118. *Diario del sureste,* 10 October 1935; *Diario de Yucatán,* 11 October 1935; circular 16 from the governor to every municipal government, 10 October 1935, AGEY PE 1010 SG 1; López Cárdenas to Lázaro Cárdenas, 11 October 1935, AGEY PE 1005 SG 1.

119. Fidencio Correa et al. to president, 11 October 1935, AGN LC 543.1/30 leg. 1; Fidencio Correa to president, 5 October 1935, AGN LC 404.1/12-1 leg. 1.

120. Lázaro Cárdenas to General Cházaro, 14 October 1935, AGN LC 543.1/30; *Diario del sureste,* 15 October 1935.

121. Luis I. Rodríguez to Orlando Herrera, 15 October 1935, AGN LC 543.1/30.

2   Left-Cardenismo and the López Cárdenas Administration, 1935–1936

1. Governor López Cárdenas to President Cárdenas, 12 February 1936, AGN LC 543.1/30 leg. 3; PSS circular, 15 December 1935, AGEY PE 1004 SG 2; *Diario del sureste,* 9, 10 November, 13, 31 December 1935.

2. *Diario del sureste,* 25, 26 October, 19, 20, 26 November 1935.

3. Miguel Martínez to governor, 22 September 1936, AGEY PE 1013 SG 1; *Diario de Yucatán,* 11, 12 October 1935; *Diario del sureste,* 12, 13 October 1935; various correspondence from AGN DGG 2.317.4 vol. 71 exp. 16 and AGN LC 543.1/30 leg. 1.

4. Circular, 12 November 1935, AGEY MA Tixkokob caja 15 leg. 41 exp. 3.

5. Partido Comunista Mexicano (PCM), *Resoluciones de la Primera Convención Estatal del Partido Comunista Mexicano: Unidos por la obra Cardenista* (Mérida: Hul-Kin, 1939), 12; Sierra and Paoli, *Cárdenas,* 88; circular, Ignacio Márquez et al., 5 November 1935, AGEY 955 SG 3.

6. Baños, "Trasfondo," 86–88.

7. Betancourt, *Memorías,* 70–71; *Memoria de la gran convención del "Partido Socialista del Sureste," celebrada la noche del 24 del mayo para elegir candidato a gobernador del estado* (Mérida: Pluma y Lápiz, 1925); AGEY PE 807 SG; *El clamor del obrero,* 27 December 1928; *Diario de Yucatán,* 21 July 1936; *Diario del sureste,* 11 January 1937.

8. Sierra and Paoli, *Cárdenas,* 84; Jorge Fernández Souza and Eric Villanueva Mukul, "Notas sobre el sindicalismo independiente en Yucatán," in *Memoria del Segundo Coloquio Regional de Historia Obrera* (Mexico City: CEHSMO, 1979), 652–53; Antonio Betancourt Pérez, "La Federación Sindical Independiente, 1934–1940," in *Memoria del Primero Coloquio Regional de Historia Obrera* (Jalapa: CEHSMO, 1977), 240–42.

9. Wells and Joseph, *Summers of Discontent;* Sally Humphries, "Modernizing Maya Agriculture: A Case Study of Peasant Entrepreneurship in North America." Diss., York University, 1989); Askinasy, *Problema agrario,* xii; Victor Manuel Canto Chán, *Los trabajadores mayas de una ex-hacienda henequenera: El ejido Ya'axkopoil, Umán, Yucatán* (Mexico City: SEP/INI/CIESAS, 1982). I am indebted to Christopher Gill for information on conditions on western haciendas.

10. Mary Kay Vaughan, "The Construction of the Patriotic Festival in Tecamachalco Puebla, 1900–1946," in *Rituals of Rule, Rituals of Resistance: Public Celebrations and Popular Culture in Mexico,* ed. William H. Beezeley, Cheryl English Martin, and William E. French (Wilmington, Del.: Scholarly Resources, 1994); *Diario del sureste,* 1 July, 9 December 1934, 29 January 1935; *Diario de Yucatán,* 9 December 1934, 26 April 1934; "Oposición sindical revolucionario de la enseñanza," 24 September 1935, AGN LC 432/219; Antonio Betancourt Pérez, "La Federación Sindical Independiente," in *Memorias del primer coloquio regional de historia oberero* (Jalapa, Mexico: CEHSMO, 1977), 240.

11. *Diario de Yucatán,* 16 April 1936; *Diario del sureste,* 1 April, 11 November 1936.

12. Pedro Echeverría, *Educación publica: Mexico y Yucatán* (Mérida: Universidad Autónoma de Yucatán, 1993), 107–9.

13. J. Galindo to president, 22 March 1935, AGN LC 542.1/765; Baños, "Trasfondo," 91–93.

14. Antonio Betancourt Pérez, interview with author, 6 November 1994; Hernán Morales Medina, interview with author, 7 June 1993; *Diario de Yucatán,* 8, 26 February 1936; *Diario del sureste,* 10 March, 26 November 1935, 18 May 1936, 1, 16 June, 11 November 1936; Pastor Ramírez to Miguel Escalante, 26 September 1936, AGEY PE 1014 SG 1; Betancourt, "Federación," 242–43; Vaughan, *Cultural Politics;* Elsie Rockwell, "Schools of the Revolution: Enacting and Contesting State Forms in Tlaxcala, 1910–1930," in Joseph and Nugent, eds., *Everyday Forms.*

15. *Diario del sureste,* 26 October 1935; *El yucatanista,* 18 January 1936; Eduardo Urzaiz, "Historia de la educación pública y privada desde 1911," in *Enciclopedia yucatanense* (Mexico City: Gobierno de Estado, 1944), 4:242–43; Echeverría, *Educación,* 114.

16. *Diario de Yucatán,* 8, 26 February 1936; *Diario del sureste,* 10 March, 26 November 1935, 18 May, 1, 16 June, 11 November 1936; Pastor Ramírez to Miguel Escalante, 26 September 1936, AGEY PE 1014 SG 1; Betancourt, "Federación," 242–43.

17. Diego Rosado to President Cárdenas, 18 August 1936, and Diego Rosado to President Cárdenas, 18 August 1936, reprinted in Fernando López Cárdenas, *Revolutionarios contra la Revolucion* (Mexico City: Lóndres, 1938), 129–35; AGN LC 432/531 and 542.1/785; Mújica, memorandum, 23 July 1936, AGN LC 404.1/12 leg. 2; *Diario de Yucatán,* 27 April 1936; *Diario del sureste,* 21 March, 15, 18, 29 May, 1 June, 31 August 1936, 26 February 1937.

18. For a full account of the struggle on Temozón, see Ben Fallaw, "The Southeast Was Red: Left-State Alliances and Popular Mobilizations in Yucatán, 1930–1940," *Social Science History* 23, no. 2 (summer 1999): 241–68.

19. Mújica, memorandum, 23 July 1936, AGN LC 404.1/12 leg. 2; AGN LC 432/531.

20. *Diario de sureste,* 6 May 1936; *Memorias del Primer Congreso Regional de Unificación Campesinos del ex-Departamento de Valladolid, Yucatán, verificado en el salón Regis de la ciudad de Valladolid, Yucatán, México, durante los días 26, 27 y 28 del junio próximo pasado* (Mérida, 1936).

21. AGEY PE 1029 sec. Mani; *Diario del sureste,* 24 October 1936; *Diario de Yucatán,* 19

January, 27 May 1937; Cayetano Castillo to governor, 6 November 1936, AGEY PE 1022 SG 1; Lorenzo López to president, 18 November 1936, AGN LC 544.5/934.

22. Ramón Berzunza Pinto, *Una chispa en el sureste (pasada y futuro de los indios mayas)* Mexico City: Talleres de la Cooperativa, 1942), 42–43, 55, 60; *Machete ilegal, 1929–1934: Edición facsimilar* (Puebla: Instituto de Ciencias Universidad Autónoma de Puebla and Centro de Estudios Históricos y Sociales, 1975), 220.

23. Betancourt, *Memorías,* 129; PCM, *Resoluciones,* 10; Informe de la Comisión de la CEN/ PNR to Yucatán, AGN DGG 2.311S; Hernán Morales Medina, interview with author, 7 June 1993; Carmen Nava y Nava, *Ideología del partido de la Revolución mexicana* (Mexico City: Centro de Estudios de la Revolución Mexicana "Lázaro Cárdenas," 1984), 262–63; Luis Alvárez Barret, *Lecturas para trabajadoras: Folleto no. 1 para ser utilizado en las escuelas nocturnas, en la campaña analfabetizante y en las organizaciones sindicales* (Mérida: Publicaciones de la Dirección de la Educación Federal en el Estado de Yucatán, 1937), 32.

24. Juventudes Socialistas Unidos de México (JSUM), *Instituto Cultural Obrero de JSUM* (Mérida: Porvenir, 1939), 19, 21.

25. Ibid., 6.

26. Peter Winn, *Weavers of Revolution: The Yarur Workers and Chile's Road to Socialism* (New York: Oxford University Press, 1986), 85–86.

27. Hernán Morales Medina, interview with author, 7 June 1993; Betancourt, *Memorías,* 130; JSUM, *Instituto Cultural Obrero,* 6, 19, 21.

28. *Diario del sureste,* 3 March 1937; Ben Fallaw, "The Life and Three Deaths of Felipa Poot" (paper presented at the Latin American Studies Association congress, Chicago, 25 September 1998); Ana Macías, *Against All Odds: The Feminist Movement in Mexico to 1940* (Westport, Conn.: Greenwood, 1982), 137–42; Antonio Betancourt Pérez, interview with author, 6 November 1994.

29. *Diario del sureste,* 3 July 1938; Alejandra García Quintanilla, *Los tiempos en Yucatán: Los hombres, las mujeres, y la naturaleza (siglo XIX)* (Mérida: Claves Latinoamericanos and Departamento de Estudios Económico y Sociales del Centro de Investigaciones Regionales "Dr. Hideyo Noguchi" de la Universidad Autónoma de Yucatán, 1986), 154–55.

30. Alvárez, *Lecturas,* 32.

31. *Diario del sureste,* 16 January, 4 March 1936, 1 April, 29 May 1938; *Diario de Yucatán,* 15 January 1936; Alvaro Pérez Alpuche to Lázaro Cárdenas, 19 October 1937, AGN LC 544.2/30; Ward M. Morton, *Woman Suffrage in Mexico* (Gainesville: University of Florida Press, 1962); Macías, *Against All Odds,* 137–42; Berzunza Pinto, *Una chispa,* 43, 48; Antonio Betancourt Pérez, interview with author, 6 November 1994.

32. Fallaw, "Life and Three Deaths"; *Diario del sureste,* 18 May, 9, 10, 16, 23 June, 15 October 1936, 3 July 1938; *Diario de Yucatán,* 27 July 1936; Fermín Pech et al. to President Cárdenas, 9 October 1936, AGN DGG 2.311M vol. 85 exp. 17.

33. William Brito Sansores, "¡Adiós maestro rural!" In *Los maestros y la cultura nacional, 1920– 1952* (Mexico City: SEP, 1987), 5:68.

34. *Diario de Yucatán,* 4 May 1936.

35. Barry Carr, *Marxism and Communism in Twentieth-Century Mexico* (Lincoln: University of Nebraska Press, 1992), 59.

36. Antonio Betancourt Pérez, interview with author, 6 November 1994.

37. *Diario de Yucatán,* 27, 30, 31 March, 1, 5, 8, 30 April 1936; *Diario del sureste,* 31 March 1936.

38. John W. Sherman, "Feuding over the Family: The Mexican Right's Critique of Soviet Russia, Republican Spain, Foreign Capitalists, and the Presidency of Lázaro Cárdenas" (paper presented at the Latin American Studies Association meeting, Chicago, 28–30 September 1995).

39. *Diario del sureste*, 18 May, 1, 23, 26, 30 June 1936; *Diario de Yucatán*, 27 April, 5, 17 June, 24 October 1936; Pastor Ramírez to Miguel Escalante, 26 September 1936, AGEY PE 1014 SG 1; Antonio Canto Vázquez to president, n.d., AGN LC 542.1/784.

40. Vaughan, *Cultural Politics*, 16.

41. *Diario de Yucatán*, 18 October 1936.

42. Sóstenes Carrillo to Miguel Cerón, 24 May 1937, AM Muna caja 2; Benítez, *Ki*, 180–84.

43. Union Magisterial Revolucionario, manifesto, 25 November 1936, AGEY PE 1018.

44. Fernández and Villanueva, "Notas," 652; *Diario del sureste*, 7 September 1936; José Cornelio Lara Tec and Edelmiro Vargas Canul, interview with author, 23 May 1993.

45. *Diario del sureste*, 11 April 1933; Felipe Montforte to National PNR, AGN DGG 2.311G (27) vol. 337.

46. *Diario del sureste*, 6 March 1934.

47. *Diario del sureste*, 26 February 1934.

48. Manuel Montes de Oca to President Comité Central Electoral Carrillo Puerto–Rogerio Chalé, 13 September 1934, AGEY AM Motul caja 26; *Diario del sureste*, 22 March 1935.

49. *Diario del sureste*, 20 April, 31 May 1935.

50. José Cornelio Lara Tec, interview with author, 23 May 1993; Baños, "Trasfondo," 87–88, and "Agrarismo," 30–34; *Diario del sureste*, 5, 27 December 1934, 8 January 1935; Chalé to Alayola, 3 April 1934, AGEY PE 974 SG 1; Genaro Polanco to Liga Central, AGEY AM Motul caja 26.

51. *Diario del sureste*, 5 December, 20 December 1934; Chalé to Alayola, 6 December 1934, AGEY PE 983 SG 1.

52. Adriano Solís to governor, 19 November 1934, AGEY PE 981 SG 1; *Diario del sureste*, 12 December 1934; Rogerio Chalé and Manuel Montes de Oca, letter, *Diario del sureste*, 11 January 1935.

53. Humberto Lara y Lara, *Sobre la trayectoria de la reforma agraria en Yucatán* (Mérida: Biblioteca Central, 1949), 30; *Diario del sureste*, 21 May 1935, 24 May 1936; Luciano May to Candelario Reyes, 17 December 1934, AGEY PE 981 SG 1; Jose Cornelio Lara Tec and Edelmiro Vargas Canul, interview with author, 23 May 1935.

54. *Diario del sureste*, 2, 9, 14 March, 20 April 1935; Rogerio Chalé, letter, *Diario del sureste*, 2 March 1935.

55. Pedro Cruz et al. to governor, 13 December 1934, AGEY PE 1004 SG 1.

56. Sierra and Paoli, *Cárdenas*, 67, 88; Antonio Betancourt Pérez, interview with author, 6 November 1994.

57. *Diario del sureste*, 20 November 1935, 19 February 1936.

58. Teodoro Azueta to governor, 8 March 1936, AGEY PE 1013 SG 1; General Francisco Mújica, memorandum, 23 July 1936, AGN LC 404.1/12 leg. 2; agreement signed by LTAH et al., Mérida, 17 June 1936, AGEY PE 1018; *Diario del sureste*, 1, 3, 24 October, 19 November 1935; 14, 27 January, 15, 25 February, 16 March, 5 May, 19, 24, 26 June 1936; *Diario de Yucatán*, 26 May 1935, 11 January, 21 February, 27 March, 20 June 1936.

59. *Sindicato* of Tebec to mayor, 17 May 1937, MA Izamal caja 35 leg. 56 exp. 1; AGN LC 432.2/245.

60. Wells and Joseph, 287–89; Gilbert M. Joseph and Allen Wells, "The Rough-and-Tumble Career of Pedro Crespo," in *The Human Tradition in Latin America: The Twentieth Century,* ed. William H. Beezley and Judith Ewell (Wilmington, Del.: Scholarly Resources, 1987), 27–40.

61. *Diario del sureste,* 14 April, 27 August, 12 November 1938, 9 May, 12 June 1939.

62. AGEY PE 1044.

63. *Diario de Yucatán,* 7 July 1936; *Diario del sureste,* 26 August 1936; AGN 2.311M vol. 85 exp. 17.

64. *Diario del sureste,* 2 January 1936; Candelario Reyes to Carlos M. Peralta, 11 January 1936, AGN LC 404.1/12-1.

65. *Diario del sureste,* 13 December 1935.

66. Ibid.

67. *Diario oficial,* 14 October 1935.

68. *Diario del sureste,* 6 December 1935.

69. Candelario Reyes to governor, 16 May 1936, AGEY PE 1022 SG 1.

70. *Diario del sureste,* 18 January, 19 February 1936.

71. *Diario del sureste,* 19 February 1936.

72. *Diario del sureste,* 30, 31 October 1935; Askinasy, *Problema agrario,* 61–62.

73. *Diario del sureste,* 31 October, 1, 3 November 1935.

74. Jovino Serna to president, 30 October 1935, and Fernando Amilpa and Rubén Magaña to president, 4 November 1935, AGEY PE 1005 SG 1.

75. *Diario del sureste,* 13, 22 December 1935.

76. Askinasy, *Problema agrario,* 70–71.

77. *Diario del sureste,* 31 October, 1, 5 November 1935; Adriano Solís Quintal to secretary of the interior, 31 October 1935, AGN DGG 2.317.4 vol. 71 exp. 9; Arcadio Lizarraga to governor, AGEY PE 992 SG 2; Luis Rodríguez to Efrain Buenrostro, 10 November 1935, AGN LC 543.1/30 leg. 2.

78. Candelario Reyes to governor, 12 October 1935, AGEY PE 1004 SG 1.

79. Various correspondence from AGN LC 404.1/12-1 leg. 2.

80. *Diario de Yucatán,* 1 January 1937; *Diario del sureste,* 8, 11 January 1936.

81. Candelario Reyes to López Cárdenas, 6 December 1935, and chief of judicial police to governor, 6 February 1936, AGEY PE 1022 SG 1.

82. *Diario de Yucatán,* 13 March, 14 June 1936.

83. Roland Chardon, "Some Geographic Aspects of Plantation Agriculture in Yucatan" (Ph.D. diss., University of Minnesota, 1961), 260–64.

84. *Diario del sureste,* 4 December 1935; Candelario Reyes to Governor Palomo, 27 July 1936, AGEY PE 1013 SG 1.

85. Sierra and Paoli, *Cárdenas,* 69; Urban Tah et al. to president, 26 December 1936, AGN DGG 2.311M vol. 85 exp. 21; Candelario Reyes to López Cárdenas, 21 October 1935, AGEY PE 1004 SG 1.

86. *Diario de Yucatán,* 8 May 1936.

87. Paulino Zúñiga et al. to president, 15 December 1935, AGN LC 404.1/12-1 leg. 2.

88. Chardon, "Geographic Aspects," 262–64.

89. *Diario de Yucatán,* 14 April 1936.

90. *Diario del sureste,* 11 December 1935, 26 January 1936; Reyes to Peralta, 11 January 1936, AGN LC 404.1/12-1.

91. Gustavo Molina Font et al. to president, 25 May 1936, AGN LC 404.1/12-1 leg. 2.

92. Fallaw, "Cárdenas," 569–74.
93. Candelario Reyes to Carlos M. Peralta, 11 January 1936, AGN LC 404.1/12-1.
94. Ibid.
95. Candelario Reyes to López Cárdenas, 13 January 1936, AGEY PE 1022 SG 1.
96. López Cárdenas to Luis I. Rodríguez, 9 April 1936, AGN LC 404.1/12-1 leg. 2.
97. *Diario de Yucatán,* 16 April 1936; *Diario del sureste,* 23 April 1936.
98. Circular dated 25 May 1936, AGEY PE 1016 SG 1.

3   Cardenismo in Crisis: Gualbertismo, the Fall of López Cárdenas, and the Rise of the Official Camarilla

1.   Adrian Bantjes, "Politics, Class, and Culture in Post-Revolutionary Mexico: Cardenismo and Sonora, 1929–1940" (Ph.D. diss., University of Texas, 1991), 563–64.
2.   Joseph, *Revolution from Without;* Paoli and Montalvo, *Socialismo olvidado.*
3.   Ilene O'Malley, *The Myth of the Revolution: Hero Cults and the Institutionalization of the Mexican State, 1920–1940* (New York: Greenwood, 1986).
4.   Samuel Brunk, "Remembering Emiliano Zapata: Three Moments in the Posthumous Career of the Martyr of Chinameca," *Hispanic American Historical Review* 78, no. 3 (August 1998): 457–90. Joseph (*Revolution from Without,* 285–87) first compared Zapata to Carrillo Puerto.
5.   Luis F. Mangas, Gualberto Carrillo Puerto, and José Luis Novelo, *Tercer Congreso Obrero del PSS: Proyectos relacionados con el Tema V Organización del PSS* (Mérida: Basso, 1930).
6.   Gualberto Carrillo Puerto to Plutarco Elías Calles, 30 June 1930, APEC "Diario de Yucatán" gav. 23 exp. 19 inv. 1485.
7.   Aurelio Velázquez, "Memorándum: Política electoral en Yucatán," 17 June 1937, AGEY PE 1022 SG 2; Acrelio Carrillo Puerto, *La familia Carrillo Puerto de Motul, con la Revolución mexicana* (Mérida, 1959), 81–82; Cardos Ruz, *Drama,* 248–51; Gualberto Carrillo to President Cárdenas, 4 August 1937, AGN LC 404.1/12 caja 201 leg. 4; *Diario de Yucatán,* 3 August 1937.
8.   Gualberto Carrillo Puerto to Lázaro Cárdenas, 6 April 1935, AGN LC 565.4/66, 26 May 1935, AGN LC 404.1/12-1 leg. 1, 23 October 1935, AGN LC 565.4/66.
9.   Poster, "Hechos, no palabras," AGN LC 544.2/30; "Manifiesto a los obreros y campesinos del estado," Mérida, 12 September 1937, AGN LC 544.2/3; *Diario de Yucatán,* 6 August 1937.
10. I must acknowledge Friedrich Katz for pointing out the tradition of the hermanos incomodos to me. On Hipólito Villa, see Friedrich Katz, *The Life and Times of Pancho Villa* (Stanford, Calif.: Stanford University Press, 1998), 268–69. On Eufemio Zapata, see Samuel Brunk, *Emiliano Zapata: Revolution and Betrayal in Mexico* (Albuquerque: University of New Mexico Press, 1995), 207–8; and John Womack, *Zapata and the Mexican Revolution* (New York: Knopf, 1968), 287. On Dámaso Cárdenas, see Gledhill, *Casi Nada.*
11. Hernán Morales Medina, interview with author, 7 June 1993; Antonio Betancourt Pérez, interview with author, 6 November 1994; Aurelio Velázquez, "Memorándum: Política," 17 June 1937, AGEY PE 1022 SG 2; Aldo Baroni, *Yucatán* (Mexico City: Botas, 1938), 124; Alvaro Pérez Alpuche to Lázaro Cárdenas, 19 October 1937, AGN LC 544.2/30; Confidential Inspector V-22 to Chief, 22 October 1937, AGN DGG 2.311G vol. 340 exp. 2.

12. *El Yucatanista,* 27 June 1933; *La metralla,* 25 September, 2 October 1937; Jesús Amaro Gamboa, *Vocabulario del Uayeismo en la cultura de Yucatán* (Mérida: Universidad Autónoma de Yucatán, 1985), 2:9.

13. *El fenix,* July 1925; E. Guerra Leal to President Cárdenas and Alvaro Pérez Alpuche to Lázaro Cárdenas, 19 October 1937, AGN LC 544.2/30; Baroni, *Yucatán,* 129; *La metralla,* 2 October 1937.

14. Gualberto Carrillo Puerto to Cárdenas, 23 October 1935, AGN LC 437/136; act of state congress, 26 May 1935; attached to López Cárdenas to Luis Rodríguez, 26 May 1935, AGN LC 544.3/30; Gualberto Carrillo to President Cárdenas, 12 November 1935, AGN LC 404.1/12; *Diario del sureste, 5,* 19 October 1937; *Diario de Yucatán,* 16 June, 13 July, 19 September 1937; Confidential Inspector v-22 to Chief, 27 October 1937, AGN DGG 2.311G vol. 340 exp. 2.

15. Betancourt, *Memorías,* 133; Sierra and Paoli, *Cárdenas,* 41–42, 99–102. My first essay on Cardenista Yucatán reflects a similar, erroneous view of Gualberto Carrillo Puerto (see Fallaw, "Rogerio Chalé: El líder caído," *Unicornio* 3:119 (4 July 1993): 3–10.

16. Lomnitz-Adler, *Exits from the Labyrinth.*

17. Marcial Sayavedro to secretary of interior, 20 April 1936, AGN DGG 2.311S(27) vol. 120 exp. 1. On Chalé's murder, see *Diario del sureste,* 24 July 1938.

18. Matthew C. Guttman, *The Meanings of Macho: Being a Man in Mexico City* (Berkeley and Los Angeles: University of California Press, 1996); Roger N. Lancaster, *Life Is Hard: Machismo, Danger, and the Intimacy of Power in Nicaragua* (Berkeley and Los Angeles: University of California Press, 1992).

19. Katz, *Pancho Villa,* 239–40.

20. Gualberto Carrillo Puerto to president, 8 April 1933, AGN DGG 2.311G(27)2 vol. 338 tomo I; Elvia Carrillo Puerto and Felipe Villamil to secretary of the interior, 20 June 1933, AGN DGG 2.311G(27)2 vol. 338 tomo II.

21. *Diario de Yucatán,* 9 August 1934; Gualberto Carrillo Puerto to Lázaro Cárdenas, 29 April 1936, AGN DGG 2.311S vol. 120 exp. 1.

22. *Diario del sureste, 5* October 1937.

23. *Diario del sureste,* 9 April 1934.

24. Schreyer, *Rancheros.*

25. B. Moreno and Pedro Sosa Leal to President Cárdenas, 23 March 1936, AGN DGG 2.311S vol. 120 exp. 1; Saturnino Cortés to Governor Alayola, 22 September 1934, AGEY PE 992; *Diario de Yucatán,* 3 August 1937.

26. *Diario de Yucatán,* 2 September 1937; Menéndez, *Directorio general,* 274.

27. Leonardo Díaz et al. to governor, 12 October 1934, AGEY PE 1007; petition dated 10 July 1936, AGN DGG 2.317.4 vol. 71 exp. 19.

28. *Diario de Yucatán,* 13 February 1936.

29. Governor López Cárdenas to Luis I. Rodríguez, 16 May 1936, AGN LC 404.1/12-1 leg. 2; Julio Chan to President Cárdenas, 30 April 1936, AGN LC 544.3/30; Elpidio López Villareal to President Cárdenas, 20 May 1936, AGN LC 544.3/30; Aurelio Velázquez and Mauro López C. to President Cárdenas, n.d., AGN LC 544.3/30.

30. Fallaw, "Life and Three Deaths"; Martín Luis Guzmán "Maestros Rurales," in *Obras Completas de Martín Luis Guzmán* (Mexico City: Compania General de Ediciones, 1971); Jesús Solís Alpuche, "El asesinato de Felipa Poot," *Diario del sureste,* 20, 21, 25–28, 31 March and 1–9 April 1986.

31. Ricardo Marín to president and Ricardo Cáceres to president, 3 February 1936, AGN LC 543.1/30 leg. 2; E. Beltrán to governor, 7 March 1936, AGEY PE 1013 SG 1; Rafael Cebada to secretary of the interior, 23 March 1936, AGN DGG 2.311S vol. 120 exp. 1; *Diario de Yucatán,* 29 January 1936, 10, 18 March 1936; *Diario del sureste,* 11 March 1936.

32. Candelario Reyes to governor, 16 May 1936, AGEY PE 1022 SG 1; Nicolas González et al. to director of the Agrarian Bank, AGEY PE 1022 SG 1; memorandum of chief of staff, 6 April 1936, AGEY MA Izamal caja 34; Alberto Cauich et al. to interior secretary, 28 March 1936, AGEY DGG 2.311G vol. 340 exp. 1; Catalino Pech et al. to President Cárdenas, 18 March 1936, AGN LC 544.3/30; *Diario del sureste,* 19 February 1936; *Diario de Yucatán,* 26 May 1936.

33. Charles Macfarland, *Chaos in Mexico: The Conflict of Church and State* (New York: Harper and Brothers, 1935), 44–45; Raquel Sosa Elízaga, *Los códigos ocultos del Cardenismo: Un estudio de la violencia política, el cambio social, y la continuidad institucional* (Mexico City: Universidad Nacional Autónoma de México and Plaza y Valdés, 1996), 79.

34. Candelario Reyes, *Apuntes para la historia de Tamaulipas en los siglos XVI y XVII* (Mexico City: Talleres Gráficos Laguna, 1944), 8.

35. *Diario de Yucatán,* 7 April 1936.

36. *Diario del sureste,* 21 May 1936; *Diario de Yucatán,* 21 May 1936.

37. *Diario de Yucatán,* 15 June 1936.

38. *Diario del sureste,* 26 June 1936; Gonzalo López Manzanero to President Cárdenas, 27 May 1936, AGN LC 544.3/30.

39. Sierra and Paoli, *Cárdenas,* 65.

40. Fernando López Cárdenas, *Revolucionarios contra la Revolucion* (Mexico: Lóndres, 1938), 40–41; General Francisco Mújica, memorandum, 23 July 1936, AGN LC 404.1/12 leg. 2; *Diccionario biográfico histórico,* Diccionario Histórico y Biográfico de la Revolución Mexicana Tomo VII (Mexico City: Instituto Nacional de Estudios Históricos de la Revolución Mexicana and Secretaría de Gobernación, 1990), 563; *Diario de Yucatán,* 21 March 1934; Echeverría, *Educación,* 19; Don Luis, *Florencio Papalomo Valencia, ¡¡ Gobernador ?? o Mi-Mi reyno por un ca-caballo: Comedia dramático-historica en un acto e infinidad de cuadros* (Mérida, 1937), 13.

41. Mújica, memorandum, 23 July 1936, AGN LC 404.1/12 leg. 2.

42. Diego M. Rosado to president, 18 August 1936, and Rogerio Chalé to president, 27 August 36, quoted in López Cárdenas, *Revolucionarios,* 129–35, 142; *Diario de Yucatán,* 14 March 1936.

43. Mújica, memorandum, 23 July 1936, AGN LC 404.1/12 leg. 2; FROC to President Cárdenas, 27 August 1936, quoted in López Cárdenas, *Revolucionarios,* 142; AGN LC 432/219; *Diario de Yucatán,* 5, 8 March, 19 April 1936; *Diario del sureste,* 7 March 1936.

44. *Diario de Yucatán,* 19, 22, 26 April, 5 May 1936; Uribe Gómez to President Cárdenas, 27 August 1936, reprinted in López Cárdenas, *Revolucionarios,* 142.

45. *Diario de Yucatán,* 28 April, 3, 12, 25 May 1936.

46. Domínguez, *Historia,* 49–50.

47. Nicolas Pech to president, 12 February 1936, AGN LC 404.1/12-1 leg. 2.

48. *Diario de Yucatán,* 18 July 1936; various correspondence from AGN LC 404.1/12 leg. 2.

49. AGN LC 432/30; Vicente Lombardo Toledano, *El llanto del sureste,* 2d ed. (México: CEHSMO, 1977); *Diario de Yucatán,* 21 February, 19, 28, 29 April, 12 May 1936; *Diario del sureste,* 22 February 1936.

50. *Diario del sureste* and *Diario de Yucatán,* 9–15 May, 1, 7, 14 June 1936; Mújica, memorandum, 23 July 1936, AGN LC 404.1/12 leg. 2.

51. *Diario de Yucatán,* 29 April, 1, 6, 8, 12, 24 May 1936.

52. *Diario de Yucatán,* 12 May, 3, 6, 9, 11, 14 July 1936; *Diario del sureste,* 29 July 1936; Macedonio Poot et al. to governor, 23 September 1936, and Liborio Kú et al. to governor, 26 September 1936, AGEY PE 1014.

53. Various correspondence from AGEY PE 1044; *Diario de Yucatán,* 28 March, 28 June, 12 July 1936; Antonio Aranda to governor, 18 May 1936, AGN DGG 2.311S(27) 13783 vol. 120 exp. 1; *El universal,* 3 July 1936.

54. *Diario de Yucatán,* 12, 14, 17 May, 1, 28, 30 June 1936.

55. *Diario del sureste,* 1 July 1936; *Diario de Yucatán,* 1 July 1936.

56. AGN LC 432/80 and 543.1/30; *Diario del sureste,* 30 June 1936; Betancourt, *Memorías,* 108.

57. *Diario de Yucatán,* 1, 2, 4 July 1936; Betancourt, *Memorías,* 107–10; AGN LC 432/80; Luis Amendolla, *La revolución comienza en los cuarentos* (Mexico City, n.p., n.d.), 231–32.

58. *Diario de Yucatán,* 1 July 1936.

59. AGN LC 432/80; Betancourt, *Memorías,* 100; Antonio Betancourt Pérez, "Se consuma la tración," reprinted in Bernardino Mena Brito, *Reestructuración histórica de Yucatán,* 3 vols. (Mexico City: Mexicanos Unidos, 1969), 3:344–50; Don Luis, *Florencio Papalomo Valencia,* 25–27.

60. López Cárdenas, *Revolucionarios,* 45–56.

61. *Diario de Yucatán,* 2 July 1936; Betancourt, "Se consuma"; López Cárdenas, *Revolucionarios,* Don Luis, *Florencio Papalomo Valencia,* 11, 27; Amendolla, *Revolución,* 232; AGN LC 544.2/30; *La metralla,* 25 September 1937.

62. Rodolfo López Sosa, *Tarjeta presidencial* (Mérida: Guerra, 1952), 50.

63. Florencio Palomo Valencia, *Los ejidos de Yucatán y el henequén* (Mexico City: Pedro Robledo, 1934); Sierra and Paoli, *Cárdenas,* 61; López Cárdenas, *Revolucionarios,* 22–24; *Diario de Yucatán,* 1 April 1936.

64. Benítez, *Kí,* 154; Baroni, *Yucatán,* 105, 130.

65. *Diario de Yucatán,* 25 November, 17 December 1936, 1 April 1937; López Cárdenas, *Revolucionarios,* 112–13; Sierra and Paoli, *Cárdenas,* 99; Villanueva Mukul, *Así tomamos,* 47–48.

66. Chalé to President Cárdenas, reprinted in López Cárdenas, *Revolucionarios,* 141–42.

67. Betancourt, *Memorías,* 109–11, 118; Manuel Ríos Thivol, "Resumen analítico de las elecciones internas del PNR, efectuadas el 4 de April último en esta entidad," 23 June 1937, AGN DGG 2, 311G vol. 339 15757; AGN LC 544.2/30; *Diario de Yucatán,* 7, 8 July, 3, 24 December 1936; *Diario del sureste,* 13, 24 March, 10, 16, 19, 21 August, 31 December 1936, 11 January, 9 July 1937.

68. Fallaw, "Chalé"; *Diario del sureste,* 28 September, 11 December 1936, 4 February 1937.

69. Reinaldo Ricalde G. to governor, 21 October 1937, AGN DGG 2.311G vol. 340 exp. 2.

70. *Diario de Yucatán,* 7, 28 July, 8 August 1936, 14, 15 April 1937; Luis Rodríguez to Silvano Barba G., 24 November 1936, AGN LC 544.5/72.

71. *Diario del sureste,* 31 December 1936, 13 March, 11 May, 28 August 1937; Jaime Orosa Díaz, *Legislación henequenera en Yucatán,* 4 vols. (Mérida: Universidad de Yucatán, 1962), 4:309–11; Palomo Valencia to Silvano Barba G., 7 July 1937, AGEY PE 1022 SG 2.

72. Carlos M. Peralta, "Apuntes," 9 September 1939, AGN LC 404.1/12 caja 201 leg. 9; Catalino Pech et al. of Izamal to President Cárdenas, 18 March 1936, AGN LC 544.3/30;

Candelario Reyes to Carlos M. Peralta, 11 January 1936, AGN LC 404.1/12-1 leg. 1; *Diario de Yucatán,* 3 October 1936, 27 March, 26 August 1937; *Diario del sureste,* 4 April, 23 June 1936, 4 September 1937; *Menzay,* November 1936.

73. *Diario de Yucatán,* 25 April, 3 May 1937.

74. *Diario del sureste,* 16 August 1937.

75. Candelario Reyes to Lázaro Cárdenas, 27 September 1937, AGN LC 404.1/12 caja 201 leg. 3; Ramón Aviléz C. to National PNR, 28 August 1936, AGN DGG 2.311 vol. 85 exp. 7; *Diario de Yucatán,* 27, 30 March 1937; *Diario del sureste,* 12 January 1937.

76. *Diario del sureste,* 28 July, 7 August, 31 December 1936; *Diario de Yucatán,* 8 July 1936; Mújica, memorandum, 23 July 1936, AGN LC 404.1/12 leg. 2.

4   The Crusade of the Mayab: Cardenismo from Above

1. *Diario de Yucatán,* 17 August 1937; AGEY 1068 sec. Hoctun.

2. *Diario de Yucatán,* 22 February 1937; *Diario del sureste,* 10 October 1937; AGEY PE 1068 sec. Kanasín.

3. Andrés Molina Enríquez, Felix F. Palavicini, and Enrique González Aparicio, *El ejido en Yucatán* (Mexico City: Mexico Nuevo, 1937), 5–6.

4. PNR, *La reforma agraria en Yucatán* (Mexico City: Talleres de "El Nacional," 1937); Lara y Lara, *Trayectoria,* 27–28; *Diario del sureste,* 9 August 1937; Humberto Canto Echeverría, "Estudio sobre la situación real de los ejidos henequeneros de Yucatán," 31 July 1939, AGN LC 404.1/12 caja 201 leg. 2.

5. PNR, *Reforma,* 9; Humberto Canto Echeverría, "Estudio sobre la situación real de los ejidos henequeneros de Yucatán," 31 July 1939, AGN LC 404.1/12 caja 201 leg. 2; *Diario del sureste,* 10, 11 September 1937.

6. PNR, *El ejido en Yucatán* (Mérida: Gobierno del Estado, 1937), 19.

7. My calculations are based on reports in *Diario del sureste* issued during the Crusade of the Mayab. PNR, *Reforma,* 35, claimed that the crusade created seventy, not fifty-six, ejidos, with 8,408, not 8,091, recipients.

   The exclusion of women from ejidal grants points to a basic contradiction in Cardenista views of women. While Cárdenas supported the vote for women, there was apparently no serious consideration of granting them the right to petition for land. While political liberation was part of the Cardenista project for women, they were to remain under the economic authority of their husbands.

8. Carlos M. Peralta, "Apuntes asunto de Yucatán: Introducción: Algunos antecedentes," 9 September 1939, AGN LC 404.1/12 caja 201 leg. 9; Humberto Canto Echeverría, "Estudio sobre la situación real de los ejidos henequeneros de Yucatán," 31 July 1939, AGN LC 404.1/12 caja 201 leg. 2; *Diario del sureste,* 29 December 1937; Fidencio Canul et al. to president, 28 August 1937, AGN LC 403/422.

9. *Genesis y formacion de henequeneros de Yucatán* (Mexico City: Al Servicio del Pueblo, 1938), 61.

10. Othón Baños Ramírez, *Neoliberalismo, reorganizacion, y subsistencia rural: El caso de la zona henequenera de Yucatán, 1980–1992* (Mérida: Universidad Autónoma de Yucatán, 1996), 119.

11. Lara y Lara, *Trayectoria,* 29; Canto Echeverría, "Estudio."

12. *Diario del sureste,* 3 September 1937, 7 January 1938.

13. Canto Echeverría, "Estudio"; General Benignos to President Cárdenas, 17 December 1937, AGN LC 404.1/12 caja 201 leg. 7.

14. Gabino Vázquez to Alayola Barrera, AGN LC 404.1/12-1 leg. 1; Candelario Reyes to Alayola Barrera, 3 October 1935, AGEY PE 1005 SG 1.

15. Escoffie, *¡Ya!* 252; Amendolla, *Revolución,* 233.

16. *Diario del sureste,* 4 September 1937; Carlos M. Peralta, "Apuntes asunto de Yucatán: Introducción: Algunos antecedentes," 9 September 1939, AGN LC 404.1/12 caja 201 leg. 9.

17. Candelario Reyes to Presidente Lázaro Cárdenas, 27 September 1937, AGN LC 404.1/12 caja 201 leg. 3; General Benignos to President Cárdenas, 17 December 1937, AGN LC 404.1/12 caja 201 leg. 7.

18. Chief of staff to attorney general, 5, 21, 23 October 1937, AGEY PE 1031 SG 2; *Diario de Yucatán,* 5 October 1937.

19. Carrillo Puerto, *Familia,* 156. *Diario del sureste,* 3 September 1937.

20. Juan de Dios Rodríguez H., *La contra-reforma agrarian en Yucatán* (n.p.: Sociedad Yucateca Andrés Quintana Roo, 1944), 18.

21. AGEY PE 1030 Sec. CLA; Lapointe, "Estado."

22. Adolfo Gilly, *El Cardenismo, una utopía mexicana* (Mexico: Cal y Arena, 1994), 212–14.

23. Edmundo Bolio Ontiveros, *Yucatán (perspectivas económicas)* (Mexico City: DAPP, 1937), 16.

24. Gamaliel Cante Canul, *La situación actual del ejidatario henequenero Maya de X-Tep'en, Yucatán* (Mexico City: SEP/INI, 1982), 134–35.

25. *Primera Convención de Sociedades Locales de los Comisariados Ejidales* (Mérida, 1937), 70.

26. *Diario del sureste,* 16, 17 August 1937; *Diario de Yucatán,* 16, 17 August 1937; Baroni, *Yucatán,* 123–25; *Primera Convención.*

27. *Diario del sureste,* 17 August 1937; *Diario de Yucatán,* 17 August 1937.

28. Baroni, *Yucatán,* 123–25.

29. *Diario de Yucatán,* 17 August 1937.

30. Ibid.

31. *Primera Convención,* 25, 29.

32. *Diario del sureste,* 17 August 1937.

33. Schuler, *Mexico between Hitler and Roosevelt,* 63–64.

34. Gustavo Molina Font, *La tragedia de Yucatán,* 2d ed. (Mexico City: Revista de Derecho y Ciencias Sociales Mexico, 1941), 125.

35. Baroni, *Yucatán,* 145–47.

36. Ibid., 151.

37. *Menzay,* September 1937.

38. *Diario del sureste,* 22 January 1937.

39. *Diario de Yucatán,* 23 August 1937.

40. Becker, *Virgin,* 104–5.

41. *Menzay,* September 1937, 4–5.

42. *Diario de Yucatán,* 23 August 1937.

43. Albert L. Michael, "The Modification of the Anti-Clerical Nationalism of the Mexican Revolution by General Lázaro Cárdenas and Its Relationship to the Church-State Detente in Mexico," *The Americas* 26 (1969): 37–46.

44. Vaughan, *Cultural Politics;* Rockwell, "Schools"; John Britton, "Teacher Unionization and the Corporate State in Mexico," *Hispanic American Historical Review* 59, no. 4

(1979): 674–90. On federal schooling in Yucatán during the Cardenista era, see Ben Fallaw, "Antonio Betancourt Pérez, la educación, y la izquierda en Yucatán, 1931–1937," *Unicornio,* 13, 20, 27 February 2000, 3–9.

45. *Menzay,* special ed., September 1937, 11, 21, 25.

46. On the importance of ceremonies in the postrevolutionary state-formation project, see Vaughan, "Construction."

47. Heidi Tinsman, "Household Patrones: Wife-Beating and Sexual Control in Rural Chile, 1964–1988," in *The Gendered Worlds of Latin American Women Workers,* ed. John D. French and Daniel James (Durham, N.C.: Duke University Press, 1997), 274–79.

48. Jeffrey Pilcher, *¡Que vivan los tamales!: Food and the Making of Mexican Identity* (Albuquerque: University of New Mexico Press), 109.

49. *Diario de Yucatán,* 15, 17 September 1937.

50. Jefe of the Departmento de Asuntos Indígenas to governor, 18 December 1936, and Jefe of the Oficina Cultura Indígena, Professor Eusebio Sánchez, to governor, 8 September 1937, AGEY PE 1016 sec. Chuburná.

51. *Diario del sureste,* 22 August 1937.

52. *Diario de Yucatán,* 20 August 1937.

53. *Diario de Yucatán,* 9 September, 26 August 1937.

54. *Diario de Yucatán,* 18 August 1937.

55. *Diario de Yucatán,* 14 August 1937.

56. *Diario de Yucatán,* 19 January, 10 October 1936.

57. AGEY, MA Izamal, caja 34, exp. 3.

58. *Diario de Yucatán,* 22 July, 10, 12 October, 13 December 1936.

59. *Diario de Yucatán,* 30 August, 3 September 1936.

60. *Diario de Yucatán,* 6 March 1936.

61. AGEY, MA Izamal, caja 34, exp. 3, 28 May 1936.

62. *Diario de Yucatán,* 27 March 1936.

63. *Diario de Yucatán,* 1 May 1936.

64. *Diario de Yucatán,* 30 May, 2 June 1937; *Diario del sureste,* 20 June 1937; interim mayor of Tizimín to governor, 22 June 1937, AGEY PE 1022 SG 1.

65. Pedro España to governor, 15 February 1937, AGEY PE 1020 SG 1.

66. *Diario del sureste,* 20, 28 April, 9 June 1937.

67. Prohibition has received very little scholarly attention outside Chiapas. See Jan Rus, "The 'Communidad Revolucionaria Institucional': The Subversion of Native Government in Highland Chiapas, 1936–1968," in Joseph and Nugent, eds., *Everyday Forms;* Stephen E. Lewis, "Chiapas' Alcohol Monopoly versus the National Indigenous Institute (INI): Lessons from a 1950s Clash between State and Federal Forces" (paper presented at the Latin American Studies Association congress, Chicago, September 1998).

5 *Alliance Failed: Cárdenas, Urban Labor, and the Open Door Election of 1937*

1. PNR, *Memoria,* 15.

2. AGN DGG 2.311S vol. 120 exp. 1.

3. Baroni, *Yucatán,* 128.

4. *Diario de Yucatán,* 7, 9, 12 September 1937; President Cárdenas to Silvano Barba G.,

24 August 1937, and Silvano Barba G. to President Cárdenas, 6, 9 September 1937, AGN LC 544.2/30.

5. *Diario del sureste,* 13 September 1937.

6. *Diario de Yucatán,* 9 October 1937.

7. Hernán Bautista to President Cárdenas, 2 October 1937, AGN DGG 2.311G vol. 339 anexa 15757; various correspondence from AGN DGG 2.311G vol. 340 exp. 2; AGN LC 544.2/30; AGEY PE 1018 SG 1.

8. *Diario de Yucatán,* 6 August 1937.

9. *Diario de Yucatán,* 19, 22 June 1937.

10. Gualberto Carrillo to President Cárdenas, 4 August 1937, AGN LC 404.1/12 caja 201 leg. 4; A. Escalante et al. to President Cárdenas, 18 October 1937, AGN DGG vol. 340 exp. 2; *Diario de Yucatán,* 24 June, 3, 6, 17 August, 9 September 1937; photo found in AGN LC 544.2/30.

11. *Diario del sureste,* 17 October, 27 September 1937; *Diario de Yucatán,* 6 August 1937; Isidro Chi et al. to President Cárdenas, 17 October 1937; AGN DGG 2.311G vol. 340 exp. 2; Gualberto Carrillo Puerto to Ignacio García Tellez, 5 October 1937, AGN LC 544.2/30; Máximo Pech to President Cárdenas, 24 September 1937, AGN DGG 2.311G vol. 339 anexa 15757 tomo II; Candelario Reyes to Lázaro Cárdenas, 27 September 1937, AGN LC 404.1/12 leg. 2.

12. AGN DGG 2.311G vol. 339 anexa 15757 tomo II; Esteban Medina et al. to President Cárdenas, 15 October 1937, AGN DGG 2.311G vol. 340 exp. 3; Alvaro Pérez Alpuche to Lázaro Cárdenas, 19 October 1937, AGN LC 544.2/30; Mayor Mérida to Miguel Lara Arcique, 6 January, AGEY MA Izamal caja 36 leg. 5 exp. 1; *Diario de Yucatán,* 24 June, 3 August 1937.

13. *Diario de Yucatán,* 12, 13 September 1937.

14. *Diario de Yucatán,* 24 June, 9, 24, 28, 30 September, 3 October 1937; Alvaro Pérez Alpuche to President Cárdenas, 19 October 1937, AGN LC 544.2/30; Renán Ricalde to governor, 21 October 1937, AGN DGG 2.311G vol. 340 exp. 2; Benito Bé to governor, 29 June 1937, AGEY PE 1031 SG 1; Alfredo Loría to governor, 10 May 1937, AGEY PE 1044 SG 1; mayor of Mérida to Miguel Lara Arcique, 6 January, AGEY MA Izamal caja 36 leg. 5 exp. 1.

15. Poster entitled "Hechos, no palabras" found in AGN LC 544.2/30; Emilio Guerra Leal to President Cárdenas, AGN DGG 2.311G vol. 340 exp. 1; Alvaro Pérez Alpuche to President Cárdenas, 19 October 1937, AGN LC 544.2/30; Confidential Inspector V-22 to Chief, 27 October 1937, AGN DGG 2.311G vol. 340 exp. 2; *Diario del sureste,* 19 October 1937.

16. *Diario de Yucatán,* 30 September 1937.

17. Inspector V-22 to Chief, 6 November 1937, AGN DGG 2.311G vol. 340 tomo II exp. 2.

18. Gualberto Carrillo to President Cárdenas, 5 October 1937, AGN LC 544.2/30; Eduardo Pech to President Cárdenas, 11 October 1937, AGN DGG 2.311G vol. 339 tomo II; *Diario del sureste,* 10 October 1937.

19. Inspector V-22 to Chief, 6 November 1937, AGN DGG 2.311G vol. 340 tomo II exp. 2; Valeria Arroyo de Rivero to President Cárdenas, 8 October 1937, AGN DGG 2.311G vol. 340 exp. 1; Central Committee pro–Cebada Tenreiro to President Cárdenas, 13 October 1937, AGN DGG 2.311G vol. 340 tomo II exp. 1; Emilio López to President Cárdenas, 4 November 1937, AGN DGG 2.311G vol. 340 exp. 2; Rafael Cebada Tenreiro to President Cárdenas, 2 November 1937, AGN LC 544.2/30; *Diario de Yucatán,* 16 October 1937.

20. AGN DGG 2.311G vol. 339 tomo II; Francisco Vázquez to governor, 22 September 1937, AGEY PE 1027 SG 1.

21. *Diario del sureste,* 6, 16 October 1937; *La metralla,* 2 October 1937; Francisco Vázquez to governor, 22 September 1937, AGEY PE 1027 SG 1; Emilio Guerra to President Cárdenas, n.d., Manuel Peraza to president, 4 October 1937, and Renán Ricalde G. to general delegate of the PNR, 12 October 1937, AGN LC 544.2/30; Máximo Pech to President Cárdenas, 24 September 1937, chief of staff to secretary of the interior, 27 September 1937, and Hernán Bautista to President Cárdenas, 2 October 1937, AGN DGG 2.311G vol. 339 anexa 15757; Emilio Guerra L. to President Cárdenas, 30 November 1937, and Renán Ricalde to governor, 21 October 1937, AGN DGG 2.311G vol. 340 exp. 2.

22. *Diario de Yucatán,* 2 September 1937; chief of staff to Mayor of Tixkokob, 27 September 1937, and Laureano Maas to President Cárdenas, 13 October 1937, AGEY PE 1027 SG 1; Gualberto Carrillo P. to Ignacio García Téllez, 5 October 1937, and Gaston Ariel Castillo et al. to President Cárdenas; and various correspondence from AGN DGG 2.311G vol. 339.

23. Rafael Aguilar Rosas to attorney general, 30 June 1937, and Inspector Ríos Thivol to governor, 21 June 1937, AGEY PE 1031 SG 1; Alfredo Loría to governor, 9 July 1937, AGEY PE 1044 SG 1; *Diario de Yucatán,* 19 September 1937; Eutimio Osorio et al. to President Cárdenas, AGEY PE 1027 SG 1; Juan Esparza to President Cárdenas, 14 October 1937, and Miguel Pérez to President Cárdenas, 14 October 1937, AGN DGG 2.311G vol. 340 exp. 1.

24. Esteban Medina et al. to President Cárdenas, 15 October 1937, AGN DGG 2.311G vol. 340 exp. 3; Máximo Pech to President Cárdenas, 24 September 1937, AGN DGG 2.311G vol. 339 anexa 15757 tomo II.

25. Hernán Bautista to President Cárdenas, 2 October 1937, AGN DGG 2.311G vol. 339 anexa 15757; Alvaro Pérez Alpuche to President Cárdenas, 19 October 1937, AGN LC 544.2/30.

26. AGN DGG 2.311G vol. 339 tomo II; *Diario de Yucatán,* 5 October 1937.

27. *Sexto censo de poblacion 1940* (Mexico City: Gobierno de México, 1941); *Yucatán revolucionario: Álbum conmemorativo de la toma de posesión del Ing. Humberto Canto Echeverría como gobernador constitutional del estado de Yucatán* (Mérida, 1938); "Memorándum: Antecedentes . . ."; Isidro Chi et al. to president, AGN DGG 2.311G vol. 340 exp. 2.

28. *Diario de Yucatán,* 9 September 1937; *Diario del sureste,* 21 September 1937. On the schedule of organizations voting, see *Diario del sureste* and *Diario de Yucatán,* 24 September–17 October 1937.

29. Adrian Bantjes, "Cardenismo: Regional Perspectives and Revisionism" (paper presented at the Latin American Studies Association congress, Chicago, 25 September 1998), 12–15.

30. Manuel Cirerol Sansores, *Historia del transporte de pasajeros en Mérida* (Mérida, 1966); Pedro Echeverría, *Los Cordeleros, 1935–1980* (Mexico City: Del Agua, 1981).

31. Lombardo Toledano's book even reprinted photographs from anti-Socialist politicians of the late 1910s and early 1920s. See Lombardo Toledano, *El llanto del sureste,* 15, 22, 29, 31. On pp. 46 and 57, he republished photographs first used by the virulently anti-Socialist writer Hugo Sol (Anastasio Manzanilla) in his *El Comunismo en México, quienes no lo incubaron . . . y quienes lo propalan,* 1st ed. (Mexico City: Hugo Sol, 1921). The photographs can be found on pp. 155 and 66, respectively, of the book's second edition.

Although more research on the subject is needed, archival evidence from the late 1920s and early 1930s suggests that some urban Socialist labor organizations were able to pressure employers to raise wages with state support. See, e.g., Juan Pérez Lara, president of Liga de Dependientes y Cocineros de Restaurantes, to governor, 16 June 1932, and related material, AGEY PE 952 SG 2. Still, Clark underscored the problems that many urban laborers in Yucatán faced during that time (see Ruth Clark, *Organized Labor in Mexico*, 2d ed. [New York: Russel and Russel, 1978], 171, 203–13).

32. Enrique Núñez González to President Cárdenas, 13 October 1935, AGN LC 404.1/12 leg. 1.

33. Enrique Núñez González to President Cárdenas, 13 October 1935, AGN LC 404.1/12 leg. 1; transcript of Liga Central meeting, 20 October 1933, AGEY PE 967 SG 1.

34. Amendolla, *Revolución*, 231–32; Enrique Núñez González to Executive Committee of the SCY, 23 May 1937, AGEY PE 1018.

35. Yuri Hulkin Balam Ramos, *La Masonería en Yucatán: El caso de La Gran Logia Unida "La Oriental Peninsular"* (Mérida: Universidad Autónoma de Yucatán, 1996), 62.

36. *Diario de Yucatán,* 9 September 1935, 26 April 1936.

37. *Diario de Yucatán,* 13 January 1937.

38. *Diario del sureste,* 13 June 1937.

39. B. Martínez to governor, 7 December 1932, AGEY PE 591 SG 1; General Francisco Mújica, "Memorándum sobre la situación de Yucatán," 23 July 1936, AGN LC 404.1/12 leg. 2.

40. Amendolla, *Revolución,* 74.

41. Betancourt, "Se consuma."

42. *Diario de Yucatán,* 14 April 1937.

43. *Diario de Yucatán,* 11 April 1937.

44. *Diario de Yucatán,* 24 February, 29 July 1936, 11, 12, 18 April 1937; report of inspector of secretary of the interior dated 29 November 1939, attached to Barba González to president, 2 December 1939, AGN LC 432/219.

45. General Francisco Mújica, "Memorándum sobre la situación de Yucatán," 23 July 1936, AGN LC 404.1/12 leg. 2; *El yucatanista,* 17 April, 29 May 1937; López Sosa, *Tarjeta,* 47.

46. The González brothers' return to power in the SFP is described in chap. 6.

47. AGN LC 432/10.

48. *Diario del sureste,* 26, 27, 28 June 1934; *El yucatanista,* 3 March 1934; Pallares to president, 4 July 1934, AGN AR 561.4/22-1; Sales Díaz to secretary of the interior, 6 June 1934, and Mario Negrón Pérez to secretary of the interior, 26 July 1934, AGEY PE 991 SG 1.

49. Lombardo Toledano, *El llanto del sureste.*

50. *Diario del sureste,* 22 February 1936; *Diario de Yucatán,* 21 February, 19, 29 April 1936.

51. *Diario del sureste,* 9, 10, 13, 14, 15 May, 1, 7 June, 28 July, 31 December 1936; *Diario de Yucatán,* 28, 29 April, 1, 6, 8, 12, 13, 15, 24 May, 14, 15 June 1936; General Francisco Mújica, "Memorándum sobre la situación de Yucatán," 23 July 1936, AGN LC 404.1/12 leg. 2; Baños, "Trasfondo," 94–95; Sierra and Paoli, *Cárdenas,* 89–90.

52. Brandenburg, "Mexico," 15, 18–20, 83–84; PNR, *Memoria,* 120–25; *Diario de Yucatán,* 5, 17 March, 5 April, 9 September 1937.

53. *Diario del sureste,* 13 March 1937; *Diario de Yucatán,* 5, 17 March 1937.

54. Ernesto Guerra Leal to President Cárdenas, 30 October 1937, AGN LC 544.2/30.

55. Florencio Avila Sánchez to President Cárdenas, 30 March 1937, Feliciano Leal and Julio

Canché to President Cárdenas, 19 February 1937, and Hernán Morales to President Cárdenas, 1 April 1937, AGN LC 544.4/30.

56. Miguel Angél Menéndez to President Cárdenas, 4 April 1937, AGN LC 544.4/30; *Diario de Yucatán,* 3, 4 April 1937.

57. Manuel Ríos Thivol, "Resumen," 23 June 1937, AGN DGG 2.311G vol. 339 annex 15757.

58. Gabriel Ferrer de M., "Historia de las comunicaciones," in *Enciclopedia yucatenense* (Mexico City: Gobierno Estado de Yucatán, 1946), 3:592–93; *Diario del sureste,* 24 March 1937.

59. *Diario de Yucatán,* 31 July 1937.

60. *Diario de Yucatán,* 23, 25 July 1937.

61. AGN LC 432/10; *Diario del sureste,* 18 August 1937; Echeverría, *Cordeleros,* 103. On "conciencia obrera," see Lázaro Cárdenas, *Palabras y documentos públicos de Lázaro Cárdenas: Informes de gobierno y mensajes presidenciales de año nuevo 1928/1940,* 2 vols. (Mexico City: Siglo XXI, 1978), 260–61.

62. Crescencio Alcocer H. to president, 10 August 1937, AGN LC 432.2/196.

63. AGN LC 432/10.

64. Angel Arias T. to president, 13 August 1937, AGN LC 432/692.

65. AGN LC 432/692.

66. *Diario de Yucatán,* 31 July 1937.

67. AGN LC 432.2/297.

68. Cárdenas, *Palabras,* 253–58, 260–61; PNR, *Reforma; Diario de Yucatán,* 18, 24 August 1937.

69. Jonathan C. Brown, "Acting for Themselves: Workers and the Mexican Oil Nationalization," in *Workers' Control in Latin America, 1930–1979,* ed. Jonathan C. Brown (Chapel Hill: University of North Carolina Press, 1997), 63–66.

70. Hamilton, *Limits of State Autonomy;* Schuler, *Mexico between Hitler and Roosevelt,* 3–4, 64–83.

71. Bantjes, *Jesus,* 110–19, 121–22.

72. Alvaro Pérez Alpuche to President Cárdenas, 19 October 1937, AGN LC 544.2/30.

73. Julio Osorio to president, 1 November 1937, AGN DGG 2.311G vol. 340 exp. 2; Ignacio García Téllez to interior secretary, 16 October 1937, AGN DGG 2.311G vol. 340 exp. 1; Gabriel Ferrer to President Cárdenas, AGN LC 544.2/30.

74. On the SFP, see Dionisio Pérez to President Cárdenas, 27 September 1937, AGN DGG 2.311G vol. 339 tomo II. On the FOP, see Juan D. Peña to President Cárdenas, Mario Recio and Demetrio Sosa to President Cárdenas, and Clemente Vázquez to President Cárdenas, 6 November 1937, AGN LC 544.2/30. On FAREYS, see *Diario de Yucatán,* 26 September 1937.

75. On the FUTV, see the report of Manual Ríos Thivol, 2 May 1937, AGN DGG 2.311G vol. 340 exp. 3. On the SCY, see *Diario del sureste,* 5 October 1937, and Luis Pereira to President Cárdenas, 25 September 1937, AGN DGG 2.311G vol. 339 tomo II; P. Avila B. of the Committee of Cordage Workers to President Cárdenas, 4 October 1937, AGN DGG 2.311G vol. 339 tomo II; and "Para conocimiento," signed Julio Osorio, 3 November 1937, AGN DGG 2.311G vol. 340 exp. 2.

76. Juan D. Peña to President Cárdenas, AGN LC 544.2/30; *Diario de Yucatán,* 9, 10 January 1937.

77. Rafael Cebada to President Cárdenas, 22 October 1937, AGN LC 544.2/30; Hernán

Bautista to President Cárdenas, 2 October 1937, AGN DGG 2.311G vol. 339 anexa 15757; Alvaro Pérez Alpuche to President Cárdenas, 19 October 1937, AGN LC 544.2/30; Gonzalo Tut to President, 28 September 1937, AGN DGG 2.311G vol. 339 tomo II.

78. In November 1940, this provision was removed (Middlebrook, 66). Kevin Middlebrook, *The Paradox of Revolution: Labor, the State and Authoritarianism in Mexico* (Baltimore: The Johns Hopkins University Press, 1995).

79. Adolfo Trujillo Dominguez, *Importantes documentos para la historia del sindicalismo en Yucatán* (Mérida, 1936), 3.

6 The Retreat of Cárdenas: The Great Ejido Plan and the New Political Equilibrium in Yucatán

1. *Diario de Yucatán,* 16 September 1937.

2. Martín Díaz de Cossio, *Henequen: Riqueza yucateca* (Mexico City: El Mundo, 1938), 74–81.

3. Schuler, *Mexico between Hitler and Roosevelt,* 91–93.

4. Benítez, *Kí,* 217, 235; *Diario del sureste,* 14 April 1938.

5. Humberto Canto Echeverría with Estebán Durán Rosado, *Cárdenas y el Gran Ejido Henequenero de Yucatán* (Mexico City: Costa-Amic, 1963), 39–43; Benítez, *Kí,* 217–18, 232; Lapointe, "Estado," 15; Sierra and Paoli, *Cárdenas,* 113–15; *Diario del sureste,* 7 April 1938.

6. *Diario del sureste,* 13, 14 February, 13 July, 7 August, 20 November, 19 December 1938.

7. *Diario del sureste,* 7 August 1938.

8. *Diario de Yucatán,* 1 January 1938; *Diario del sureste,* 3 January, 14 February, 8, 13 July 1938; Carlos M. Peralta, "Apuntes," 9 September 1939, AGN LC 404.1/12 caja 201 leg. 9; "Acta," AGN LC 404.1/12 caja 201 leg. 7.

9. Lapointe, "Estado," 15; *Diario del sureste,* 12 April, 8 July 1938.

10. Sierra and Paoli, *Cárdenas,* 117; *Diario del sureste,* 12, 17 April 1938; Peralta, "Apuntes," 9 September 1939, AGN LC 404.1/12 caja 201 leg. 9.

11. Sierra and Paoli, *Cárdenas,* 117–18.

12. *Diario del sureste,* 1 January, 11, 12 February, 22 June 1938; Vicente Salgado Paez to secretary general of the FSI, 26 September 1938, AGEY PE 1032 SG 1; Tomás Briceño to President Cárdenas, 11 February 1938, AGN LC 404.1/12 caja 201 leg. 8.

13. Canto Echeverría to President Cárdenas, 3 April 1938, AGN LC 404.1/12 caja 201 leg. 4; *Diario del sureste,* 3, 9, 10, 12, 16, 17 April 1938.

14. Fernando Eduardo Cásares et al. to President Cárdenas, 20 January 1939, AGN LC 404.1/12 caja 201 leg. 8; Lapointe, "Estado," 15.

15. Emilio Pacheco to President Cárdenas, 25 November 1938, AGN DGG 2.311M vol. 85 exp. 52; José María Esquivel Fernández to interior secretary, 22 July 1940, AGN DGG 2.311 vol. 17 exp. 4; Miguel Angel Menéndez to Lázaro Cárdenas, 2 September 1940, AGN LC 544.5/72.

16. *Diario del sureste,* 3 March, 14 April, 12 November 1938; AGEY PE 1032 SG 1; AGEY PE 1039 SG 1; AGEY PE 1044 SG 1.

17. Hamilton, *Limits of State Autonomy,* 241–48; Alicia Hernández, 181–83.

18. Alvaro Pérez Alpuche to president, 19 October 1937, AGN LC 544.2/30; *Diario del sureste,* 9 March 1940.

19. CCM in Yucatán Foundation, 17 September 1935, AGEY PE 1022 SG; AGN LC 702.1/93; *Diario de Yucatán,* 31 March 1938.

20. *Diario del sureste,* 24 May 1938.

21. *Diario del sureste,* 13 January 1940; PCM, *Resoluciones,* 9–10; Santiago Pérez, president PRM, circular, 30 March 1939, AGEY PE 1049 SG 1; Sierra and Paoli, *Cárdenas,* 109; Brandenburg, "Mexico," 91.

22. *Diario del sureste,* 11 August, 26 August 1938; Florentino May et al. to President Cárdenas, 5 September 1938, AGN DGG 2.311 vol. 85 exp. 24; Emilio Pacheco to CNC, 23 February 1939, AGN DGG 2.311M vol. 83 exp. 13.

23. Diego Rosado to Carlos Erosa Peniche, 11 October 1939, AGEY PE 1044 SG 1; Florentino May to President Cárdenas, 5 September 1938, AGEY DGG 2.311M vol. 85 exp. 24; Marcelino Tuz to governor, 7 March 1938, AGEY PE 1045 sec. Chichimila; Pedro Romero to President Cárdenas, 8 January 1938, AGN DGG 2.311G; *Diario official,* 14, 16 February, 10 March, 21 April, 2, 7 May, 16, 17 June, 22 July, 13, 22, 25 August 1938; *Diario del sureste,* 17 February, 16 March, 30 April 1938, 13 January 1939; *Diario de Yucatán,* 5, 17 March, 7 April 1938, 23 March 1940.

24. Lapointe, "Estado," 15–16.

25. There are some parallels between Cárdenas's belief that peasants should have greater control over the running of ejidos in Yucatán and the guarded endorsement that Cárdenas at times gave to urban workers' attempts to control the workplace, as described by Jonathan Brown (see Jonathan C. Brown, introduction to Brown, ed., *Workers' Control,* 12–13).

26. Baroni, *Yucatán,* 123–25.

27. *Diario del sureste,* 2 January 1938; "Acta de la Primera Convención de Ejidos Autónomos," AGN LC 404.1/12 caja 201 leg. 7.

28. *Diario del sureste,* 26, 27, 28, 29 April 1939.

29. *Diario del sureste,* 28, 29 August 1939.

30. "Camaradas ejidatarios," AGN LC 541/2368; AGEY AM Tixkokob caja 15 leg. 41 exp. 3; Monforte to governor, 15 June 1933, AGEY 973; AGN LC 541/2368; *Diario del sureste,* 4 April 1936, 6, 22 September 1939.

31. *Diario de Yucatán,* 20 November 1939.

32. *Diario de Yucatán,* 24, 27 August 1939.

33. Of fifteen directors of the CPEE, Umán supplied four, Acancéh two, Mérida two, and Conkal three (*Diario del sureste,* 4 September 1939).

34. *Diario de Yucatán,* 23 March, 4 April 1940.

35. *Diario del sureste,* 1 September 1939.

36. Minutes of the Syndical League of Samahil, 24 September 1939, AGEY PE 1038 SG 1.

37. Diego Rosado to Carlos Erosa Peniche, 11 October 1939, AGEY PE 1044 SG 1; Diego Rosado to Coronel Beteta, 12 September 1939, AGEY LC 404.1/12 caja 201 leg. 8; *Diario del sureste,* 26 September 1939.

38. *Diario de Yucatán,* 14 September, 18 December 1939; *Diario del sureste,* 16, 22, 24, 26 September 1939; "Puntos," 14 September 1939, AGN LC 404.1/12 caja 201 leg. 10; Bartolomé García Correa to Fernando Vargas Ocampo, 8 September 1939, AGN LC 404.1/12 caja 201.

39. Gobierno del Estado, *El ejido,* 338–39; *La prensa,* 1, 2, 4, 6, 7, 8 September 1939; Bartolomé García Correa to Fernando Vargas Ocampo, 8 September 1939, AGN LC 404.1/

12 caja 201 leg. 7; Miguel Angél Menéndez to President Cárdenas, 28 June 1939, AGN LC 404.1 / 12 caja 201 leg. 9.

40. "Puntos," 14 September 1939, AGN LC 404.1/12 caja 201 leg. 10; *Diario del sureste,* 13 September 1939; Amendolla, *Revolución,* 238.

41. *Diario del sureste,* 22 September 1939; *Diario de Yucatán,* 22, 23, 24 September 1939; Vicente Salgado Páez to Coronel Beteta, 23 September 1939, AGN LC 404.1/12 caja 201 leg. 10; Arsenio Lara to president, AGN LC 404.1/12 caja 201 leg. 9.

42. *Diario de Yucatán,* 6 November 1939.

43. *Diario de Yucatán,* 15, 27, 29 September 1939; *Diario del sureste,* 26, 28, 30 September 1939.

44. *Diario del sureste,* 12, 13 September 1939; AGEY PE 1042 SG 1; Gobierno del Estado, *El ejido en Yucatán* (Mérida: Gobierno del Estado, 1937), 338–39.

45. *Diario del sureste,* 21, 22, 23 November, 9 December 1939; Amendolla, *Revolución,* 239–41.

46. *Diario de Yucatán,* 7 December 1939.

47. Diego Rosado to Carlos Erosa Peniche, 11 October 1939, AGEY PE 1044 SG 1.

48. *Diario de Yucatán,* 2 November 1939.

49. *Diario de Yucatán,* 4 December 1939.

50. AGEY PE 1044 Sec. CLA.

51. *Diario de Yucatán,* 28 September, 4 November, 7 December 1939; AGEY PE 1068 sec. Kanasín.

52. Chief of state to military chief of Thirty-second Zone, AGEY PE 1042 SG 1; *Diario de Yucatán,* 4 November, 7 December 1939, 13 April 1940.

53. *Diario del sureste,* 24, 31 July, 7 August 1940; *Diario de Yucatán,* 2 December 1939, 18 July, 10, 13, 21, 24 August 1940; AGEY PE 1068 Sec. Hoctun.

54. *Diario de Yucatán,* 4–12 December 1939; *Diario del sureste,* 8 December 1939; Gobierno del Estado, *El ejido,* 345.

55. *Diario de Yucatán,* 18 December 1939; *Diario del sureste,* 17, 19 December 1939.

56. *Diario de Yucatán,* 25 September, 11 November, 9 December 1939; *Diario del sureste,* 30 December 1939, 5 January 1940; *Diario oficial,* 9 May 1939.

57. AGN LC 432/219; Gobierno del Estado, *El ejido,* 324–25, 327.

58. Gobierno del Estado, *El ejido,* 341–48; *Diario del sureste,* 17 November 1939.

59. Gobierno del Estado, *El ejido,* 341–48, 339–40; *La prensa,* 24 February 1940; *Diario de Yucatán,* 7, 10 April, 23 May, 13 July 1940; *Diario del sureste,* 22 November 1939, 7 October 1940; Santiago Cab to governor, 16 August 1939, AGEY 1051 SG 1; A. Escalante to President Cárdenas, 8 July 1940, AGN LC 544.1/30; Diego Rosado to governor, 26 July 1939, AGEY PE 1068 Sec. Tecoh & Timucuy; private secretary of the governor to Interior Ministry, 9 November 1939, AGN LC 404.1/12 caja 201 leg. 8; Canto Echeverría to President Cárdenas, 7 October 1940, AGN LC 404.1/12 caja 201 leg. 6. Sosa Elízaga, *Códigas ocultos,* 500, dismisses rumors that the federal military commanders in Yucatán were linked to Almazán and qualifies them as among the generals most loyal to Cárdenas.

60. Inspector of the Interior Ministry, 29 November 1939, attached to Barba González to President Cárdenas, 2 December 1939, AGN LC 432/219.

61. Adrian Bantjes, "Politics, Class and Culture in Post-Revolutionary Mexico: Cardenismo and Sonora, 1929–1940" (Ph.D. diss., University of Texas, 1991).

62. *Diario de Yucatán,* 21, 23 March 1940.

63. Porfirio Pech et al. to President Cárdenas, 12 April 1940, AGN LC 541/2368; *Diario de Yucatán,* 21, 23 March, 11 April, 2 June 1940; *Diario del sureste,* 11 April, 8, 9, 10 May 1940.

64. AGN LC 541/2368; *Diario de Yucatán,* 8, 11 May 1940; *Diario del sureste,* 10 May 1940.

65. *Diario de Yucatán,* 8 May 1940; *Diario del sureste,* 11 May 1940; AGN LC 541/2368.

66. Gobierno del Estado, *El ejido,* 421–27; Betancourt, *Memorías,* 135; Lázaro Cárdenas to General Augustín Castro, 9 May 1940, AGN LC 556.63/143; *Diario del sureste,* 9 June 1940; *Diario de Yucatán,* 11, 12 May 1940.

67. Echeverría, *Política,* 95; *Diario de Yucatán,* 14 May 1940; Gobierno del Estado, *El ejido,* 415–16.

68. *Diario de Yucatán,* 23 May 1940.

69. *Diario de Yucatán,* 20 May 1940.

70. Gobierno del Estado, *El ejido,* 416–17; *Diario de Yucatán,* 14, 26 May, 13, 17, 29 June, 8, 19 July 1940.

71. Gobierno del Estado, *El ejido,* 417–20; AGN DGG 2.317.4 vol. 8 exp. 7; congressional decrees, 6 July 1940, AGEY PE 1064 SG 1.

72. Roberto Sarlat et al. to President Cárdenas, 12 July 1940, AGN DGG 2.311M vol. 17 exp. 4; José María Esquivel Fernández et al. to interior secretary, 22 July 1940, AGN DGG 2.311 vol. 17 exp. 4; *Diario de Yucatán,* 7–10, 13 July 1940.

73. Schreyer, *Rancheros,* 92–98.

74. Ronfeldt, *Atencingo,* 47.

75. *La prensa,* 24 February 1940; Diego Rosado to governor, 26 July 1939, AGEY PE 1068 Sec. Tecoh & Timucuy.

76. Alberto Jiménez to Rafael Lugo Gruintal, 31 August 1939, AGEY PE 1027 Sec. Judicial.

77. *Diario del sureste,* 12, 15, 27, 29 July, 1, 6, 9 August 1940; Cab Baz to Governor Cardos Ruz, 29 July 1940, AGEY PE 1065 SG 1.

78. Gobierno del Estado, *El ejido,* 428–40.

79. *Diario del sureste,* 29 July, 13 August 1940.

80. *Diario de Yucatán,* 23 July, 18 August, 3, 4 September 1940; *Diario del sureste,* 24 July, 4 September 1940; Pedro Carrillo to governor, 21 July 1940, AGEY PE 1060 SG 1.

81. *Diario del sureste,* 28 July, 3, 8 August 1940.

82. *Diario del sureste,* 3 August 1940.

83. Cárdenas's initial indecision forced Cardos Ruz to come to Mexico City on 4 August 1940 to plead his case before the minister of the interior (the chief political officer of the cabinet), Ignacio García Tellez, who politely ignored his pleas and announced that Cardos Ruz's key supporter, General Izaguirre, was being transferred in a "purely military move." This suggests that Cárdenas had made up his mind to restore Canto Echeverría to power even before the two men met on 5 August. To add insult to injury, during his trip to Mexico City, Cardos Ruz's car collided with a statue on the Paseo de la Reforma after a night on the town. On 9 August, Cardos Ruz accepted the inevitable and resigned. See Betancourt, *Memorías,* 137; J. Zavala Reyes to President Cárdenas, 22 October 1940, AGN LC 404.1/12 caja 201 leg. 6; *Diario del sureste,* 5, 9, 10, 21 August 1940.

Canto Echeverría's return was assured when President Cárdenas publicly called his right to rule a "simple fact" and criticized the way in which Cardos Ruz had taken power. By this, he implied that General Izaguirre had exceeded the legal bounds of the federal military by interfering in politics—while conveniently omitting the role of the new federal commander of the state, General Aureo Calles, in ejecting Cardos Ruz and installing Canto Echeverría. *Diario del sureste,* 24 August 1940.

84. AGN DGG 2.317.4 vol. 8 exp. 7.

85. Rigoberto Vázquez to President Cárdenas, 7 August 1940, AGEY DGG 2.331 vol. 17 exp. 4.

86. *Diario de Yucatán,* 13, 16, 21, 22, 24 August, 8, 13, 25 September 1940; *Diario official,* 10 September 1940; Félix Vallejos F. to President Cárdenas, 22 August 1940, AGN DGG 2.317.4 vol. 8 exp. 7; Gobierno del Estado, *El ejido,* 449–63; Gonzalo López Manzanero to Congress, 20 August 1940, AGEY PE 1057 SG 1.

87. *Diario de Yucatán,* 9 October 1940; Gobierno del Estado, *El ejido,* 474–75, 493; various correspondence from AGN LC 404.1 / 12 caja 201 leg. 6; "Ejidos," 14 November 1940, AGN LC 544.4/30.

88. *Diario de Yucatán,* 24, 26 September, 2 October, 28 December 1940; *Diario del sureste,* 5 October, 20 November 1940.

89. Canto Echeverría to Lázaro Cárdenas, 30 September 1940, AGN LC 544.5/72.

90. *Diario del sureste,* 9–20 October 1940.

91. *Diario de Yucatán,* 22 December 1940; Miguel Angél Menéndez to president, 28 September 1940, AGN LC 544.5/72.

92. *Diario del sureste,* 15, 16 October 1940; Arsenio Lara Puerto to President Cárdenas, 10 October 1940, AGN LC 404.1 / 12 caja 201 leg. 6.

93. *Diario de Yucatán,* 10 October 1940; *Diario del sureste,* 14 October 1940.

94. Voting figures for the FDI candidates were never released. Canto Echeverría to President Cárdenas, 23 October 1940, AGN LC 544.4/30.

95. Governor Canto Echeverría to President Cárdenas, 18 November 1940, AGN LC 544.4/30.

96. Humberto Canto Echeverría to President Cárdenas, 23 October 1940, AGN LC 544.4/ 30.

97. *Diario de Yucatán,* 25 October 1940; STERM Sección 31 to President Cárdenas, 24 October 1940, AGN LC 544.4/30.

98. *Diario del sureste,* 17, 25 November 1940.

99. *Diario del sureste,* 18, 19 November 1940.

100. *Diario del sureste,* 25 November 1940; Camp, *Mexico's Leaders,* 959.

101. *Diario del sureste,* 17, 18, 23 November, 10 December 1940.

102. *Diario de Yucatán,* 24 November 1940.

103. Various correspondence from AGN DGG 2.311 vol. 83 exp. 69; *Diario del sureste,* 9 November 1940.

104. *Diario del sureste,* 22 November 1940; *Diario de Yucatán,* 25 November 1940; Arsenio Lara P. et al. to Graciano Sánchez, 23 November 1490, AGN LC 544.3.

105. *Diario del sureste,* 22 November, 1 December 1940; *Diario de Yucatán,* 13, 25–27 November, 10, 13 December 1940; Arsenio Lara P. et al. to Graciano Sánchez, 23 November 1940, AGN LC 544.3; Mario Negrón Pérez, 16 November 1940, AGN DGG 2.311 vol. 83 exp. 69.

106. *Diario de Yucatán,* 1, 20 December 1940.

107. *Diario del sureste,* 26 November 1940.

108. *Diario de Yucatán,* 5 December 1940; Canto Echeverría to González Gallo, 17 December 1940, AGEY PE 1057 SG 1.

109. *Diario de Yucatán,* 24, 28 December 1940; *Diario del sureste,* 25 December 1940.

110. *Diario del sureste,* 28, 29 November 1940.
111. David Raby, *Educación y revolución social en México (1921–1940),* trans. Roberto Gómez Ciriza (Mexico City: Sep-Setentas, 1974), chap. 7.
112. Bantjes, *Jesus.*
113. Vaughan, *Cultural Politics,* 72–75.
114. Guillermo Guzmán Flores, "El Cardenismo y la nueva democracia," in *Historia de la cuestion agraria mexicana, estado de Zacatecas,* vol. 2, *1940,* ed. Ramón Vera Salvo (Mexico City: Juan Pablos, 1992), 243–56.

7   Cárdenas Compromised: Cardenismo's Legacy in Yucatán

1. Bantjes, *As If Jesus Walked on Earth: Cardenismo, Sonora, and the Mexican Revolution* (Wilmington, Del.: Scholarly Resources, 1998), 195.
2. Bantjes, *As If Jesus.*
3. Othón Baños Ramírez, *Yucatán: Ejidos sin campesinos* (Mérida: Ediciones de Universidad Autónoma de Yucatán, 1989), 118.
4. Jim Handy, *Revolution in the Countryside: Rural Conflict and Agrarian Reform in Guatemala, 1944–1954* (Chapel Hill: University of North Carolina Press, 1994), 112–17.
5. Schuler, *Mexico between Hitler and Roosevelt,* 63–71.
6. Saúl Escobar Toledo, "El Cardenismo más allá del reparto: Acciones y resultados," in *Historia de la cuestión agraria mexicana,* vol. 5, *El Cardenismo: Un parteaguas histórico en el proceso agrario (primera parte), 1934–1940,* ed. Everardo Escárcega López and Saúl Escobar Toledo (Mexico City: Siglo XXI, 1991), 435. No national statistics were published for the year 1939, but there is no evidence that federal spending in Yucatán was exceptionally high.
7. Antonio Rodríguez, *El henequén: Una planta caluimniada* (Mexico City: Costa-Amic, 1966), 280; Benítez, *Kí;* Eric Villanueva Mukul, *El henequén en Yucatán: Industria, mercado, y campesinos* (Mérida: Maldonado, 1990), 109, 133.
8. Sierra and Paoli, *Cárdenas,* 73.
9. Baños, "Trasfondo," 95; Sierra and Paoli, *Cárdenas,* 108.
10. Bantjes, *As If Jesus,* 224–25, 351–95.
11. Sierra and Paoli, *Cárdenas,* 114: "el sector más retardario de la burguesía."
12. Rosemary Louise Lee, "The Tourist Industry in Yucatan: A Case Study in the Interaction between Class Structure and Economic Development" (Ph.D. diss., University of California, Irvine, 1977), 154–55, 162.
13. Asael Hansen and Juan Bastarrachea M., *Mérida: Su transformación de capital colonial a naciente metrópoli en 1935* (Mexico: INAH, 1985), 162–65.
14. Jeffrey Brannon and Eric N. Baklanoff, *Agrarian Reform and Public Enterprise in Mexico: The Political Economy of Yucatán's Henequen Industry* (Tuscaloosa: University of Alabama Press, 1987).
15. Roque Armando Sosa Ferreyro, *Cosas de Yucatan* (Mexico City: Costa-Amic, 1969), 24; Armando Flores Beltrán, *Regiones ganaderas del estado de Yucatán: Estudio económico social agropecuario de la Zona Número 68* (Mérida: Secretaria de Agricultura y Fomento, Dirección General de Ganaderia, 1943), 92.
16. Benítez, *Kí,* 140.
17. Humphries, "Modernizing Maya Agriculture," 179–80.

18. Lee, "Tourist Industry," 153–54, 171.

19. Rubén García Clark, "Tripartisimo y nueva geografía electoral," *El cotidiano* 65 (November 1994): 33–38.

20. Rosa Albina Garavito Elías, "Vencer sin convencer," *El cotidiano* 65 (November 1994): 23.

21. Karl Schmitt, *Communism in Mexico: A Study in Political Frustration* (Austin: University of Texas Press, 1965).

22. Menéndez, *Lucha social,* 157.

23. Ibid., 145–49.

24. Eric Villanueva Mukul, *Crisis henequenera y movimientos campesinos en Yucatán, 1966–1983* (Mexico City: INAH, 1985).

LIST OF ABBREVIATIONS

ADIH Associación de Defensa de la Industria Henequenera Political front formed by the hacendados to oppose agrarian reform. It was disbanded after the Cardenista reform in the fall of 1937.

APY Alianza Popular Yucateca Umbrella organization founded by Governor Palomo Valencia and his group to co-opt syndical federations and urban unions.

ASDC Alianza Sindical de Defensa Colectiva Federation of urban unions that joined the CDE in opposing Canto Echeverría in 1939–40. Members of the ASDC included the SFP and the old Bartolista truckers' cooperative, which wanted to regain lucrative rights to transport henequen that the governor had given to the FUTV. The SCY also joined it, as did other independent unions.

CCA Confederación de Comunidades Agrarias Peasant organization founded by Gualbertistas in the 1937 gubernatorial campaign. It collapsed soon afterward.

CCM Confederación Campesina Mexicana National peasant federation founded by Portes Gil in 1936. It was later superseded by the Confederación Nacional Campesina (CNC).

CDE Comité Pro-Defensa Ejidal Political organization founded by the Tixkokob camarilla.

CdT Camara de Trabajo Founded by the CGT to unify labor nationally, it was taken over by the PNR in 1933 but never achieved much strength. Its Yucatecan branch functioned as the urban wing of the PSS.

CESOC Comité Estatal Social Obreros y Campesinos Popular organization supported by Governor Canto Echeverría.

CGOCM Confederación General de Obreros y Campesinos de México National labor federation founded by Lombardo Toledano, Fidel Velázqez, and the other labor leaders who controlled ex-CROM syndicates of Puebla and Mexico City. It became the parent organization of the CTM.

CGT Confederación General de Trabajadores National anarchosyndicalist federation. In spite of its radical ideology, its leaders in Yucatán were often corrupted by landowners.

CLGOC Confederación de Ligas Gremiales de Obreros y Campesinos Official title adopted by the PSS in 1934 to signify its transformation from political party to socioeconomic, syndical organization.

CNC Confederación Nacional Campesina National peasant federation created in 1938 by the PRM.

CPEE Comité Pro-Equidad Ejidal Group created by Governor Canto Echeverría and the official camarilla to oppose the CDE.

CROM Confederación Regional Obreros Mexicanos National labor federation created in the 1920s but largely displaced by the CTM during the Cárdenas administration.

CRY   Confederación Revolucionario de Yucatán   Political front created by the official camarilla after the PRM recognized the FDI's triumph in internal PRM elections in the fall of
1940.

CTM   Confederación de Trabajadores de México   National labor federation founded in early
1936 by Lombardo Toledano from the merger of the CGOC, regional FROCs, and other
elements.

FAREYS   Filarmónicos, Actores, Restaurentes, Espectáculos y Similar de Yucatán   Union of
entertainers and service workers formed on 7 March 1936.

FDI   Frente Democrática Independientiente   Political front formed by opposition groups to
challenge the official camarilla in the municipal and congressional elections in the fall of 1940.

FDOC   Frente Defensor de Obreros y Campesinos   Popular organization supported by
Governor Canto Echeverría and headed by old Bartolista politicians.

FOP   Federación Obrera de Progreso   Federation of syndicates of the port of Progreso,
founded in the late 1910s.

FROC   Federación Regional de Obreros y Campesinos   Regional labor and peasant syndi-
cate federations founded by Lombardo Toledano and the CGOC, later absorbed by the
CTM.

FSI   Frente Sindical Independiente   Communist federation of urban and rural peon syndicates founded in 1934.

FTY   Federación de Trabajadores de Yucatán   CTM branch in Yucatán.

FUPDM   Frente Unica Pro-Derechos de Mujeres   National feminist organization affiliated
with the PCM and the PNR/PRM.

FUTV   Frente Unico de Trabajadores de Volante   Union of truckers and taxi drivers founded
in 1936.

JSUM   Juventud Socialista Unida de México   Communist youth organization founded in
late 1935.

LCA   Liga de Comunidades Agrarias   Peasant organization sponsored by the Agrarian Bank.

PAN   Partido de Accíon Nacional   Right-center opposition party founded in 1939.

PCM   Partido Comunista Mexicano   Mexican Communist Party.

PNR   Partido Nacional Revolucionario   The national party founded by Plutarco Elías Calles
in 1929 as a confederation of regional caudillos and key generals. It changed its name to
Partido Revolucionario Mexicano (PRM) in 1938.

PRD   Partido de la Revolucíon Demócratica   Left-center opposition party that emerged out
of Cuauhtemóc Cárdenas presidential campaign in 1987.

PRI   Partido de la Revolución Institutionalizado   State Party's name adopted in 1946 when
PRM changed name.

PRM   Partido de la Revolución Mexicana   Name adopted by the PNR in 1938 under Cárdenas, accompanied by a transformation of the party structure to the corporate structure
of worker (CTM), peasant (CNC), military, and "popular" affiliates.

PRUN   Partido Revolucionario de Unificación Nacional   Opposition party that ran Almazán for president in 1940.

PSS   Partido Socialista del Sureste   Founded by Felipe Carrillo Puerto in 1918, it controlled
elected offices in Yucatán until the mid-1930s, when it merged with the PNR and changed
its name to the CLGOC.

SCY   Sindicato de Cordeleros de Yucatán   Union of cordage factory workers founded in
1933.

SFP   Sindicato de Ferrocarrilleros Peninsular   Railroad workers' union.

STERM   Sindicato de Trabajadores de Enseñanza Revolucionario Mexicano   Teachers' union formed by uniting state and federal teachers' unions.

UMR   Unión de Maestros Revolucionarios   State teachers' union affiliated with the Communist Party of Mexico.

UTEY   Unión de Trabajadores de Enseñanza de Yucatán   Federal teachers' union covertly linked to the Communist Party of Mexico.

BIBLIOGRAPHY

Books, Articles, and Interviews

Aboites, Luis. "El socialismo en el oriente de Yucatán: Un caso de historia regional." Departamento de Antropología, Universidad Autónoma Metropolitana, 1980. Typescript.

Alonzo Caamal, Bartolomé. *Los Mayas en la política, a través de Chichimilah, Yucatán.* Mexico City: SEP / INI, 1982.

Alvarado Mendoza, Arturo. *El Portesgilismo en Tamaulipas.* Mexico City: Colegio de México, 1992.

Alvárez Barret, Luis. *Lecturas para trabajadoras: Folleto no. 1 para ser utilizado en las escuelas nocturnas, en la campaña analfabetizante y en las organizaciones sindicales.* Mérida: Publicaciones de la Dirección de la Educación Federal en el estado de Yucatán, 1937.

Amaro Gamboa, Jesus. *Vocabulario del Uayeísmo en la cultura de Yucatán.* Mérida: Universidad Autonoma de Yucatán, 1985.

Ancona Riestra, Roberto. *Arquitectura de las haciendas henequeneras.* Mérida and Bogotá: Universidad Autónoma de Yucatán and Escala, 1996.

Anguiano, Arturo. *El estado y la política obrera del cardenismo.* Mexico City: Ediciones Era, 1975.

Ankerson, Dudley F. *Agrarian Warlord: Saturnino Cedillo and the Mexican Revolution.* DeKalb: Northern Illinois University Press, 1984.

El asesinato de Carrillo Puerto (discursos y articulos en elogio del ilustre martir, y protestas contra sus infames asesinos). Mexico City, 1924.

Askinasy, Siegfried. *El problema agrario de Yucatan.* 2d ed. Mexico City: Ediciones Botas, 1936.

Ayuso Cachón, Andrés. *Crónica de Teabo.* Mérida: Impremer, 1976.

Aznar Mendoza, Enrique. *El problema económico de Yucatán: La crisis henequenera: Sus causas, la solución.* Mérida: El Porvenir, 1931.

——. *El problema económico de Yucatán: Segunda parte: Renovarse o morir.* Mérida: Imprenta Universal, 1932.

——. "Historia de la industria henequenera desde 1919 hasta nuestros dias." In *Enciclopedia yucatense,* 3:727–87. Mérida: Estado de Yucatán, 1947.

Balam Ramos, Yuri Hulkin. *La masonería en Yucatán: El caso de la gran logia unida "la oriental peninsular."* Mérida: Universidad Autónoma de Yucatán, 1996.

Baños Ramírez, Othón. "Agrarimo estatal y poder en Mexico (1915–1940): El caso de Yucatán." *Revista de la Universidad Autónoma de Yucatán* 165 (1988): 20–39.

——. *Yucatán: Ejidos sin campesinos.* Mérida: Ediciones de Universidad Autónoma de Yucatán, 1989.

——. "El trasfondo politico de la reforma agraria: El caso de Yucatan, 1933–1937." *Revista de la Universidad Autónoma de Yucatán* 172 (1990): 80–95.

——. *Neoliberalismo, reorganizacion, y subsistencia rural: El caso de la zona henequenera de Yucatán, 1980–1992.* Mérida: Universidad Autónoma de Yucatán, 1996.

Bantjes, Adrian. "Politics, Class, and Culture in Post-Revolutionary Mexico: Cardenismo and Sonora, 1929–1940." Ph.D. diss., University of Texas, 1991.

——. "Burning Saints, Molding Minds: Iconoclasm, Civic Ritual, and the Failed Cultural Revolution." In *Rituals of Rule, Rituals of Resistance: Public Celebrations and Popular Culture in Mexico,* ed. William H. Beezley, Cheryl English Martin, and William E. French. Wilmington, Del.: Scholarly Resources, 1994.

——. *As If Jesus Walked on Earth: Cardenismo, Sonora, and the Mexican Revolution.* Wilmington, Del.: Scholarly Resources, 1998.

——. "Cardenismo: Regional Perspectives and Revisionism." Paper presented at the Latin American Studies Association congress, Chicago, 25 September 1998.

Baroni, Aldo. *Yucatán.* Mexico City: Botas, 1938.

Batt, Laura. "La burguesía de espita, Yucatán (1900–1924)." In *Sociedad, estructura agraria, y estado en Yucatán,* ed. Othón Baños Ramírez. Mérida: Universidad Autonoma de Yucatán, 1990.

Becker, Marjorie. "Black and White and Color: *Cardenismo* and the Search for a *Campesino* Ideology." *Comparative Studies in Society and History* 29 (1987): 453–66.

——. *Setting the Virgin on Fire: Lázaro Cárdenas, Michoacán Peasants, and the Redemption of the Mexican Revolution.* Berkeley and Los Angeles: University of California Press, 1995.

Benítez, Fernando. *Ki: El drama de un pueblo y de una planta.* 2d ed. Mexico City: Fondo Cultura Economica, 1962.

Berzunza Pinto, Ramón. *Una chispa en el sureste (pasado y futuro de los indios mayas).* Mexico City: Talleres de la Cooperativa, 1942.

Betancourt Pérez, Antonio. "La Federación Sindical Independiente." *Memorias del primer colquio regional de historia obrero.* Jalapa: CEHSMO, 1977.

——. *Memorias de un combatiente social.* Mérida: Instituto de Cultura de Yucatán, 1991.

——. Interview by author. 30 October 1994.

Bolio Ontiveros, Edmundo. *De la cuna al paredón.* Mérida, 1931.

——. *Yucatán (perspectivas económicas).* Mexico City: DAPP, 1937.

——. *Diccionario historico, geografico, y biografico de yucatán.* Mexico City, 1944.

——. *Yucatán en la dictadura y en la Revolución.* Mérida, 1967.

Bracamonte Sosa, Pedro. *Amos y sirvientes: Las haciendas de Yucatán, 1789–1860.* Mérida: UNAM, 1993.

Brandenburg, Frank. "An Experiment in One-Party Democracy." Ph.D. diss., University of Pennsylvania, 1955.

Brennan, Thomas. *Public Drinking and Popular Culture in Eighteenth-Century Paris.* Princeton, N.J.: Princeton University Press, 1988.

Brannon, Jeffrey, and Eric N. Baklanoff. *Agrarian Reform and Public Enterprise in Mexico: The Political Economy of Yucatán's Henequen Industry.* Tuscaloosa: University of Alabama Press, 1987.

Brito Sansores, William. "¡Adiós maestro rural!" In *Los maestros y la cultura nacional, 1920–1952* (5 vols.). Mexico City: SEP, 1987.

Britton, John. "Teacher Unionization and the Corporate State in Mexico." *Hispanic American Historical Review* 59 (1979): 674–90.

Brown, Denise Fay. "Yucatec Maya Settling, Settlement, and Spatiality." Ph.D. diss., University of California, Riverside, 1993.

Brown, Jonathan. "Acting for Themselves: Workers and the Mexican Oil Nationalization." In *Workers' Control in Latin America, 1930–1979,* ed. Jonathan Brown. Chapel Hill: University of North Carolina Press, 1997.

————. Introduction to *Workers' Control in Latin America, 1930–1979,* ed. Jonathan Brown. Chapel Hill: University of North Carolina Press, 1997.

Brunk, Samuel. "Remembering Emiliano Zapata: Three Moments in the Posthumous Career of the Martyr of Chinameca." *Hispanic American Historical Review* 78 (1998): 457–90.

Bustillos Carrillo, Antonio. *Los Mayas ante la cultura y la Revolución.* Mexico City, 1957.

Bustillos Méndez, Rafael. *El Gran Kanxoc: José María Iturralde Traconis.* Mérida, 1987.

Camp, Roderic Ai. *Mexico's Leaders: Their Education and Recruitment.* Tuscon: University of Arizona Press, 1980.

————. *Mexican Political Biography, 1935–1981.* Tuscon: University of Arizona Press, 1982.

Campbell, Federico. *La invención del poder.* Mexico City: Aguilar, 1994.

Cante Canul, Gamaliel. *La situación actual del ejidatario henequenero Maya de X-Tep'en, Yucatán.* Mexico City: SEP/INI, 1982.

Canto Chán, Victor Manuel. *Los trabajadores Mayas de una ex-hacienda henequenera: El ejido Ya'axkopoil, Umán, Yucatán.* Mexico City: SEP/INI/CIESAS, 1982.

Canto Echeverría, Humberto, with Esteban Durán Rosado. *Cárdenas y el Gran Ejido Henequenero de Yucatán.* Mexico City: Costa-Amic, 1963.

Cárdenas, Lázaro. *Palabras y documentos públicos de Lázaro Cárdenas: Informes de gobierno y mensajes presidenciales de año nuevo 1928/1940.* 2 vols. Mexico City: Siglo XXI, 1978.

Cardos Ruz, Laureano. *El drama de los Mayas: Una reforma social traicionada.* Mexico City: Editorial Libros de México, n.d.

Carey, James C. *The Mexican Revolution in Yucatán, 1915–1924.* Boulder, Colo.: Westview, 1984.

Carlos, Manuel L. "Peasant Leadership Hierarchies: Leadership Behavior, Power Blocs, and Conflict in Mexican Regions." In *Mexico's Regions: Comparative History and Development,* ed. Eric Van Young. San Diego: Center for U.S.-Mexican Studies, 1992.

Carr, Barry. *Marxism and Communism in Twentieth-Century Mexico.* Lincoln: University of Nebraska Press, 1992.

Carrillo Puerto, Acrelio. *La familia Carrillo Puerto de Motul, con la Revolución mexicana.* Mérida, 1959.

Censo 1920: Censo general de habitantes, Estados Unidos Mexicanos, edo. de Yucatán. Mexico City: Departamento de Estadística Nacional México, 1928.

Censo 1930: Quinto censo de población, 15 de Mayo de 1930, edo. de Yucatán. Mexico City: Secretaría de la Economía Nacional, Dirección General de Estadística, 1934.

Censo 1940: Sexto censo población–1940, Estados Unidos Mexicanos, Yucatán. Mexico City: Secretaría de la Economía, Dirección General de Estadística, 1943.

Chardon, Roland Emanuel Paul. *Geographic Aspects of Plantation Agriculture in Yucatan.* Washington, D.C.: National Research Council, 1961.

Cirerol Sansores, Manuel. *Ushmal.* Mérida, 1952.

————. *Historia del transporte de pasajeros en Mérida.* Mérida, 1966.

Clark, Ruth. *Organized Labor in Mexico.* 2d ed. New York: Russel and Russel, 1978.

Córdova, Arnaldo. *La política de masas del Cardenismo.* Mexico City: Era, 1974.

Craig, Ann. *The First Agraristas: An Oral History of a Mexican Agrarian Reform Movement.* Berkeley and Los Angeles: University of California Press, 1983.

de la Peña, Guillermo. "Poder local, poder regional: Perspectivas socioantropológicas." In *Poder local, poder regional,* ed. Jorge Padua and Alain Vanneph. Mexico City: Colegio de México/CEMCA, 1993.

Díaz de Cossio, Martín. *Henequen: Riqueza yucateca.* Mexico City: El Mundo, 1938.

Diccionario histórico y biográfico de la Revolución mexicana: Tomo VII. Ed. Mauricio Bretón González, Maricela Concha Radillo, Gustavo Adolfo Cubero Piña, and Olga Cárdenas Trueba. Mexico City: Instituto Nacional de Estudios Históricos de la Revolucion Mexicana y Secretaria de Gobernacion, 1990.

Domínguez Aké, Santos. *La vida de Felipe Carrillo Puerto y su memoria en Muxupip.* Mérida: Maldonado, Consejo Nacional para la Cultura y las Artes, Culturas Populares, 1992.

———. *La historia de la sociedad ejidal de Muxupip.* Tlahuapan: INI /Sedesol, 1994.

Domínguez Tacú, Diego. "Mis recuerdos como campesino henequenero." In *Memoria historia de los henequeneros yucatecos,* ed. Concejo Nacional para la Cultura y las Artes. México City: Dirrección General de la Cultura Popular, 1992.

Don Luis, *Florencio Papalomo Valencia, ¡¡ Gobernador ?? o Mi-Mi reyno por un ca-caballo: Comedia dramático-historica en un acto e infinidad de cuadros.* Mérida, 1937.

Echeverría, Pedro. *La politica en Yucatán en el siglo XX: 1900–1964.* Mérida: Máldonado, 1985.

———. *Educación publica: Mexico y Yucatán.* Mérida: Universidad Autónoma de Yucatán, 1993.

El ejido henequenero de Yucatán: Su historia desde el 10 de febrero de 1938 hasta el 30 de noviembre de 1940. Mexico City: Editorial Cultura México, 1941.

Escobar Toledo, Saul. "El Cardenismo más allá del reparto: Acciones y resultados." In *Historia de la cuestión agraria mexicana,* vol. 5, *El Cardenismo: Un parteaguas histórico en el proceso agrario (primera parte), 1934–1940,* ed. Everardo Escárcega López and Saúl Escobar Toledo. Mexico City: Siglo XXI, 1991.

Escoffie Zetina, Manuel. *¡Ya!: Libro de los buenos yucatecos.* Mérida, 1954.

Falcon, Romana. "El surgimiento del agrarismo Cardenista—una revisión de las tesis populistas." *Historia Mexicana* 27 (1978): 333–86.

Fallaw, Ben. "Cárdenas and the Caste War That Wasn't: Land, Ethnicity, and State Formation in Yucatán, 1847–1937." *The Americas* 53 (1997): 551–77.

———. "The Life and Three Deaths of Felipa Poot." Paper presented at the Latin American Studies Association congress, Chicago, 25 September 1998.

———. "The Southeast Was Red: Left-State Alliances and Popular Mobilizations in Yucatán, 1930–1940." *Social Science History* 23, no. 2 (summer 1999): 241–68.

———. "Antonio Betancourt Pérez, la educación y la izquierda en Yucatán, 1931–1937," *Unicornio,* 13, 20, 27 February 2000, 3–9.

Fernández Souza, Jorge, and Eric Villanueva Mukul. "Notas sobre el Sindicalismo Independiente en Yucatán." In *Memoria del segundo coloquio regional de historia obrera.* Mexico City: CEHSMO, 1979.

Ferrer de M., Gabriel. "Historia de las Comunicaciones." In *Enciclopedia yucatenense* (vol. 3). Mexico City: Gobierno de Estado de Yucatán, 1946.

Flores Beltrán, Armando. *Regiones ganaderas del estado de Yucatán: Estudio económico social agropecuario de la zona número 68.* Mérida: Secretaria de Agricultura y Fomento, Dirección General de Ganaderia, 1943.

Fowler-Salamini, Heather. *Agrarian Radicalism in Veracruz, 1920–1938.* 2d ed. Lincoln: University of Nebraska Press, 1978.

French, William. *A Peaceful and Working People: Manners, Morals, and Class Formation in Northern Mexico.* Albuquerque: University of New Mexico Press, 1996.

Frente Ideológico Revolucionario. *El ejido en Yucatán.* N.p., 1935.

Friedrich, Paul. *The Princes of Naranja: An Essay in Anthrohistorical Method.* Austin: University of Texas Press, 1986.

Gamboa Ricalde, Alvaro. *Yuctan desde 1910: Tomo I (1910–1914).* Veracruz: Imprenta Standard, 1943.

Garavito Elías, Rosa Albina. "Vencer sin convencer." *El cotidiano* 65 (November 1994): 21–32.

García Clark, Ruben, "Tripartisimo y nueva geografía electoral." *El cotidiano* 65 (November 1994): 33–38.

García Correa, Bartolome. *Como se hizo su campaña política.* Mérida: Imprenta Gamboa Guzman, 1930.

García Quintanilla, Alejandra. *Los tiempos en Yucatán: Los hombres, las mujeres, y la naturaleza (siglo XIX).* Mérida: Claves Latinoamericanos and Departamento de Estudios Económico y Sociales del Centro de Investigaciones Regionales "Dr. Hideyo Noguchi" de la Universidad Autónoma de Yucatán, 1986.

Garrido, Luis Javier. *El partido de la Revolución institucionalizada: La formación del nuevo estado en México.* Mexico City: Secretaría de al Educación Publica, 1986.

Genesis y formacion de henequeneros de Yucatán. Mexico City: Al Servicio del Pueblo, 1938.

Gilly, Adolfo. *El Cardenismo, una utopía mexicana.* Mexico City: Cal y Arena, 1994.

Gledhill, John. *Casi Nada: A Study of Agrarian Reform in the Homeland of Cardenismo.* Austin, Texas: Institute for Mesoamerican Studies, 1991.

Gobierno del Estado. *El ejido en Yucatán.* Mérida: Gobierno del Estado, 1937.

Goldkind, Victor. "Social Stratification in the Peasant Community: Redfield's Chankom Reinterpreted." *American Anthropology* 67 (1965): 863–80.

Gómez Sánchez, Pedro. "El Cardenismo en Zacatecas." In *Historia de la cuestion agraria mexicana, estado de Zacatecas,* vol. 2, *1940,* ed. Ramón Vera Salvo. Mexico City: Juan Pablos, 1992.

González Navarro, Moisés. *La Confederacion Nacional Campesina: Un grupo de presión de la reforma agraria mexicana.* Mexico City: Costa-Amic, 1968.

———. "La obra social de Lázaro Cárdenas." *Historia Mexicana* 34 (1984): 353–74.

González Padilla, Beatriz. "La dirigencia política en Yucatán, 1909–1925." In *Hacienda y cambio social en Yucatán,* ed. Luis Millet et al. Mérida: Maldonado, 1984.

González Rodríguez, Blanca. "Cuatro proyectos de cambio en Yucatán." In *Hacienda y cambio social en Yucatán,* ed. Luis Millet et al. Mérida: Maldonado, 1984.

Graham, Richard. *Patronage and Politics in Nineteenth-Century Brazil.* Stanford, Calif.: Stanford University Press, 1990.

Guttman, Matthew. *The Meanings of Macho: Being a Man in Mexico City.* Berkeley and Los Angeles: University of California Press, 1996.

Guzman, Martin Luis. *Obras completas de Martín Luis Guzmán.* Mexico City: Compañia General, n.d.

Guzmán Flores, Guillermo. "El Cardenismo y la nueva democracia." In *Historia de la cuestion agraria mexicana, estado de Zacatecas,* vol. 2, *1940,* ed. Ramón Salvo Vera. Mexico City: Juan Pablos, 1992.

Haber, Stephen. *Industry and Underdevelopment: The Industrialization of Mexico, 1890–1940.* Stanford, Calif.: Stanford University Press, 1989.

Hamilton, Norah. *The Limits of State Autonomy.* Princeton, N.J.: Princeton University Press, 1982.

Handy, Jim. *Revolution in the Countryside: Rural Conflict and Agrarian Reform in Guatemala, 1944–1954.* Chapel Hill: University of North Carolina Press, 1994.

Hansen, Asael, and Juan Bastarrachea M. *Mérida: Su transformación de capital colonial a naciente metrópoli en 1935.* Mexico City: INAH, 1985.

Hart, John. *Anarchism and the Mexican Working Class, 1860–1931.* Austin: University of Texas Press, 1978.

Henderson, Timothy. "Unraveling Revolution: Yucatán, 1924–1930." M.A. thesis, University of Texas, 1988.

Hernández, Alicia. *Historia de la Revolución Mexicana, 1934–1940.* Vol. 16, *La Mecanica Cardenista.* Mexico City: El Colegio de Mexico, 1979.

Hernández Rodríguez, Rogelio. *Amistades, compromisos, y lealtades: Líderes y grupos políticos en el estado de México, 1942–1993.* Mexico City: El Colegio de México, 1998.

Historia documental del partido de la Revolución. Mexico City: PRI, 1981.

Holmes, Barbara Ellen. "Women and Yucatec Kinship." Ph.D. diss., Tulane University, 1978.

Ianni, Octavio. *El estado capitalista en la epoca de Cárdenas.* Mexico City: Serie Popular Era, 1977.

Jacobs, Ian. *Ranchero Revolt: The Mexican Revolution in Guerrero.* Austin: University of Texas Press, 1982.

Joseph, Gilbert. *Revolution from Without: Yucatán, Mexico, and the United States, 1882–1923.* 2d ed. Durham, N.C.: Duke University Press, 1988.

Joseph, Gilbert, and Allen Wells. "The Rough-and-Tumble Career of Pedro Crespo." In *The Human Tradition in Latin America,* ed. William Beezley and Judith Ewell. Wilmington, Del.: Scholarly Resources, 1987.

Joseph, Gilbert, and Daniel Nugent. *Everyday Forms of State Formation: Revolution and the Negotiation of Rule in Modern Mexico.* Durham, N.C.: Duke University Press, 1994.

Juventudes Socialistas Unidos de México. *Instituto Cultural Obrero de JSUM.* Mérida: El Porvenir, 1939.

Katz, Friedrich. *The Life and Times of Pancho Villa.* Stanford, Calif.: Stanford University Press, 1998.

Knight, Alan. *The Mexican Revolution.* 2 vols. Lincoln: University of Nebraska Press, 1986.

——. "Cardenismo: Juggernaut or Jalopy?" In *Texas Papers on Mexico.* Austin: Institute of Latin American Studies, University of Texas at Austin, 1990.

——. "Racism, Revolution, and *Indigenismo:* Mexico, 1910–1940." In *The Idea of Race in Latin America, 1870–1940,* ed. Richard Graham. Austin: University of Texas Press, 1990.

——. "Revolutionary Project, Recalcitrant People." In *The Revolutionary Process in Mexico,* ed. Jaime E. Rodríguez O. Berkeley and Los Angeles: University of California Press, 1990.

——. "Popular Culture and the Revolutionary State in Mexico, 1910–1940." *Hispanic American Historical Review* 74, no. 3 (1994): 393–444.

——. "Habitus and Homicide: Political Culture in Revolutionary Mexico." In *Citizens of the Pyramid: Essays on Mexican Political Culture,* ed. Wil Pansters. Amsterdam: Thela, 1997.

Krauze, Enrique. *Reformar desde el origen: Plutarco E. Calles.* Mexico City: Fondo de Cultura Económica, 1987.

Kubli, Luciano. *Sureste proletario: Apuntes de una jira fecunda.* Mexico City, 1935.

Lancaster, Roger. *Life Is Hard: Machismo, Danger, and the Intimacy of Power in Nicaragua.* Berkeley and Los Angeles: University of California Press, 1992.

Lapointe, Marie. "El estado mexicano y las elites del henequen en Yucatan (1935–1980)." *Gazeta universitaria* 12 (1991): 13–30.

Lara Tec, José Cornelio, and Edelmiro Vargas Canul. Interview by author. 23 May 1993.

Lara y Lara, Humberto. *Sobre la trayectoria de la reforma agraria en Yucatán.* Mérida: Zamna, 1949.

Lee, Rosemary Louise. "The Tourist Industry in Yucatan: A Case Study in the Interaction between Class Structure and Economic Development." Ph.D. diss., University of California, Irvine, 1977.

Lombardo Toledano, Vicente. *El llanto del sureste.* 2d ed. Mexico City: CEHSMO, 1977.

Lomnitz-Adler, Claudio. *Exits from the Labyrinth: Culture and Ideology in the Mexican National Space.* Berkeley and Los Angeles: University of California Press, 1992.

López Cárdenas, Fernando. *Revolutionarios contra la Revolucion.* Mexico City: Lóndres, 1938.

López Sosa, Rodolfo. *Tarjeta presidential.* Mérida: Guerra, 1952.

Loret de Mola, Carlos. *Los caciques.* 3d ed. Mexico City: Grijalbo, 1979.

Loyola Díaz, Rafael. *La crisis Obregón-Calles y el estado mexicano.* 4th ed. Mexico City: Siglo XXI, 1991.

MacFarland, Charles. *Chaos in Mexico: The Conflict of Church and State.* New York: Harper and Bros., 1935.

Machete ilegal, 1929–1934: Edición facsimilar. Puebla: Instituto de Ciencias Universidad Autónoma de Puebla and Centro de Estudios Históricos y Sociales, 1975.

Macías, Ana. *Against All Odds: The Feminist Movement in Mexico to 1940.* Westport, Conn.: Greenwood, 1982.

Manero, Enrique. *Anarquía henequenera.* Mexico City, 1960.

Mangas, Luis F., Gualberto Carrillo Puerto, and José Luis Novelo. *Tercer Congreso Obrero del PSS: Proyectos relacionados con el tema V organización del PSS.* Mérida: Basso, 1930.

Martínez Assad, Carlos, Mario Ramírez Rancaño, and Ricardo Pozas Horcasitas. *Revolucionarios fueron todos.* Mexico City: Secretaría de Educación Pública, 1982.

Medin, Tzvi. *Ideología y praxis política de Lazaro Cárdenas.* Mexico City: Siglo XXI, 1972.

————. *El minimato presidencial: Historia política del Maximato (1928–1935).* 5th ed. Mexico City: Era, 1991.

Memoria de la Segunda Convencio Nacional Ordinaria del Partido Nacional Revolucionario, relatores. Mexico City: Partido Nacional Revolucionario, 1934.

Memoria historica de los henequeros yucatecos. Unidad Regional Yucatan de Culturas Populares. Mexico City: Direcion General Consejo Nacional para la Cultura y las Artes, 1992.

Memorias del Primer Congreso Regional de Unificación Campesinos del ex-Departamento de Valladolid, Yucatán, Verificado en el Salón Regis de la Ciudad de Valladolid, Yucatán, México, durante los días 26, 27 y 28 del Junio próximo pasado. Mérida, 1936.

Mena Brito, Bernardino. *Reestructuración histórica de Yucatán.* 3 vols. Mexico City: Mexicanos Unidos, 1969.

Menéndez, Gabriel Antonio. *Directorio general.* Mérida: Impresora Popular, 1941.

Menéndez, Hernán R. "H²O, el virus historiográfico que ha contaminado la investigación regional: Herencia oligárquica e historia oficial." *Unicornio,* 24 March 1996, 3–7.

Menéndez, Ivan. *Lucha social y sistema político en Yucatán.* Mexico City: Grijalva, 1981.

Meyer, Jean. *Historia de la Revolución mexicana.* Vol. 11, *Periodo 1928–1934: Estado y sociedad con Calles.* Mexico City: Colegio de Mexico, 1977.

Meyer, Lorenzo. *Historia de la Revolucion mexicana.* Vol. 12, *Periodo 1928–1934: Los inicios de la institucionalizacion la política del Maximato.* Mexico City: Colegio de Mexico, 1978.

——. "La Revolución mexicana y sus elecciones presidenciales: Una interpretation (1911–1940)." *Historia mexicana* 32 (1982–83): 143–97.

Michaels, Albert. "The Modification of the Anti-Clerical Nationalism of the Mexican Revolution by General Lázaro Cárdenas and Its Relationship to the Church-State Detente in Mexico." *The Americas* 26 (1969): 36–53.

——. "Crisis of Cardenismo." *Journal of Latin American Studies* 2 (1970): 51–79.

Michaels, Albert. "La elecion de 1940." *Historia mexicana* 21 (1971–72): 81–134.

Molina Enríquez, Andrés, Felix F. Palavicini, and Enrique González Aparicio. *El ejido en Yucatán.* Mexico City: Mexico Nuevo, 1937.

Molina Font, Gustavo. *El problema agrario en la zona henequenera de Yucatán.* Mexico City, 1934.

——. *La tragedia de Yucatán.* 2d ed. Mexico City: Revista de Derecho y Ciencias Sociales Mexico, 1941.

Morales Medina, Hernán. Interview by author. 7 June 1993.

Morton, Ward. *Woman Suffrage in Mexico.* Gainesville: University of Florida Press, 1962.

Narváez Ek, Venancio. *San Antonio Too: Historia de una hacienda henequenera.* Mérida: Programa de Apoyo a la Cultura Municipal y Comunitaria y Consejo Nacional Para la Cultura y las Artes, 1992.

Nava y Nava, Carmen. *Ideología del partido de la Revolución mexicana.* Mexico City: Centro de Estudios de la Revolución Mexicana "Lázaro Cárdenas," 1984.

Nugent, Daniel, ed. *Rural Revolt in Mexico: U.S. Intervention and the Domain of Subaltern Politics.* 2d ed. Durham, N.C.: Duke University Press, 1998.

O'Malley, Ilene. *The Myth of the Revolution: Hero Cults and the Institutionalization of the Mexican State, 1920–1940.* New York: Greenwood, 1986.

Orosa Díaz, Jaime. *Legislación henequenera en Yucatán.* 4 vols. Mérida: Universidad de Yucatán, 1962.

Pacheco Cruz, Santiago. *Recuerdos de la propaganda constitucionalista en Yucatan.* Mérida: Talleres Gráficos y Editorial Zamná, 1953.

Pacheco Méndez, Guadalupe, Arturo Anguiano Orozco, and Rogelio Vizcaíno A. *Cárdenas y la izquierda mexicana: Ensayo, testimonios, documentos.* Mexico City: Juan Pablos, 1975.

Palomo Valencia, Felipe. *Los ejidos de Yucatán y el henequen.* Mexico City: Pedro Robredo, 1934.

Partido Comunista Mexicano. *Resoluciones de la Primera Convención Estatal del Partido Comunista Mexicano: Unidos por la obra Cardenista.* Mérida: Hul-Kin, 1939.

Partido Nacional Revolucionario. *La reforma agraria en Yucatán.* Mexico City: El Nacional, 1937.

Payne, Stanley G. *Spain's First Democracy: The Second Republic, 1931–1936.* Madison: University of Wisconsin Press, 1994.

Pilcher, Jeffrey. *¡Que vivan los tamales! Food and the Making of Mexican Identity.* Albuquerque: University of New Mexico Press, 1998.

Pimentel, María Guadalupe. "Recuerdos del 36." In *Los maestros y la cultura nacional, 1920–1952* (vol. 2). Mexico City: SEP, 1978.

Purnell, Jennie. *Popular Movements and State Formation in Revolutionary Mexico: The Agraristas and Cristeros of Michoacán.* Durham, N.C.: Duke University Press, 1999.

Primer informe anual que rinde el Comite Ejecutivo Nacional del Partido Nacional Revolucionario a todos los sectores sociales del pais, Junio 1936. Mexico City: PNR, 1936.

Primera convención de sociedades locales de los comisariados ejidales. Mérida, 1937.

Redfield, Robert. *The Folk Culture of Yucatan.* Chicago: University of Chicago Press, 1941.

Restall, Matthew. *The Maya World: Yucatec Culture and Society, 1550–1850.* Stanford, Calif.: Stanford University Press, 1997.

Reyes, Candelario. *Apuntes para la historia de Tamaulipas en los siglos XVI y XVII.* Mexico City: Talleres Gráficos Laguna, 1944.

Rockwell, Elsie. "Schools of the Revolution: Enacting and Contesting State Forms in Tlaxcala, 1910–1930." In *Everyday Forms of State Formation: Revolution and the Negotiation of Rule in Modern Mexico,* ed. Gilbert Joseph and Daniel Nugent. Durham, N.C.: Duke University Press, 1994.

Rodríguez, Antonio. *El henequén: Una planta calumniada.* Mexico City: Costa-Amic, 1966.

Rodríguez H., Juan de Dios. *La contra-reforma agrarian en Yucatán.* N.p.: Sociedad Yucateca Andrés Quintana Roo, 1944.

Ronfeldt, David. *Atencingo: The Politics of Agrarian Struggle in a Mexican Ejido.* Stanford, Calif.: Stanford University Press, 1973.

Rubin, Jeffrey. *Decentering the Regime: Ethnicity, Radicalism, and Democracy in Juchitán, Mexico.* Durham, N.C.: Duke University Press, 1997.

Rugeley, Terry. *Yucatán's Maya Peasantry and the Origins of the Caste War.* Austin: University of Texas Press, 1996.

Rus, Jan. "The 'Comunidad Revolucionaria Institucional': The Subversion of Native Government in Highland Chiapas, 1936–1938." In *Everyday Forms of State Formation: Revolution and the Negotiation of Rule in Modern Mexico,* ed. Gilbert Joseph and Daniel Nugent. Durham, N.C.: Duke University Press, 1994.

Saragoza, Alex. *The Monterrey Elite and the Mexican State, 1880–1940.* Austin: University of Texas Press, 1988.

Savarino, Franco. *Pueblos y nacionalismo, del régimen oligárquico a la sociedad de masas en Yucatán, 1894–1925.* Mexico City: INEH, 1997.

Schmitt, Karl. *Communism in Mexico: A Study in Political Frustration:* Austin: University of Texas Press, 1965.

Schreyer, Frans J. *The Rancheros of Pisaflores: The History of a Peasant Bourgeoisie in Twentieth-Century Mexico.* Toronto: University of Toronto Press, 1980.

Schuler, Friedrich. *Mexico between Hitler and Roosevelt: Mexican Foreign Relations in the Age of Lázaro Cárdenas, 1930–1940.* Albuquerque: University of New Mexico Press, 1998.

Shattuck, George. *The Peninsula of Yucatan: Medical, Biological, Meteorological, and Sociological Studies* (Washington: The Carnegie Institute, 1933).

Shulgovski, Anatol. *México en la encrucijada de su historia.* 2d ed. Mexico City: Fondo de Cultura Económica, 1963.

Shuman, Malcolm Karl. "The Town Where Luck Fell: The Economics of Life in a Henequen Zone Pueblo." Ph.D. diss., Tulane University, 1974.

Sierra Villarreal, Jose Luis. "Reflexiones en torno a las aportaciones del Profr. Antonio Betancourt Pérez en materia filosófica." In *Antonio Betancourt Pérez: Premio excellencia academica, 1992–1993.* Mérida: Academia Yucatanense de Ciencias y Artes, 1993.

Sierra Villareal, Jose Luis, and Jose Antonio Paoli Bolio. *Cárdenas y el reparto de los henequenales.* Mérida: Gobierno Estado de Yucatán, 1986.

Sol, Hugo (Anastasio Manzanilla). *El Comunismo en México, quienes lo incubaron . . . y quienes lo propalan.* 2d ed. Mexico City: Hugo Sol, 1955.

Sosa Elízaga, Raquel. *Los códigos ocultos del Cardenismo: Un estudio de la violencia política, el cambio social y la continuidad institucional.* Mexico City: Universidad Nacional Autónoma de México and Plaza y Valdés, 1996.

Sosa Ferreyro, Roque Armando. *Cosas de Yucatan.* Mexico City: Costa-Amic, 1969.

Spenser, Daniela. "Workers against Socialism? Reassessing the Role of Urban Labor in Yucatecan Revolutionary Politics." In *Land, Labor, and Capital in Modern Yucatan: Essays in Regional History and Political Economy,* ed. Gilbert Joseph and Jeffrey Brannon. Tuscaloosa: University of Alabama Press, 1991.

Sullivan, Paul. "Ethnicity." In *Ethnology: Supplement to Handbook of Middle American Indians, Vol. 6,* ed. John Monaghan and Barbara Edmunson. Austin: University of Texas Press, 2000.

Taylor, William B. *Drinking, Homicide, and Rebellion in Colonial Mexican Villages.* Stanford, Calif.: Stanford University Press, 1979.

Thompson, Richard Allen. "Status, Ethnicity, and Mobility in a Yucatec Town." Ph.D. diss., University of Texas, 1970.

Tinsman, Heidi. "Household Patrones: Wife-Beating and Sexual Control in Rural Chile, 1964–1988." In *The Gendered Worlds of Latin American Women Workers,* ed. John D. French and Daniel James. Durham, N.C.: Duke University Press, 1997.

Torres, Manuel A. *Verdadero Socialismo.* Mérida: Universal, 1922.

Trujillo Dominguez, Adolfo. *Importantes documentos para la historia del Sindicalismo en Yucatán.* Mérida, 1936.

Tutino, John. *From Insurrection to Revolution in Mexico: Social Bases of Agrarian Violence, 1750–1940.* Princeton, N.J.: Princeton University Press, 1986.

Urzaiz, Eduardo. "Historia de la educación pública y privada desde 1911." In *Enciclopedia yucatanense* (vol. 4). Mexico City: Gobierno de Estado, 1944.

Valdes Acosta, José María. *A traves de las centurias: Obra especial: Que contiene apuntes historicos, relatos genealogicos, reseñas biograficas, paginas literarias, antiguos documentos y retratos.* Mérida: Pluma y Lapiz, 1923.

Vaughan, Mary Kay. "The Construction of the Patriotic Festival in Tecamachalco, Puebla, 1900–1946." In *Rituals of Rule, Rituals of Resistance.* Wilmington, Del.: Scholarly Resources, 1994.

———. *Cultural Politics in Revolution: Teachers, Peasants, and Schools in Mexico, 1930–1940.* Tuscon: University of Arizona Press, 1997.

Velázquez, Aurelio. *Desde la casa del pueblo.* Mexico City: Editorial de Izquierda de la Cámara de Diputados, 1936.

Villanueva Mukul, Eric. *Así tomamos la tierras.* Mérida: Maldonado, 1984.

———. *Crisis henequenera y movimientos campesinos en Yucatán, 1966–1983.* Mexico City: INAH, 1985.

———. *El henequén en Yucatán: Industria, mercado, y campesinos.* Mérida: Maldonado, 1990.

Wasserman, Mark. *Persistent Oligarchs: Elites and Politics in Chihuahua, Mexico, 1910–1940.* Durham, N.C.: Duke University Press, 1993.

Weldon, Jeffrey. "Congress, Political Machines, and the Maximato: The No-Reelection Reforms of 1933." Paper presented at the Latin American Studies Association congress, Atlanta, 10 March 1994.

Wells, Allen. *Yucatán's Gilded Age: Haciendas, Henequen, and International Harvester, 1860–1915.* Albuquerque: University of New Mexico Press, 1984.

Winn, Peter. *Weavers of Revolution: The Yarur Workers and Chile's Road to Socialism.* New York: Oxford University Press, 1986.

Yucatán revolucionario: Album conmemorativo de la toma de posesión del Ing. Humberto Canto Echeverría como Gobernador Constitutional del Estado de Yucatán. Mérida, 1938.

Periodicals and Archival Materials

Diario del sureste.
Diario de Yucatán.
El eco socialista.
El heraldo de Yucatán.
El hombre libre.
El clamor del obrero: Organo de la Liga Calos Marx.
El constituyente: Organo del bloque consituyentes del PSS.
El fenix.
Joven guardia: Organo de JSUM.
Menya.
La metralla.
Obrero.
La rafaga.
Tribuna revolucionaria.
Vibracion.
El yucatanista.
Yucateco socialista.
Archivo General de la Nación. Mexico City, Mexico.
Archivo General del Estado de Yucatán. Mérida, Yucatán, Mexico.
Archivo de la Secretaría de Educación Pública. Mexico City, Mexico.
Archivo de Plutarco Elías Calles y Fernando Torreblanco. Mexico City, Mexico.

Index

Ben Fallaw is Assistant Professor of History and Latin American Studies at
Colby College.

Library of Congress Cataloging-in-Publication Data
Fallaw, Ben.
Cárdenas compromised : the failure of reform in postrevolutionary
Yucatán / Ben Fallaw.
p. cm.
ISBN 0-8223-2758-9 (cloth : alk. paper)
ISBN 0-8223-2767-8 (pbk. : alk. paper)
1. Cárdenas, Lázaro, 1895–1970. 2. Mexico — Politics and
government — 1910–1946. 3. Yucatán (Mexico : State) — Politics and government.
4. Land reform — Mexico — History. I. Title.
F1234.C233 F35 2001   972.08′25 — dc21   2001028666